BN
MERRY
HALL
McLaren

MERRY HALL

Beverley Nichols with Four, the cat, on the front steps of Merry Hall, photograph by George Konig courtesy of the Bryan Connon Collection

MERRY HALL

Beverley Nichols

With a Foreword by Ann Lovejoy

TIMBER PRESS
Portland, Oregon

Photographs of Beverley Nichols are the property of Bryan Connon, reproduced with permission

Drawings by William McLaren

First published in 1951 by Jonathan Cape

TIMBER PRESS, INC.
The Haseltine Building
133 S.W. Second Avenue, Suite 450
Portland, Oregon 97204, U.S.A.

Printed in Hong Kong

Sixth printing 2002

Library of Congress Cataloging-in-Publication Data

Nichols, Beverley, 1899–
Merry Hall / Beverley Nichols ; with a foreword by Ann Lovejoy.
p. cm.
Facsim. reprint of: London : Cape, 1951.
Includes index.
ISBN 0-88192-417-2
1. Gardening—England. 2. Nichols, Beverley, 1899—Homes and haunts—England. I. Title.
SB455.N57 1998
635'.09422—dc21 97-47253
CIP

CONTENTS

Beverley Nichols and "Oldfield," his gardener, regarding "t'chrysanthe-mums" in the greenhouse of Merry Hall, photograph courtesy of the Bryan Connon Collection

FOREWORD

LIKE so many other readers, I discovered Beverley Nichols by picking up a dogeared copy of *Down the Garden Path* at a secondhand bookstore. Now a classic, it was Nichols's first garden book. When it was published in 1932, it created a huge new readership for Nichols, who was then known chiefly as a reporter and novelist. Such popularity was completely understandable, for as I quickly found, reading one Nichols book leads one irresistibly to seek out another and yet another.

Merry Hall was the second Nichols book I came upon. I was thrilled to learn that it was the first of a trilogy, and that another Nichols trilogy and several singletons remained to be savored. Nichols's writing affects many people this way, each work creating a terrific appetite for more. Finding his garden books became a favorite pastime on road trips, when I could ransack used bookstores across the country. I was forced to search these books out one by one, for, despite his long and successful career, which spanned over fifty years and encompassed more than fifty books, Nichols's work had fallen almost entirely out of print by the mid 1980s.

Most of his books were so timely as to belong utterly to their period. Few of them read as well now as they did in their day, when Nichols's bons mots were widely quoted and his exploits followed like those of film stars or politicians. His fame, or perhaps notoriety, was in a way his undoing, for fond as the English are of their eccentric and talented countrymen, they are also merciless toward any perceived self-promotion.

A debonair hero who shrugged off acclaim with understated modesty would be adored for life, but let any inclination to inflate his own status appear, and the populace could turn against a fellow overnight.

Despite his lengthy string of hits in every attempted field, Nichols's essential insecurity caused him to revel in his own glory in a way that repeatedly put his public off. With each new endeavor, he would win fresh kudos, yet sooner or later his egotistical transgressions would remove him once again from general favor. This cycle grew more pronounced toward the end of his life, when his increasing propensity for melodramatic autobiography exposed him to severe (if deserved) criticism.

Nichols would probably be astounded by the fact that his most lasting literary legacy would consist of his garden writing. Tossed off quickly, the garden books were composed as Nichols composed his garden beds, each idea leading to and intertwining with the next. Indeed, he described writing *Down the Garden Path* as being "like arranging a bunch of mixed flowers, here a story, here a winding paragraph, here a purple passage, and suddenly there was a book."

There was indeed a book, one that made him enormously famous not only in England (where the great boom in gardening had not gone unnoticed by Nichols, who was quick to delve into any promising new arena) but also across the water. In England, garden greats such as Constance Spry and Vita Sackville-West (whose own garden writing has long outlasted her novels and poetry) heaped Nichols's garden books with praise, calling him a pioneer in exploratory flower arranging and in promoting the possibilities of winter bloom.

The garden books, however, succeeded so well not because Nichols was a plantsman or a formidable horticulturist (he was neither, and assiduously avoided the practical side of gardening) but because they seemed so refreshing when set against Nichols's more serious works. Light, bright, and effortlessly amusing, his garden writing perfectly balanced his ardent (and sometimes sentimental) delight in plants with the playful spirit and sometimes quite brilliant malice that characterized so many of his human relationships.

Indeed, some people claim with a certain amount of justice that his garden books are not garden books at all. As much about his houses and cats and friends and neighbors as about plants and garden making, these books have a deliciously gossipy quality, with just a taste of naughtiness that might well prove unpalatable in greater quantity. They also live as his other works do not. Their lasting success is due in part to his knack for capturing the universals of garden making. All of us have entertained the kind of garden visitors, pleasant or obnoxious, that delight or plague Beverley Nichols. All of us have watched with horrified fascination as simple garden plans take on a life of their own, implacably expanding to overwhelm all constraints of time or budget. All of us have fallen heavily for unsuitable plants and paid a stiff price for our foolishness, or left dearly beloved ones behind with undying regret. Nichols knew what it was to adore the idea of a plant or a garden as much as the thing itself. He understood the seductive quality of the unbridled imagination and, despite knowing exactly what was to come, left it unbridled anyway. In this, he is to be applauded, for not through common sense and timidity are limited horizons expanded and unlikely dreams realized.

Fortunately for his fellow gardeners, Nichols was a tirelessly productive author who found time to write ten garden books among his many other pursuits. For much of his adult life, Nichols traveled the world as a political and general news correspondent for a number of English newspapers and journals. He wrote for a great many magazines and reviews as well, both as a regular columnist and occasional contributor.

In his lifetime, he published six novels, five detective stories, four children's books, four political works, two travel books, two collections of short stories, two sets of religious essays, two sets of essays on popular culture, six dramas, some dozen popular show tunes, a few librettos, and a dozen miscellaneous collections and anthologies (including a series of cat books). He also wrote no fewer than six autobiographies, most of which might be considered as works of fiction to some degree. This self-absorption will come as no surprise to readers who enjoy his disarming habit of watching himself with great fascination. Luckily, we join him in his admiration and are equally interested (or nearly so) in his adventures and responses.

Rereading *Merry Hall* for the third or fourth time, I was as always reminded of my favorite E. F. Benson stories, in which Lucia and her archrival, Miss Mapp, battle for social supremacy. Nichols's portraits of his neighbors, Miss Emily, the locally bred Termagant, and "Our Rose," the trendy florist, are every bit as juicy. His learned friend Marius has devotees as well, as does Merry Hall's stern and stubborn gardener, Oldfield. Given the choice of which character one would most like to know in real life, however, everybody I ask always unhesitatingly plumps for Gaskin, Nichols's manservant, whose poise and perfection give Bunter a run for his money.

Like Nichols's other garden books, *Merry Hall* is full of deliberately quotable tidbits, the most persistently popular of which runs, "It is only to the gardener that Time is a friend, giving each year more than he steals." If time has treated

Nichols's reputation a bit roughly in some respects, time has been a friend to his garden writing, which remains as lively and rewarding today as it did half a century ago. If this is your first excursion into Nichols country, welcome. Prepare to be amazed, and amused as well. If you are returning here, welcome back. The pleasures of this land, you will find, do not pall but only increase with age, like those of our gardens.

Ann Lovejoy
Bainbridge Island, Washington

MERRY HALL

Facsimile of the Original Edition of 1951

EARTH

BEVERLEY NICHOLS

With drawings by
William McLaren

JONATHAN CAPE
THIRTY BEDFORD SQUARE
LONDON

CONTENTS

To

Mr. A. E. NEWBY

A Great Gardener

and

A Gentleman of the Old School

Bind me, ye woodbines, in your twines;
Curl me about, ye gadding vines;
And oh so close your circles lace,
That I may never leave this place;
But, lest your fetters prove too weak,
Ere I your silken bondage break,
Do you, O brambles, chain me too,
And, courteous briars, nail me through.

ANDREW MARVELL,
on Appleton House,
to the Lord Fairfax

CHAPTER I

OVER THE HEDGE

SOME fall in love with women; some fall in love with art; some fall in love with death.

I fall in love with gardens, which is much the same as falling in love with all three at once.

For a garden is a mistress, and gardening is a blend of all the arts, and if it is not the death of me, sooner or later, I shall be much surprised. A pleasant sort of death, I venture to suggest, which runs in the family. One of my grandfathers died of a clump of *iris stylosa*; it enticed him from a sick bed on an angry evening in January, luring him through the snow-drifts with its blue and silver flames; he died of double pneumonia a few days later. It was probably worth it.

Then there was a great-uncle who expired because of his passion for pears – not the fruit, but the blossom. He could not, quite rightly, have enough pear blossom; he wanted to hug it, bees and all, as a nice old gentleman should. So he took to climbing up into the branches, and sitting among the wild white spray of the flowers, for hours on end, with none but the bees for company. And one day a branch broke, and they found him out there in the orchard, lying on his back, staring up to the April sky, with an expression on his face of the greatest serenity.

I cannot forecast, with any accuracy, the probable nature of my own horticultural demise; at the moment, in view of the fact that the water garden is claiming most of my attention, it will probably take the form of drowning. Indeed, by the time these words are published, I may already have been discovered floating under a clump of James Brydon *nymphaeas*, a variety of water-lily which is described in the catalogues as *a deep old rose pink that sometimes seems flushed with crimson.* That sounds a good description of the prose in which many of the passages in this book will doubtless be written. When I begin to write about flowers I lose all sense of restraint, and it is far, far too late to do anything about it.

You cannot say you have not been warned.

§ II

We begin, oddly enough, with a wealth of old oak. This unpleasant phrase will be found engraved on the hearts of all those who, in contemporary Britain, have ever bought, or tried to buy, or thought of buying a house.

I was one of those who were trying to buy a house. This was six years ago. The war was over . . . at least, it was fashionable to suggest that the war was over, though one had not noticed it. I had returned to London after doing a job in India, and as soon as I set foot in that most melancholy and desolate of cities I knew that if I did not get back to a garden I should die.

You have to be a gardener to understand that the expression of such a feeling is not a mere figure of speech; it is, quite literally, a matter of life or death. I believe that if it were possible to take what might roughly be described as a 'psychic photograph' of a gardener, you would find that there would be ghostly tendrils growing from the tips of his fingers, and shadowy roots about his feet, and that there would be a pattern of ectoplasmic lines that linked him in a natural rhythm with the curve and sway of the branches about him. And I believe that if this same picture were taken when he was removed from his natural environment, it would be the picture of a dying man – the frail tendrils and roots would be starved and stunted, the rhythm broken. 'Green fingers' is not only a flash of poetry; it is a fact in physiology.

So I had to buy a house in the country. Buy, not rent. It is ridiculous to rent things if you are a gardener; it fidgets you. Even a very long lease is upsetting. I once owned a house with a 999 years lease, and it gave me an unbearable sense of being a sort of week-end guest; it hardly seemed worth while planting the hyacinths. Only a freehold will do, because when you plant a tree you want to think of its roots stretching down and down for ever, and its branches reaching up and up for all time, till in the end the blossom mingles with the stars.

Therefore I went around the London house agents, as one demented, in search of a 'desirable' country freehold. And all I found was a wealth of old oak.

It was quite extraordinary – the way in which this

phrase crept into every catalogue, loomed over every prospectus, and dominated every discussion. It was a house agent's 'must'. Was there something peculiar – not to say bizarre – about the drains? Never mind; there was a Wealth of Old Oak. Was the garden small, triangular, and entirely surrounded by large red trams, which, in their turn, were filled with large red women in mackintoshes? Maybe. But there was a Wealth, a Veritable Treasury, of Old Oak. Did it face North, was it Edwardian Gothic, was there a lunatic asylum over the wall, and would a sensitive spaniel have howled itself to death at the mere sight of it on a rainy night? Yes, sir. It did. And there was. And it would. All quite correct. But kindly remember, there was a Wealth of Old Oak. Or, as I began to think of it, a W. of O.O.

After a time I developed a technique which saved a great deal of time. Perhaps, if you are searching for a house, you may care to adopt it.

This is what happens.

Leaning over the counter, and speaking in hushed tones, as though he were imparting some fascinating secret, the house agent will begin. . . .

'There is a wealth of . . .'

Instantly you must reply ' . . . oldoak'. But you must not be too anxious to get it in first, or the words will get glued together in a sound like 'dloak'. That is unwise because it means that one has to repeat oneself, which spoils the effect. It is better, if you decide to adopt this method, to spit the words out very distinctly, being very sure to enunciate the consonants . . . thus, 'olD oaK'. Like Demosthenes with the pebbles. Once, in desperation, I replied 'Oldy oakey', but that, again, is not to be recommended. It introduces an atmosphere of farce.

And really, it was not a farce at all; it was a tragedy. Here was I, craving for a garden, with the sap dying in me and the last traces of green fading from my fingers, and I was shut out by an apparently impenetrable barrier of old oak. And I did not like old oak; in fact, I loathed it.

That may seem a strange confession from one who once had a love affair with a Tudor cottage. But though it may seem sad, one grows out of Tudor cottages. Little by little, the charm of being stunned and sent reeling to the wall, six times a day, by the low beams on the ceiling, is apt to pall; one no longer darts gaily up to the bathroom for the sticking plaster, chortling with amusement at the nice Tudore bumpe on one's forehead. Nor, as season gives way to season, and as the bedroom floor sinks more sharply, tilting at an even acuter angle, does one take so much pleasure in emerging from bed, as it were, on skis, and sliding down a highly polished slope towards a lattice window through which the dawn comes but faintly. It would be pleasant, one feels, to be able to stand up straight, from time to time; it would be even pleasanter to be able to read a book without crouching in a draught under the aforesaid lattice.

As it is with comfort, so it is with taste; to linger in the Tudors is merely a sign of aesthetic adolescence; one must move on to the eighteenth century, and if one has any sense, stay there. There comes a time, or there should come a time, in the life of every civilized man, when he realizes that the eighteenth century said the last word worth saying in absolutely everything connected with the domestic arts. Sometimes this realization comes by chance; he may be standing in a Georgian doorway, and the sun may shine on it, and he may look up and suddenly perceive that he is standing in a frame that is as perfect as a melody by Mozart. Sometimes it comes painfully, by long study and application. In my case it came when I inherited four William and Mary chairs of the school of Daniel Marot. Those chairs altered my life. By their elegance, their assurance, and their chastity, they were a silent reproof to everything in their vicinity, including myself. I was not sufficiently elegant; I was not sufficiently assured; and we will skip the rest. But those chairs did persuade me, at least, to try. It is very foolish to laugh at the memory of Oscar Wilde, vowing to live up to his blue china. If he had kept that vow, he would not have had so intimate an acquaintance with Reading Gaol, and at least a hundred boring little scribblers would not have made a fortune by twisting the mask of his tragedy into an even uglier shape than he twisted it himself.

That, however, is by the way (a sentence which had better be 'set up in type', for everything in this book is by the way).

To resume. I wanted a house. And I wanted a Georgian house. And I wanted a garden of at least five acres. A garden which, for preference, should be wrecked and lost and despairing. A garden riddled with brambles, stung almost to death with nettles, and eaten to the bone with blight – a garden locked in a mortal struggle with every sort of weed and pest and horror. I was in a rescuing mood, and if you were to translate this rather odd paragraph into terms of ballet, you would have to go to the third act of Tchaikovsky's 'Sleeping Beauty'.

I could not find that garden. Sometimes it seemed that I had found it, but then the house would be wrong. The two were never to be had together, in spite of all the glowing promises of the advertisements. Often as I returned to London, disconsolate after a fruitless errand of some hundreds of miles, I felt that it might be profitable to compile a glossary of house-agents' jargon and to translate this jargon into fact. Thus –

Usual offices These, only too often, proved to be far from 'usual', unless one were accustomed to staggering out into shrubberies in search of malevolent sheds.

Well Laid Out Garden This implied an 'artistic' rockery, containing a small pool, in the centre of which a very spiky pelican glared, with justified distaste, at a mass of the more repulsive forms of aubretia.

Excellent Conservatory This was only to be interpreted as a warning. It should have been followed by – 'Beware'. I never viewed a house with a conservatory that was not falling down, with half its panes missing and its heating system in ruins.

Fittings at Reasonable Valuation This meant that one was expected to buy strips of tattered linoleum at a price which would have been exorbitant for Aubusson rugs. It meant that one was required to pay for roller blinds which, when unrolled, emitted showers of moths and woodlice. It meant – but never mind. For the house is just round the corner.

§ III

One day, when I had almost given up hope, and was thinking of passing the rest of my life in a tent, or a caravan, or if the worst came to the worst, the Ritz, I happened to turn to the back page of *The Times* and my eye caught the following advertisement.

> EASY REACH OF LONDON. Charming Georgian Manor House in quiet leafy lane. Five acres. Outbuildings. Excellent condition. Freehold. Reasonable price for quick sale. Sole agents Stanhope & Filgate, Meadowstream 339.

Had one been in the habit of making sounds of mocking laughter this would have been an occasion for doing so. The advertisement rang false in every syllable. From bitter experience I knew only too well how it should be interpreted:

Easy Reach of London meant the suburbs of Glasgow.

Georgian meant early Victorian with a neo-Tudor garage.

Leafy Lane meant a dark brick alley looking out on to the football ground of an orphanage.

Outbuildings meant three small sheds, roofed with corrugated iron.

As for the 'excellent condition' and the 'reasonable price', that was just too silly to think about.

None the less I rang up Meadowstream 339. And immediately three very astonishing things happened. Firstly, I got Meadowstream 339. Secondly, I had a conversation with a charmingly voiced young lady who, for some obscure reason, did not appear outraged by the fact that I had answered the advertisement. Thirdly, the house – after being in the market for at least two hours – had not yet been sold. These three omens struck me as so significant that I decided to go down to Meadowstream that very afternoon.

§ IV

My companion on this eventful journey was Bob R—. The R— conceals the name of one of the great Jewish families of England, a family with ancient roots and honourable traditions. Bob belongs to the younger branch of the R—s; 'I am the poor relation,' he always says, by which we are to understand that he is not a millionaire – quite.

Bob is in his early forties; he has grey hair, restless hands, and dark, melancholy eyes which look vague but are, in fact, as keen as a hawk when any *objet d'art* looms on the horizon. He has impeccable taste, and to see him in an antique shop is a liberal education. He pushes open the door, stares around him, pauses with his hands on his hips, and sniffs. And then, if there is anything to pounce upon, he pounces. It may be a little dusty piece of Meissen at the back of a shelf, or a Louis Quinze clock with the ormolu painted over, or a fragment of Queen Anne needlework that everybody else has overlooked. Whatever it is, he sniffs it out. And then he buys it, heaving deep sighs, and prophecying ruin and destruction.

Bob is proud, and he despises those of his brethren who seek to deny their origins. Not that he is a bore about it; indeed, he constantly seeks to give to the tragedy of his race a mordant twist of humour. 'You see, my dear,' he will say to a woman friend, 'I belong to the Race, and am therefore not quite normal.' If he hears me bargaining in an antique shop he will raise his eyebrows and exclaim, 'Really, my dear fellow, one would think you had a Touch of the Blood.' There is only one thing about him – materially – which might suggest to an outsider that he was not entirely Aryan. That is his watch-chain. It is only a slender thread of gold, barely noticeable on his waistcoat, but at the end of it, concealed in his trouser pocket, is a fabulous assortment of golden objects which are produced when he wishes to light a cigarette. Apart from the gold lighter, which is studded with sapphires, there are two solid gold latchkeys, a gold ring, a golden guinea, a gold champagne 'twizzler', a gold seal, several gold charms, and a gold compass – ('to be used in concentration camps, my dear').

Bob seems unaware of the sensation which is invariably produced whenever this glittering horde is dragged out of his pocket, and the only comment I have ever heard him make on it was when he said 'it ought to come in handy in a pogrom'. I think that his main use for it is that it gives him something to rattle when he is emotionally disturbed. He was going to rattle it a good deal, during this particular expedition.

So there we were, the two of us, on a sunny afternoon in June, and precisely where our journey took us there is no need to indicate. It is enough to say that though the village of Meadowstream lay only an hour from London, it proved to be sheltered on the north by a deep and ancient forest and swept from the west by the wind over a lonely heath. And when at last we found the 'leafy lane', it was indeed a leafy lane, quiet and winding, with meadows on one side and a few little cottages on the other, that seemed to have strayed away from the rest of the village, like children playing truant.

We drove slowly, for the lane was very narrow. Then it suddenly widened beneath the branches of an immense copper beech. It was so beautiful a tree that I slowed down the car in order to get a better view of it. As I did so, I noticed, through the dark, waving branches, an old Georgian house, standing further down the lane.

'How very pretty that looks,' I said to Bob. 'The red brick, and the red shadows of the leaves, and the . . .'

Then I sat up. 'You don't think . . .'

'What?'

'That couldn't possibly be the house we're looking for?'

'That? That's a *mansion*. Don't be ridiculous.'

But it was.

§ V

We parked the car and walked down the lane.

To describe the house as a 'mansion' was one of Bob's customary exaggerations, but it was certainly larger than I had expected. It was sheltered from the road by a tall hedge of the ugliest evergreens known to man – speckled laurels, variegated holly and rank, untrimmed laurestinus, but through the gaps one could see that it had immense 'possibilities'. The original structure was a simple Georgian square, with all the Georgian perfection of line, and to this square had been added another wing which was reasonably symmetrical. But certain things had been done to the façade which were so architecturally outrageous that one longed, there and then, to take a pick-axe and hack them away. Chief among these was a large square bow window, bleak and uncompromising, which jutted out from the centre of the house, to the right of the door. I stared at this bow window through the hedge; it stared back; we knew each other for enemies.

'That would have to be one of the first things to go,' I muttered to myself.

'You're not *seriously* considering it?'

Bob's voice made me jump. 'Why not?'

'It's far too large; it's falling to pieces; it's bang on the road . . .'

'It's not too large; it's not falling to pieces; and it isn't on a road, it's on a lane, with a very pretty ten-acre meadow to look out on.'

'People could glare in at you. And further down the lane there's a farm, and you know what you are about farm noises.'

'Do stop crabbing for a minute.'

There was an elaborate shrug from Bob, and a sharp rattle of the gold chains, which, as we have seen, was always a bad sign.

I put my hand on the gate, and looked up at the house, trying to think. It was a very important moment in one's life. This was the first house I had seen which could possibly be regarded as a potential home. If one were to take it – life being what it is and 'things' being what they are – it would certainly be the last home I should have, on this side of the grave.

As I stood there I had a curious feeling about this house which was unlike any feeling I had ever had about a house before. It was a sort of pity. I felt that the house was lonely – desolate and cold in spite of the gentle afternoon sunlight – and that it desperately needed somebody to come and cheer it up. The sunlight should have made it smile, but how could it possibly smile in its present condition? It looked at once starved and stifled; starved because of the thin, blistered paint, the patched roof, and the cracked, dirty glass; stifled because of the rank and gloomy hedge which had thrust its way almost through the very windows.

'Come on, Bob. I'm going to explore.'

With another shrug from Bob, and another rattle of gold chains, we pushed open the gate and walked up the steps. I rang the bell. Silence. Another ring. Still silence.

While we were waiting Bob said – rather grudgingly – 'This is a very beautiful door.'

I looked up at it and nodded. It was indeed a perfect door.

'About 1770 I should say,' continued Bob. 'And whoever it was who put that coloured glass in the fanlight should have been popped into Dachau.'

'There's nobody here so let's go round to the back and see if we can get in.'

I love breaking into deserted houses, climbing in through the larder, tiptoeing round in the silence, with only the sound of the sparrows chirping in the ivy outside the grimy windows . . . and wondering, all the time, if some awful man is going to surprise one and ask one what the hell one is doing. One should never go for a country walk without an order to view a deserted house.

But this house was different. I did not feel that I was intruding, I felt I was entering into my rightful inheritance. Nor did we have to break in, for the kitchen door was open.

The kitchen was immense. Very lofty, with all sorts of corridors leading out of it, and vast cupboards and dressers.

'This would make a wonderful rehearsal room for the flying ballet,' sniffed Bob.

I made no comment. I was wondering what Gaskin would say about it.

'The servants' hall,' Bob added, 'is perhaps a *trifle* small . . .' he pointed to a moderately sized sitting-room on the left '. . . considering that you would need a staff of at least *fourteen*. . . .'

'You know very well, Bob, that I have a staff of one. And only one.'

'In which case . . . ' He finished the sentence with a positive fusillade of gold rattlings. His patience was evidently wearing very thin. And it was to the accompaniment of these rattlings that we made the tour of the house – tiptoeing round in the silence, talking, as one does on these occasions, *sotto voce*.

Perhaps you had better come with us, though I warn you that I am not much good at describing the layout of a house. Who is? Don't you find that whenever you read descriptions of the plans of houses in novels you get hopelessly lost? I do. Even in detective stories, when it is vital that one should remember that the conservatory door was on the *left* of the cloakroom, which, in its turn, was on the *right* of the dining-room – (because otherwise the body would have got stuck in the serving-hatch) – I get flustered and go round in circles and find myself wandering into all sorts of rooms where Agatha Christie had no intention to lead me.

So we will not attempt a formal plan. Better to jot down a few rough impressions.

The Hall. Large, dark and of incredible gloom. The lower part of all the walls was covered with a dado like a skin disease. This extended for about three feet from the floor. Above this was a wallpaper which, if not actually designed with the set purpose of inducing maniac despondency, was well calculated to have this effect. Its motif was a whirl of black cabbages – or so they seemed – against a background of acid blue petunias.

'This should be stripped,' I said to Bob, with some obviousness.

'It should be psychoanalysed,' he retorted.

Drawing-room. Huge. Two rooms knocked into one. Breathtaking possibilities, with windows facing south, west and east. A lovely old floor of polished oak.

'That floor would cost three hundred to put in today,' I said to Bob.

'And three hundred a year to keep polished,' he snapped.

Dining-room. Possibilities terrific. Visions of candle-lit parties, bare shoulders reflected in gesso mirrors, Sheraton sideboards, Tio Pepe in Georgian decanters, spinach soufflés, nectarines from the walled garden, Chateau Yquem with walnuts . . . (Was one *mental*? But yes. For the year was 1946 and the place was England. And that meant that if one ever had a candle-lit party it would be because the power had been cut, and if one's guests ever had bare shoulders it would be because they had no coupons left to cover them with calico.)

But it was nice to dream.

Staircase. Perfection. Just a line, and a curve, and another line, and another curve. In short, a Georgian staircase. When one has said this, one has said all that is necessary to say.

By the way, this lovely feature – as delicate as a cadenza by Rossini – had been painted an aggressive orange.

Bedrooms. There were five or six on the first floor and about five more on the floor above, and when we got on the landing, and when Bob noticed this extra staircase, stretching into an architectural infinity, there was an almost deafening rattle of chains, because he really could not bear the thought of my going on with the folly of inspecting such an immense property.

However, I told him that the five bedrooms on the top were really attics and did not 'count'.

'What do you mean . . . not *count*? They're *there*, aren't they?'

'So what?'

'How are you going to furnish them?'

'I shan't.'

'It would drive me mad . . . all those empty rooms.'

I can't see why. I could easily run the Vatican with one servant. . . .'

'*No?* Have you told the Pope?'

'Merely because one has a lot of rooms one needn't use them.'

'I can only repeat it would drive *me* mad. I should come up at night and prowl round and mutter, and feel like a ruined earl.'

'Why not? One's a ruined something-or-other, whatever one is. So why not be a ruined earl?'

More chain-rattling, and a resumption of the tour.

The bedrooms were – potentially – gay and charming, but they had been transformed by previous owners into a succession of chambers of horror. The main excruciation in each room was the fireplace. There are certain shades of pink which should come under the Obscenities Act – (if there is such a thing) – shades so arch and so evil that they turn the stomach. All these shades were in evidence in the brilliantly tiled beastlinesses that greeted us as we opened every door. But I noticed that the outlines of the original fireplaces were still visible beneath the sickly wallpaper.

I smiled to myself; the very monstrosity of it all was an inspiring challenge; my fingers itched for a pickaxe.

We went downstairs again, crossed the hall, turned right, and found ourselves in a little conservatory that led to a very large room indeed. This room seemed to be an addition to the rest of the house, and as I peered through the door I saw, from the hanging lights, that it had been used as a billiards-room. If I were crazy enough to take the house, it should be turned into a music-room; it was ideally situated for long, secret struggles with arpeggios and violent arguments with cadenzas.

But now, music was forgotten, for through the lofty windows we could at last get a proper view of the garden.

I almost dreaded to go outside; so much depended on it. But it was now or never. We opened the door and stepped into the sunlight.

§ VI

There is a certain dialogue which must be familiar not only to everybody who has ever owned a garden, but also to everybody who has ever been shown over one.

It begins with the words . . . '*But you should have seen it when we came!*'

Do you recognize it? You are standing in the porch, with your hostess and her daughter by your side, looking out on to a trim lawn and a neat herbaceous border, and you make some polite little remark about how beautifully everything is kept up. That starts them off.

'But you should have seen it when we came!' cries the hostess, clasping her hands. 'Shouldn't he, Ada?'

'He should indeed,' agrees Ada. 'He could have NO IDEA!'

'None! *Nobody* could have any IDEA!'

'It was a WILDERNESS!' cries Ada.

'It was worse than a wilderness. It was a SHAMBLES!'

'The nettles were as high as one's shoulder!'

'As for the brambles . . .'

'And the bindweed . . .'

'And the ground-elder . . .'

'Oh, my dear, that ground-*elder*!'

It is almost certain, at this stage, that one of the ladies will observe that when she dies, the word 'ground-elder' will be found written on her heart. 'Like Mary Queen of Scots and Calais,' she adds tactfully, in case one had forgotten.

I will not attempt to deny that in the past five years I myself have very frequently initiated this dialogue. '*But you should have seen it when we came!*'

For when Bob and I stepped out of the house, we stepped, not into a garden, but into a field. Indeed, it was worse than that. If it had just been a field, pure and simple, one could have said: 'Well, we'll scythe it and plough it and plant it, and get some sort of design into it, and it'll all be very naked for a year or two, but at least it will have begun on the right lines, and it'll be terrific fun watching it mature.'

But it wasn't nearly as simple as that. For as we stood there, staring out on to about three acres of knee-high grass, at the end of which there seemed to be some sort of orchard, it was immediately apparent that Somebody had been Up To Something in that field, and that what he had been Up To was very nasty indeed.

Immediately opposite us was a large and slimy pond. It lay at only a few feet from the billiards-room; its surface was alive with mosquitos, and it exuded a very sickening odour. When Bob threw a stone into it to see how deep it was, a smell came out that seemed to me to be positively mauve. Then, as we moved hurriedly away, we saw looming ahead of us a huge mound, overgrown with docks and nettles, which had obviously been formed by the earth that came from the pond. As if this were not bad enough, the mound had been plastered over with angry little rocks made out of cement with pebbles stuck into them – the sort of thing one sees in the gardens of railway stations.

Worse was to come. As we threaded our way down a ruined path that led in the direction of the orchard, we constantly encountered evidences of previous occupation, and all these evidences were horrible. For instance, there suddenly loomed out of a clump of cow-parsley an awful sort of plaster dwarf; somebody had stuck him on to a block of cement that had been carved to imitate a log of wood; the effect was very painful indeed. Then we came to an unexpected clearing in which there were six small flower-beds; the centre one was shaped like a star and the others were shaped like crescents; they were filled with a very petulant variety of double pink begonia, and they were quite as nasty as it is possible to be. And there were odd flights of steps that seemed to lead to nowhere at all, except to shrubberies of speckled laurel and golden privet, neither of which is my favourite form of vegetation.

The orchard – as far as we could judge from a hasty tour of it – was in pretty good shape; there were some fine old Cox's Orange and some really magnificent pears. But even here I had forebodings, for the whole orchard was shadowed by towering ranks of giant elms which seemed, indeed, to have been planted round the whole estate. And if you have ever had to do with elms and their suckers, you will agree that they are one of the vilest curses that a gardener can inherit.

We wandered back through the long grass, and I must admit that I was beginning to feel somewhat disconsolate. One had tackled some big jobs in one's time, but nothing approaching this. However, I was not going to admit as much to Bob – not yet. For there was still a lot to see. Through a gap in the wall, behind a rambling old barn that had been converted into a garage, we caught a glimpse of yet another garden.

We stepped through the gap. . . .

§ VII

That was the moment when I first saw the lilies.

And that was the moment when, having seen them, I mentally signed the contract to buy the house. The acres of wilderness behind me were forgotten. The size of the house itself, the cost of repairing it, to say nothing of keeping it up – all these sordid details seemed to have no significance. I had to possess those lilies. Which may sound temperamental and tiresome but it happens to be true.

The lilies were of the variety known as Regale, and

they stood in rows of glistening white down the whole length of one side of the kitchen garden. A faint breeze was stirring, and as they nodded their heads there drifted towards us a most exquisite fragrance. Never before, in any garden of the world, have I seen such lilies; their loveliness was literally dazzling; the massed array of the white blossom was like sunlit snow. Nor was this shining, shimmering beauty merely the result of mass, for as I walked closer I saw that each individual blossom was a perfect specimen, with a stem that was often four feet high, bearing on its proud summit no less than a dozen blossoms.

I turned to Bob and grinned. I can't remember saying anything, and if I could, it would be unwise to repeat it. But I remember that he grinned back, and made a gesture which I had seen him make before on occasions when he had been deeply moved by something beautiful – when, for instance, Menuhin had just finished the slow movement of the Elgar violin concerto. It was only a shrug of the shoulders and a flick of the wrists but it meant . . . well, it just meant that there was nothing to say.

So we will assume a pause of some minutes while we recover our equilibrium. Having done so, I looked around me and saw that I was standing in a kitchen garden of exceptional neatness and fertility. It was the sort of kitchen garden one sees attached to Dutch houses, in which every pea is in its right place, and each individual Brussels sprout looks as if it had been personally shampooed. Against the old brick walls the peach trees had been trained by a master hand; each shoot was delicately tied with bass. (A well trained peach tree is as pretty as a piece of jewellery, I always think.)

In the corner were a couple of greenhouses, each of

them much bigger than any greenhouse I had ever owned. I was about to go over to them to see what was inside when the door of the larger greenhouse was opened, and out stepped an old man. He was wearing a floppy straw hat, and he was carrying a basket of vegetables. For a moment he paused, staring in our direction. Then he walked towards us, holding himself very erect and looking very stern.

I went to meet him.

'Good afternoon,' I said.

He halted, like a soldier.

'Good afternoon . . . sir.'

He stared at me with an expression of extraordinary disapproval. I felt like a recruit being ticked off by the sergeant-major. I felt like any common trespasser, confronted by the law. But I liked the old man, and I was very anxious that he should like me.

I managed a grin.

Reluctantly he touched his hat.

'I've been looking over the place,' I said.

'Yes, sir?'

'It's possible that I might be taking it.'

As I said these words a positive tattoo was rattled on Bob's golden chains. The very thought of such a folly was causing him to feel explosive. The rattle was so fierce and sudden that the old man blinked, but he said nothing.

'Are you the gardener here?'

'Yes, sir.'

'Been here long?'

A deep sigh. 'Nigh on forty years.'

I wondered what that sigh meant. The memory of happiness? Regret for times past?

'That's a wonderful lot of Regales you've got there.'

For the first time the old man seemed, ever so faintly, responsive.

'Aye,' he said. 'They're pretty good.'

'Have they been established for long?'

'Thirty years or so.'

'Where did you get the bulbs?'

'Boolbs?' A snort. '*Boolbs?* I didn't get boolbs. I grew 'em from a handful of seed.'

'Does that take long?'

'Three years. Of course, garden book says seven. But I don't allus hold wi' garden books.' He paused and glanced at the lilies. 'Mr. Stebbing couldn't abide 'em,' he observed. 'Wouldn't ever have 'em in t'house. Said they made him think of funerals.'

'He must have been a funny sort of person.'

The old man drew himself up and looked at me very straight. For the first time I noticed that he had only one good eye. 'Mr. Stebbing was a gentleman' – a slight emphasis on the 'gentleman' – 'as knew his own mind.'

And so, my friend, I thought, do you.

'Was he here for long?'

'Thirty years.'

'And before that?'

'Before that there was Doovz.'

I write the name as he pronounced it, in his soft, gentle Lancashire accent. I have not much talent for writing dialect, so the reader must try to fill in his own phonetics. The word Doovz baffled me. It sounded Russian.

'Was he a foreigner?' I asked.

'Doovz? Foreigners?' The old man snorted. 'Mr. and Mrs. Doove were as Lancashire as they make 'em. 'Twas they who liked the lilies.'

'Well, I certainly like them myself. You'd have to pay a pretty price for those in London.'

'Aye.'

The old man made no other comment. I was longing for him to ask me if I would care for a bunch, but he made no offer to do so. I was glad he didn't. It was a sign that he put the care of other people's property above the chance of earning a tip.

A warning rattle of chains came from Bob in the background. The conversation was beginning to bore him.

'Well,' I said, 'I must be going. I'll let you know if anything happens. By the way, what is your name?'

'Oldfield, sir.'

'Perhaps we may be working together before long.'

Again he made no comment. But when I held out my hand, he shook it like a man.

§ VIII

As soon as we got back into the car to go home, Bob exploded.

'It's sheer stark raving lunacy,' he declared.

'What is?'

'The whole idea.'

'You don't like the place?'

'*Like* it? Of course I like it. I also like Blenheim. I

also like the Chateau de la Garoupe. And the Villa Borghese is quite charming. But I should find them rather a tax on my resources.'

'I don't think it would be as bad as all that.'

'It would be worse. Look at the garden alone. It needs bulldozing. It needs ploughing up. It needs an *army* . . . even to get it into any sort of shape. And after you've done that, it needs another army to keep it going.'

'I think you exaggerate.'

'My dear fellow, you don't know – you just don't *know*. You haven't *had* a garden since the war; things are different.'

'Surely not so different as all that? You can still buy packets of seeds. The sun still shines and the rain still falls.'

'I'm not talking about the elements; I'm talking about gardeners. How many gardeners did I have at Hill Farm?' (Hill Farm had been Bob's extremely luxurious little place in Kent.)

'I don't know, Bob.'

'I had six. Yes – *six*. And what did I get out of them? Misery and incompetence and robbery and frustration. A few sticks of rancid seakale. A bundle or two of rhubarb that had to be *sawn* before one could bite it. Rows and rows of broad beans that one was never allowed to eat before they were the size of *cricket* balls . . .'

'You used to have some lovely flowers.'

'Flowers! Really . . . *flowers*! All stuck in from pots at *fabulous* expense. Brought down in lorries from Covent Garden. Even if I wanted a row of polyanthus the plants had to be bought and *drenched* in liquid manure and if

I didn't have an armed *guard* over them all night the entire lot would be eaten by rabbits.'

'But Bob . . .'

'The lawns alone,' he continued, with mounting passion, 'were enough to drive one mental. *Quarryfuls* of sand. *Reservoirs* of water. Bags and bags of "selective" weed-killer that completely destroyed all the grass and made the plantains grow the size of *hollyhocks*. It would have been infinitely cheaper, but *infinitely*, to have carpeted the entire area with Bokhara. You just don't *know*.'

'But Bob . . .'

'I tell you, you don't *know*. Everything's different. Utterly different. When you had *your* garden it was just a little cottage, and the world was comparatively sane, and there were still young men walking about the country who would do a day's work and didn't expect to be massaged and positively *fanned* before they'd consent to pluck up a very small piece of groundsel at five pounds an hour . . .'

But Bob . . .'

'And now, you propose to buy a practically derelict mansion in the middle of acres and acres of chaos . . . it's too much. I can't bear it. Let's change the subject.'

But of course, we didn't. We went on and on, all the way to London. And it was not till we were crossing Putney Bridge that we came to any conclusion.

'Well,' said Bob with an elaborate shrug, 'have it your own way. You can't say I haven't warned you. However, I don't think you *will* take the place, for one very simple reason.'

'What's that?'

'Gaskin.'

(Gaskin, in case the reader is not acquainted with this celebrated person, is the factotum who has looked after my interests and indulged my follies ever since I came of age.)

'What's Gaskin got to do with it?'

'As soon as he sees the house he'll tell you it's totally impossible for one person to run it.'

'I wonder.'

'There's no wondering about it. After all, Gaskin's only *human*. I know he sometimes seems to have at least *six* pairs of hands, and he must have the constitution of a *herd* of oxen to do all he does, but there *are* limits. To try to keep that house even dusted would be a perpetual *steeplechase* . . .'

'It would be very good for his figure.'

'I bet you five pounds he'll say no.'

'Taken.'

'Fifty if you like.'

'Five's quite enough.'

So that was that.

We will snap this story to a close.

When I got home I told Gaskin about the house; I also told him about the wager. And I added, with serpentine cunning: 'By the way, Gaskin, if you do feel you can manage it I think you ought to have the fiver yourself.'

Gaskin went down on the following day, and he had not been in the house twenty minutes before he had fallen in love with it and worked out a complete schedule for running it single-handed.

When I rang up Bob to tell him this, I added, somewhat maliciously, that Gaskin was so far from being intimidated by the prospect of running the house that he was afraid that time might hang heavy on his hands. Could Bob suggest any suitable hobby with which he might fill in his idle hours? The answer, over the telephone, was the fiercest of gold rattlings. But the fiver arrived by return of post.

And I bought the house.

CHAPTER II

JUNGLE WARFARE

IT was not till I rang up the agents on the following day that I found out what the house was called.

'By the way,' I said to the nice girl on the telephone, 'there wasn't any name on the prospectus – just a plan. I suppose it has got a name?'

'Yes,' she replied. 'A very pretty one, too. Its name is Merry Hall.'

'Merry Hall! Is that really its name?'

'Certainly. Don't you like it?'

'I love it. But . . . but . . .' It was difficult to explain what I meant. 'Hall' sounded so very grand. It made one think of landed estates, and tenants touching their caps, and going out in dog-carts on frosty mornings to pour soup into elderly widows. It made one think of being a squire in gaiters, and I hadn't got any gaiters. It made one think of smoky inns and old men with clay pipes, muttering to themselves . . . 'They dew say as 'ow there dew be a new squoire up at 'All' – 'Aye, and some noice goings-on there'll be there, you mark moi word.'

What *had* one let oneself in for?

'Has it been called Merry Hall for long?' I asked the girl on the telephone.

'I think so – at any rate for nearly two hundred years. 'Merry' seems to be a local name. There's a 'Merry Lodge' on the outskirts of the village, and the wood at the back of the church was called 'Merry Wood' as far back as 1700.'

I thanked her and rang off. It was all rather alarming. However, the mere fact that one lived in a house called a 'Hall' did not necessarily mean that they would double one's income-tax. (Or did it? One could not be too sure in these days.) After all, as Mr. Squeers once observed to Nicholas Nickleby, a man could call his house an island, if he was so inclined. And it was nice to know that Merry Hall really *was* its proper name. To have invented it would have been rather pretentious.

I hurried out to find Gaskin, who was in the kitchen, giving 'One' a liver pill ('One', my Siamese cat, will shortly weave his way into these pages).

'Gaskin,' I said, 'do you know what the house is called?'

'No, sir?' (A deft flick and the pill was in and 'One' jumped down, looking outraged.) 'Merry Hall? Well! We *are* going up in the world!'

'Don't you like it?'

'It'll look nice on the notepaper,' said Gaskin, with disarming directness.

It is extraordinary how often Gaskin anticipates my own feelings. For I must confess that this was exactly what I had been thinking myself. As clearly as if it were already before me I could see the printed legend:

MERRY HALL

MEADOWSTREAM

We would have it done by Smythson's of Bond Street on their most expensive blue paper, and as soon as it arrived I would sit down and write letters to people whom I wanted to impress or to annoy. (Bob would certainly be one of the first recipients.) Perhaps one might ask Smythson's to print in the left-hand corner some of those charming little symbols of engines and telephones and letter-boxes which used to be fashionable on the stationery of some of the stately homes of England. On the other hand, perhaps not. People might think one had opened a tea-garden.

At any rate, I ordered the notepaper, there and then, long before I had signed the contract, or done any of the legal things one has to do when one buys houses. It was obviously a case of putting the cart before the horse . . . but then, putting carts before horses has always been one of my favourite occupations.

§ II

It is at this point that the book really begins. And it begins with a fire.

Or perhaps it doesn't. Perhaps it begins with the Urns.

Or perhaps it doesn't even begin with the Urns. Perhaps it begins with Miss Emily.

For the fire, and the Urns, and Miss Emily, are all mixed up in my memory in a sort of midsummer haze, and it is difficult to decide which came first. So let us try, very quickly, to sketch in the background of these exciting events.

We arrived in July – 'we' being, in order of importance, Gaskin, 'One' and 'Four' – (my two cats) – an ex-naval type whom we will call Cyril – (chosen for amiability and a capacity for lifting heavy weights) – and myself. There ensued some weeks of chaos.

When the van oozed up the lane, with a great deal of crashing of branches from the trees overhead, and when my furniture was taken out and distributed round the house, there was nothing to do but to sit down on a packing-case and laugh. For really, it was all too ridiculous. The whole lot could easily have been put into the billiards-room – which, as we have seen, was to be the music-room. True, we each had a bed, with a chair by the side of it, and there was a dining-room table with four more chairs, and there was my desk and immense quantities of books, and a few ornaments, but that was all.

(I need hardly say that during the whole of this period Bob was constantly on the telephone, making the gloomiest prognostications and asking the most embarrassing questions.

'But my dear Beverley, what about the drains?'

'They're superb drains.'

'How do you know? Have you had them examined?'

'Of course' (a lie).

'And what do they say?'

'Everybody's in raptures about them.'

A pause and a suspicious sniff. 'And what are you going to do about *furniture*?'

'We shall manage to squeeze it in somehow.'

Etc. etc. It always ended with Bob ringing off with a rattle of chains.)

But we must return to the fire, and the Urns, and Miss Emily.

The fire was the direct result of our frenzy to get things done in a hurry. As you may remember from our first glimpse of the house, Merry Hall was originally a charming Georgian 'shell' to which all sorts of horrors had been added. There was the square bow window, which we nicknamed 'The Wart'. There was also, on the south front, a weird sort of summer-house, *circa* 1900, which we nicknamed 'The Excrescence'. It had a roof of green [*sic*] tiles, and a lot of woodwork arranged in a frenzy of rusticity. We could not do anything about the Wart for the moment, because it would have meant knocking down half the house, and Mr. Young – the local builder and a most valued friend – went quite pale at the thought of all the licences and permits that would be needed.

But we could and did do something about the Excrescence. We did it with pickaxes and whoops of glee.

If you had happened to stroll down the lane, on any sunny afternoon during those first few weeks, and if you had chanced to stand on tiptoe and look over the old brick wall, you would have seen a remarkable assembly. You would have seen a number of young men in a minimum of clothing hurling themselves with a savage joy at the Excrescence, rending it apart and chucking it into wheelbarrows. You would also have seen a number of young women aiding and abetting, clutching great curling stems of ivy and lugging them across the lawn, brandishing hatchets and leaping into clumps of Portuguese laurel, and only pausing every five minutes to reinvigorate themselves with the necessary ration of lipstick.

You see, it was so impossible to get labour that one simply had to call in one's friends. And life being what it was and London being pretty dreary, they seemed only too anxious to help, particularly when one told them that their main function was to be destructive. 'Darling, you don't mean to say you want me to pull something *down*? And to root something *up*? Oh, I can't *wait* . . . how do I get there?'

So I told them how to get there, and since one of the main directives was the village inn, which bore the haunting name of the Leg of Mutton and Cauliflower, they often arrived in a state of some exhilaration.

At last we can come to the fire. This was how it happened.

It was about seven o'clock on a warm summer's evening. The day's work was done. The young males and females who had been crashing round the garden had departed in a series of battered old sports cars, leaving behind them a trail of havoc and destruction, to which they promised to return on the following day.

'I think they're open, don't you?' said Cyril. Which, in case you don't know, is the naval way of suggesting that it is time for a drink.

'I'm sure they are. Will you get it or shall I?'

'I will.'

'What d'you want?'

'Let's be very grand and open the bottle.'

It should be explained that 'the' bottle was our one and only bottle of champagne, which had been lurking in the background, on the point of explosion, for several months.

'O.K.'

He departed, very briskly. When the navy is on the track of champagne, the speed with which it moves is quite exceptional.

I sat down on the grass and stared around me. There was still a tremendous amount to be done, indeed, there was everything to be done. And as far as I could see, I should have to tackle it alone, for up till now I had made small progress with Oldfield.

Indeed, it was only a few days ago that I had learned,

for certain, that he was prepared to stay on in my service at all. He would 'see', he said, when I first broached the matter to him. With that I had to be content. I did not attempt to plead or argue; he was obviously of a fiercely independent nature, and any attempt to cajole him might have been fatal. When he told me that he would be glad to stay on, I could have embraced him, but I avoided any display of enthusiasm. All I said was that we must 'get together and have a long talk'.

But we did not get together, and we did not have a long talk, or even a short one. Oldfield remained locked, as it were, in the kitchen garden, apparently oblivious to what was going on outside. Not that he was idling; I had never met such a man for work; at this very moment, at a time when most gardeners would long ago have gone home to tea, I saw him in the distance, dipping his watering cans into the old rain-water tank, on his way to the tomato bed. (I had already learned that he rightly despised those who do their watering from the tap; the water must have fallen straight from the skies, and must, if possible, be of the same temperature as the air around it. All through the summer, along the wall under the peach trees, he used to set a dozen cans of rain-water every morning, to be used at nightfall.)

No, it was not that he was idle; indeed, I wished that he could be persuaded to take things more easily in this heat, for it was quite impossible for even such a hungry household as mine to devour the glistening piles of vegetables which he daily heaped upon the kitchen table. Gaskin was shelling peas, bottling tomatoes and salting beans till he was purple in the face; every meal was a vegetarian's banquet; as for the salads – never have I known such a profusion of rare and succulent herbs. They were like lucky dips, with always something fresh in them . . . little sprigs of tarragon, baby nasturtium leaves, layers of cold sliced aubergines, shredded fennel, tiny yellow tomatoes the size of grapes and as sweet as nuts. The ingredients for those salads were always arranged by Oldfield in a special basket, lined with leaves from the fig tree.

But though he worked like a black, he remained aloof. And . . . haunted. Yes, that was the word. He was haunted by Mr. Stebbing. Every topic of conversation, however remote, led back to the ghost of his former master.

Consider the pond. This was really the first big gardening job – if it can be called a gardening job – which I attempted. It was a priority number one, for as long as it existed it was impossible to open the windows of the music-room. One would march in, grimly determined, and stalk to the piano with one's fingers ready for an hour's mortal combat with one of Chopin's more devilish cadenzas, and then . . . one would gulp, and feel sick and pale, and hurry to the window to shut out the fearful effluvia that drifted up from it.

It had to be filled, and at first we tried to fill it ourselves, using for the purpose the speckled concrete stones with which Mr. Stebbing had adorned the mound, under the illusion that he was creating a rockery. But every time that we threw in a stone it was as though a devil shot up and wreathed towards us, breathing the sickly odours of the grave. So I told Gaskin to go into the village and get some odd men to do it.

'They'll need extra beer money for a job like that,' he

observed. They would indeed, I agreed. I could only hope that they did not catch some awful disease and send me lawyer's letters.

When I mentioned to Oldfield that the pond was being filled up, he said:

'Mr. Stebbing had that pond dug.'

'It seems rather a funny place for a pond, just outside the window of the largest room in the house.'

' 'Twas a fine pond. 'Twas a pond for dooks.'

Oldfield's accent is so soft and gentle that I really did think he meant that it was a pond for dukes. It seemed a curious playground for such exalted persons, so I waited eagerly for more.

'Then dooks was chased away by Pomeranians,' he continued.

I had a momentary vision of quantities of elderly gentlemen in coronets fleeing wildly across the lawn, clutching towels round their waists, pursued by the savage cries of a barbaric tribe. It was like a scene from *Iolanthe*. Then I realized what he meant. Ducks.

'Did Mr. Stebbing really have Pomeranians?' I inquired, with little sympathy, for I am not pro-Pomeranian.

'Fourteen of 'em. They was too much for dooks.'

Which I could well believe.

'Too much for begonias, too,' he chuckled. 'They just worried begonia bed to death.' That, I thought, was rather sensible of the Pomeranians. Begonias are not flowers, they are a state of mind, and a regrettable state into the bargain. 'But that wouldn't have mattered to Mr. Stebbing if one of 'em hadn't bitten him on t'chin. And seeing as he wore a beard . . .'

I could bear no more. Beards, begonias, Pomeranians . . . what could be less alluring? The beard was the last straw. For surely it must be universally admitted that beards, except on sailors, minor prophets and persons suffering from advanced erysipelas, are obscene.

This was the only sort of co-operation I was getting from Oldfield. It could hardly be called a partnership, as yet. But I still had hopes.

§ III

As usual, we have digressed. We must go back to the moment when at the end of a hot and tiring day, we were sitting on the grass surrounded by the ruins of the Excrescence, feeling rather low at the thought of all the labour ahead, of the months and maybe years that would be needed before we could get rid of all the horrors and start planning a real garden.

Consider that speckled holly hedge alone, which was looming over me at this very moment, shutting out the sunlight. It stretched all round the front of the house, roughly following the crescent of the charming little Georgian wall. It was huge, dark and ragged, and at least a third of it was dying. Its only merit was that it partially concealed an exceptionally sinister cast-iron railing.

'What *are* we to do about that eyesore?' I asked Cyril when he returned with the bottle of champagne.

'Get rid of it, of course.'

'It would take weeks. And I don't think Oldfield would be too pleased.'

'Why not?'

'Mr. Stebbing planted it. And he adored Mr. Stebbing.'

'So what?'

'One must consider these things. Oldfield's a marvellous gardener, but he's haunted by Mr. Stebbing. And we've already done heaps of things he must hate. After all, it was Mr. Stebbing who built the Wart. Mr. Stebbing also built the Excrescence. Mr. Stebbing also dug the pond and made the mound and bought that awful plaster dwarf that we found lurking in the nettles.'

'To hell with Mr. Stebbing. May he rot!'

'If you say that he'll probably come swishing out of the holly making rattling noises.'

'That's probably what he did in real life.'

'Anyway, I think we'll leave the hedge for the moment.'

'Here's to its downfall!'

We raised our glasses. Champagne invariably shoots to my head like a rocket, exploding in beautiful, singing stars. When I looked at the hedge, a few moments later, I noticed to my surprise that it had suddenly become at least a foot higher, and several shades darker.

'You know, I think we really *must* take that hedge down.'

'When?'

'Quite soon.'

Another sip. Simultaneously the hedge leapt up another foot and became so dark that it shadowed the whole house.

'In fact, now.'

We rose to our feet with great dignity, and floated, rather than walked, towards the tool shed. As we went, I found myself reflecting on the great importance, in moments like this, of a glass of champagne. Not a 'drink'. It is not a question of an alcoholic shot-in-the-arm; to depend on alcohol for inspiration is the surest way to madness. But a glass of champagne, for some mystic reason, is different; it is to wine what Shelley was to poetry; it gives wings to the spirit. And now, it was to give wings to us.

Armed with hatchets, we charged full tilt at the hedge, singing 'Heigh-ho the holly, this life's most jolly', to the admirable setting of Mr. Roger Quilter. But soon it ceased to be so jolly, for the old trunks were as hard as steel, and the branches seemed to be made of resilient rubber. After five minutes' chopping Cyril threw his hatchet to the ground.

'This damned thing'll take years,' he growled.

I felt inclined to agree, but continued to chop away.

'My hands are torn to ribbons,' he continued. 'If we go on like this we shall bleed to death. There's only one thing to do. Burn it.'

I was still sufficiently in control of my senses to realize the folly of this procedure.

'It would be madness,' I observed coldly. 'The flames would go as high as the roof.'

'So what? There isn't any wind. They wouldn't touch the house.'

'Even if they didn't the heat would be so terrific that all the windows would crack.'

'No, they wouldn't. Anyway, aren't you insured?'

'Not against arson.'

'This isn't arson. It's common sense.'

I took the last sip of my champagne. Maybe it was common sense. Maybe it was better than common sense, maybe it was inspired lunacy. Who cared? Heigh ho the holly! Life, again, was most jolly.

'All right. Let's start at this end.'

Cyril bent down, scooped up a pile of dead leaves, and struck a match. There was a splutter, a thread of smoke, and a thin flame crept into the hedge.

Then it happened. There was a sound like the crackle of fireworks, a swift uprush of light, and the whole hedge was ablaze. If it had been saturated in petrol it could not have caught more swiftly, more dramatically. We staggered back aghast; the house was lit in a garish light, the window-panes were painted a lurid red. The heat was appalling.

I have a confused memory of the next five minutes. I seem to recollect a frenzied rush across the lawn for buckets of water, and the agitated figure of Gaskin beating at the hedge with a broom; Cyril, in the meantime, was doing various naval things with grim efficiency and no effect. How could there be any effect? We were caught up in an inferno.

But ten minutes later the hedge had disappeared. Only two of the lower windows were cracked. The front door, doubtless, could be repainted for a fiver. Eventually the scarred lawn would be green again. Sooner or later . . . probably later . . . my blisters would heal.

Cyril – calm and naval to the last – leapt triumphantly on to the wall. He put his heel against one of the railings, which must have been nearly red-hot. He brought it crashing to the ground. I had a sudden vision of the wall, and the semi-circle, free of holly, denuded of its degrading cast-iron crown.

We went in to wash, and to apply such soothing

ointments as could be found. I had pains in the head, in the back, and over a large surface of my skin. But they did not seem to matter, because the aforesaid vision remained, and I knew that it would be only a matter of days before it was translated into reality.

CHAPTER III

MISS EMILY AND THE URNS

WHEN you buy an old house, you buy not only bricks and mortar, tiles and chimneys, trees and lawns; you also buy ghosts. Of this I am firmly convinced. You buy an ectoplasmic mass of loves and hates and ardours and regrets, lingering on from the past, and some of these influences are still so potent that you will gradually discover that the house has spots that are either happy or sad for no apparent reason, that there is a room which can never be serene even though the sunlight streams into it, and that, conversely, there is some little dark corridor, twisted and narrow, which is always permeated with an extraordinary sense of delight.

With the ghosts of the past one can deal, as I was learning to deal with Mr. Stebbing. It is the ghosts of the present who are more difficult – the previous owners who, though they have moved into some other part of the county, seem to imagine that their former tenancy gives them a right of interference; the middle-aged men and women who played on your lawns when they were children; and of course, the locals, who watch every move you make, and study every alteration with a profound misgiving and – one sometimes suspects – a secret hope that it will all go wrong.

With one of these ghosts I was now confronted.

§ II

From time to time, in my converse with Oldfield, I had heard mysterious references to a certain 'Miss Emily', who had frequently been a guest at Merry Hall in the past. Needless to say, she did not compete with Mr. Stebbing, who remained, and always would remain, the bright star in Oldfield's particular universe; nor could she be regarded as a rival to the Doves – (Doovz) – though she was once mentioned in connection with them. Oldfield had been talking of Doovz' arrival, and how the neighbours had called. 'And Miss Emily called too,' he observed, 'but she never came but once.'

'Why was that?' I asked.

'Well, she was an Honourable. So I reckon Doovz weren't oop enuff for 'er.'

From which I gathered that Miss Emily might perhaps have been something of a snob.

Otherwise she remained a shadowy figure. I learned that she had a soft spot for those large speckled calceolarias which always put me in mind of a tropical disease, that she was a glutton for King William pears, that she could not abide cats, and that she undertipped the servants. None of these qualities seemed to me to be endearing, and so whenever Oldfield mentioned her, I endeavoured to change the subject.

However, she was now to appear in the flesh.

It was a lovely morning in early September when Miss Emily first came into my life. I was lying back on the one and only sofa, watching 'One' and 'Four', who were prowling in and out of the packing cases, when Gaskin entered with a note. 'This was pushed through the letter-box,' he said. 'And if those cats don't keep away from those cases I shall have to Hoover the whole place for the third time.' With which, abruptly, he departed. Gaskin was evidently beginning to feel the strain.

I opened the note. This was what I read.

DEAR MR. NICHOLS,

I hope you will forgive a total stranger for writing to wish you a very warm welcome to 'Merry Hall'. Such a pretty name, I have always thought, and I have no doubt that *you* will make sure that it lives up to that name!

To me, the old house used to feel like a second home, for I often stayed there in the days of dear Mr. Stebbing – such a *gentleman*, of the real old school, and such perfect *taste*. And always so patient with poor Mrs. Stebbing, who was an invalid, as I expect you know (Heart). I often think that her illness really shortened his life, for she was able to do very little in the garden, and was exhausted after lifting heavy weights.

What a joy it will be for you to carry on Mr. Stebbing's tradition! And how fortunate you are to step into a house and garden where *no alterations* are necessary, particularly in these days when everything is so difficult! If you will allow me, I should so like to call, as soon as you are settled, and if there are any of

Mr. Stebbing's ideas which you would like to hear about, I shall be so happy to tell you of them.

And now I come to the real point of my letter. I am a vegetarian, with only a quite small garden, which is entirely given over to flowers. (One *must* have one's flowers – but I am sure I need not remind *you* of that!) This means that I am at the mercy of my local greengrocer, who is most exorbitant, and not always fresh. Might I therefore ask if we could come to a little arrangement? I happened to be passing Merry Hall the other day and ventured to peep through the hedge, and I noticed that the kitchen garden was *brimming* with the most wonderful vegetables (Dear Oldfield – I am so glad you are keeping him on). Might I be allowed to purchase some from you? It would be most convenient to me, and I dare hope that it might also be helpful to you. One cannot afford to neglect any source of income nowadays, can one?

I trust you will forgive me for writing so informally, but I am sure you will understand. Yours sincerely,

EMILY KAYE.

P.S. I am afraid that I should not be able to fetch the vegetables myself, so I hope it would not be too inconvenient to you to deliver them – preferably on Saturdays, between three and four? I took the liberty, when I was passing, of walking up the dear old drive, and I saw that you are running your car. Such a luxury, nowadays! My own, alas, is soon to be laid up, or I would not have troubled you with this request.

My first impulse on reading this letter was to tear it up. Long experience as a writer has taught me that this is the best procedure in ninety-nine cases out of a hundred. One receives sheaves of impossible requests and ridiculous criticisms, and if one attempts to answer them one is lost, and involved in all sorts of acrimonious exchanges.

But this letter was not quite so simple. A glance at the address – 'The Lilacs, Little Heatherington' – informed me that Miss Emily lived only a few miles away; for all I knew she might have some sort of power to annoy me if she were offended; besides, she might well be a valuable source of information about the history of the old house, and I was beginning to love it so much that I cherished every scrap of information I could gather about its past.

So I sat down and wrote my reply.

DEAR MISS KAYE,

Thank you so much for your kind letter. I should have been glad to help you, but . . .

Here I paused. But what? But I was not a greengrocer? But I was a hard-worked author who liked his Saturday afternoons? But I thought she had a damned cheek?

However, one did not wish to appear discourteous. For all I knew she might – in spite of Oldfield's remarks – be a nice old thing, living in the past, eating barrowloads of leeks and dreaming of Mr. Stebbing, for whom it was obvious that she had entertained a secret passion. So I continued . . .

. . . but I am afraid that I should not be able to undertake the delivery of any vegetables. Like all the rest of us, I have only a limited amount of petrol, and I have to conserve it for essential business. Yours sincerely,

BEVERLEY NICHOLS.

I read the letter through again. It seemed to meet the case. It was very short, but it was not actually rude.

And that, I thought, would finish the matter.

§ III

Now that I come to retell this story, I see how perfectly it fulfilled the requirements of the Unities, how it sped swiftly along its appointed groove towards an inevitable climax.

For the morning of the arrival of Miss Emily's letter was also the morning after the fire which destroyed the holly hedge; indeed, Miss Emily had probably been writing it at the very moment when Cyril and I had been making our unkind remarks about her beloved Mr. Stebbing.

It all fitted together – not that I realized it at the time. As soon as I had written my reply, I went out to survey the damage of the night before. As I stepped back into the lane to get a better view, I quickly forgot about Miss Emily and her vegetables and Mr. Stebbing and his horrors. It was evident that something very extraordinary and very delightful had happened. True, the whole entrance looked as though it had been blitzed, with the cracked windows, the blistered door, the broken railings, and the black line of charred holly stumps. But that did not matter. All that mattered was that the original design of the house had suddenly been revealed in the naked simplicity of its creators. What had previously been a dark, unholy mess was now seen as a simple curve of low brick wall, not one inch too high or too low or too short or too long, but drawn in a single masterly sweep that served as the essential foundation for the plan of the whole house. It was a perfect example of Georgian 'rightness'. Even as I stood there I could imagine how Mr. Stebbing must have hated it, how he must have gnashed his teeth with impatience, till he had erected his hideous cast-iron railings on top of it, and half-throttled it with the speckled holly.

I noticed something else. At each end of this lovely little wall there were two brick pillars. They stood there, perfectly poised, exactly the right height, exactly the right width. But in spite of their architectural rightness they were wrong, or rather, they were incomplete. They had obviously been built to hold something – carved pineapples, or stone balls, or . . . or . . . or Urns.

It was when the word Urns came into my head that the garden was born.

§ IV

Yes, the garden began with those Urns. They were destined to form the first splash of colour on a canvas that was hitherto blank. They were to have the honour of holding aloft the first flowers in a procession which, as I grew older, was to swell into a carnival of blossom.

They must be found at once, without a moment's delay. They would have to be Georgian, of course, and probably of lead, and it would be permissible for them to be rather ornate, with swags of grapes and heads of satyrs and all sorts of twinings and twistings in the details.

And they could be filled with flowers before the day

was out. One could almost certainly find some pots of trailing things in the market – geraniums, clematis and the like – and stick them in there and then. It might be 'cheating', but I did not care. If the worst came to the worst I could put buckets of water in them and fill them with huge bunches of cut flowers, and then go back to the house and hide behind a curtain and glare out to see the effect they had on anybody who might walk up the lane.

So I hurried out to the kitchen to tell Gaskin that I was going out to find some urns.

'Urns?' he said, with singular lack of enthusiasm. 'Whatever for?'

'For the pillars outside.'

He sniffed. 'There's a hundred and one things we want more than urns. We've hardly got two tea-cups left to match. There's only one coffee pot that isn't cracked. The Hoover's on its last legs. You ought to be putting first things first.'

I told Gaskin that I was very sorry, and made soothing suggestions about going up to Harrods for the day, and then I hurried out, got into the car, and drove off.

I was bound for Crowther's, which, as you will see in a moment, is one of the most alluring establishments in the whole of Britain.

As I trundled along, feeling about as happy as it is possible to feel, at the thought of the adventure ahead, I indulged in a little mental argument with Gaskin. 'First things first,' he had said, and no doubt most people would have agreed with him, particularly if they had seen Merry Hall. There were a thousand and one essentials clamouring for attention. There were walls falling down and cellars flooding and windows sticking, and there was a most peculiar smell in the woodshed. This latter, alone, was a 'first thing' of major importance.

But then, I have never believed in Gaskin's philosophy. Surely – in all matters appertaining to elegance – the most important thing to do first is the *last* thing? If one is learning a Chopin nocturne, for example, in which the melody glides smoothly along for three pages, and then, on the fourth page, suddenly falls in a shimmering cataract of cadenzas, it seems to me important to master these pianistic rapids before enjoying the calm waters that preceded them. Most people adopt the opposite course; they learn the easy first three pages, and play them over and over again till everybody in the house is sick to death of them, and then when they come to the cataract they plunge in head first and flounder about in a whirl of sharps and flats, after which they slam down the lid of the piano and stalk out of the house with a sullen expression, convinced that Chopin put in these things merely to be annoying (which is probably the case).

It is the same when you are furnishing a house. If you have only just enough money to buy a bed, a chair, a table and a soup-plate, you should buy none of these squalid objects; you should immediately pay the first instalment on a Steinway grand. Why? Because the aforesaid squalidities are essentials, and essentials have a peculiar way, somehow or other, of providing for themselves. 'Look after the pennies and the pounds will look after themselves' . . . that is the meanest, drabbest little axiom that ever poisoned the mind of youth. People who look after pennies deserve all they get. All they get is more pennies.

These profound but anti-social reflections were suddenly interrupted by a loud hiss and a sharp jerk of the steering wheel. I had a puncture. It seemed a rather cold comment on my philosophy, for if the first thing you have to do is to change a tyre . . . well, the first thing you have to do is to change a tyre, and that is all there is to it.

§ V

It was well on in the afternoon before I reached Syon Lodge, which is the home of Bert Crowther; however, the hour did not seem to matter, for this is a place where time stands still. When you visit it you are caught up in a dream.

It is a real place, lying on the outskirts of Isleworth, a mile or so over the bridge from Kew. (I think I ought to state that I have no sort of business connection with it, though I should very much like to have, and if Mr. Crowther ever reads this the least he can do is to send me a present of a faintly bloated cupid.) If you did not know about Crowther's, and were merely to walk past the high brick walls, you would think that here was a private house, inhabited by some person of great distinction and taste. But if you do know about it, you step through a little door in the wall, and. . . .

And you walk into the strangest garden in the world, or rather, a whole series of gardens, leading to leafy groves and shadowed lawns and trellised walks, crowded with the strangest collection of creatures that can ever have met together. Battalions of leaden cupids flock under the trees and sport on the old stone parapets; fauns and satyrs grimace from the undergrowth; round the ancient fountains a chorus of grey stone figures extend their arms and point their toes, gazing at the dancing water with eyes that see nothing and yet see everything, as they gazed, long ago, in the gardens from which they have been transported . . . the gardens of Versailles, of Rome, of Athens, and of many of the stately homes of England. There are scores of sundials, some of them thickly encrusted with moss, for whole decades have passed since the sun filtered through the mulberry branches to tell them the time of day; there are Palladian summer-houses, dusty and deserted; there are plinths and porticoes and balustrades and marble columns; and there is a whole Noah's Ark of animals, from elegant Chinese cockerels to plaster Victorian dogs, which, even in their mouldy dissolution, under the laurels, still manage to look respectable.

And there are urns. And urns. And still more urns. There are so many urns, in fact, urns of lead and marble and stucco and porphyry and terracotta, that one could walk off with a cartload of them without anybody being any the wiser. Indeed, that is one of the charms of Crowther's; nobody ever seems to be there. It takes ages before you find some young man in a shed who is reassembling an Adam mantelpiece and ask him the price of – say – an iron gate, and he never knows, and has to wander off to find our Mr. Smith, and then you spend a delightful hour waiting for our Mr. Smith who, at last, comes drifting along, and delivers a long and graceful exposition on Georgian ironwork, and finally, with the utmost reluctance, informs you of the sum for which the gate may be yours.

So I went to Crowther's, and walked through the groves and the alleys to the sunken garden where most of the urns were grouped together. For nearly half an hour I prowled about among them; it was like stepping through the pages of a fairy-tale, so quiet was the garden, so rich the influences of the past. At last I found the pair I wanted. They were lying on the grass in the shadow of one of the old mulberries; the fruit from the branches had fallen on them and around them so thickly that they were stained with the juice, and the lips of the maidens engraved on them glistened scarlet in the dying sunlight. They were delicately carved in lead, and on the sides of each urn four heads were embossed, two of youths and two of maidens. The faces of the maidens were placid and resigned, but the faces of the youths were scowling and passionate, maybe because they had been condemned by their creator to stare in front of them for all time, with never a chance to turn their heads to glance at their fair companions. Round the lips of the urns were clusters of grapes and at the base a frieze of acanthus leaves.

They had to be mine. Whatever they cost they had to be mine. Repairing the roof could wait; mending the cracks in the ceiling could wait; the peculiar smell in the woodshed could, and almost certainly would, wait. I had to have those urns. And after the customary search for our Mr. Smith, who seemed even vaguer and more distant than usual, a bargain was struck, the urns were reverently placed in the back of the car, and I drove off.

That, you might think, was the end of the adventure. In fact, it proved to be only the beginning.

§ VI

It was growing dark when I returned to Merry Hall, for I had to make a number of calls on the way. A harvest moon was rising behind the poplars, and there was a silvery mist of autumn over the fields. The old house looked lonely and deserted. So much the better. I should be able to put up the urns on their pillars, all by myself, and gloat over them in the moonlight, without being distracted by human company.

Putting them up proved rather more difficult than I had anticipated. The wall was shaky with age, the pillars were high, and the urns were extremely heavy. However, at last I managed it. As I stepped back into the lane to see them on their setting, I knew that they were right. They were not only right, they were inevitable. They 'belonged'. Although they had only been there for a few moments, they might have been there for ever. They had become part of the house and all its ancient elegance; they spoke the same language. I began, in imagination, to fill them with flowers, roses and lilies and dreamy sprays of honeysuckle. . . .

As I stood there, I heard a car coming up the lane. A moment later I was dazzled by a pair of powerful headlights. There was an impatient hooting. Damn! I had left the car in the middle of the road. I hurried over to move it out of the way. As I did so, the hooting stopped, the headlights dimmed, and the engine was switched off. From the inside of the car there came a feminine voice, on a gentle note of interrogation.

'Mr. Nichols?'

'Yes?'

'May I introduce myself? I am Emily Kaye.' As she

spoke, she opened the door and stepped out, extending her hand. 'Good evening.'

'Good evening.'

To say that I was embarrassed would be an understatement.

'I'm afraid my car is in your way,' I said.

'Please don't trouble. I can easily reverse and go round by another road.'

'But I insist.'

I hurried to my own car, thankful for a moment's respite.

During our not very sparkling dialogue I had been forming a swift impression of my companion. She was tall and very slim, and she carried herself very erect. In spite of her greying hair I guessed that she was in her late thirties; I also guessed that in spite of her appearance of frailty she had more than her share of wiry vigour. There was a steely glint in those heavy-lidded eyes, for all their wistful candour.

I drove my car close to the hedge and returned to Miss Emily.

'I wish I could ask you to come inside . . .' I began.

'Oh, but I wouldn't *dream* of it,' she interrupted. 'I know what it is, settling in. I expect you're still at sixes and sevens.'

'Yes, we are.'

'Things are *so* difficult to get nowadays, are they not?'

'They are indeed.'

I would not waste paper on reproducing these banalities were it nor for the fact that every word made me think of vegetables. 'Sixes and sevens' suggested six cauliflowers and seven beetroots. 'Difficult to get' made me think of sitting like a miser on a pile of leeks.

Apart from this, our conversation had another subtle interest, if you could only have been standing by our side. For as we murmured our platitudes – ('People don't really *want* to work nowadays, do they?' . . . 'Such *shoddy* materials, not at all like they used to be.') – all the time that we intoned these well-worn phrases, Miss Emily was very evidently 'putting on an act'. This act was expressed in a series of flinches.

Let me explain. Miss Emily would say something like – 'so sad that so many of our old houses are falling into the wrong hands' – and then she would glance at the house, and flinch. Having flinched, she immediately recollected herself, and assumed a brave smile. Then she looked at the house again, and flinched once more. Another brave smile. Another flinch. And so on.

I knew quite well why she was doing it. She was Flinching, with a capital 'F', because the house no longer belonged to dear Mr. Stebbing, and she wished to let me know, beyond any shadow of doubt, that her heart was broken. And she was Smiling, with a capital 'S', because she also wished to let me know that in spite of everything she was Bearing Up. The sweet holly hedge might be burnt to bits, the beautiful cast iron railings might be tumbled into the dust, sacrilege and desecration might be all around her, but she would rise above it. And who could tell whether, by her delicate feminine influence (coupled with the matchless taste of the late Mr. Stebbing, gently trickling down from the clouds) she might not convince me of the error of my ways, and lead me back into the paths of light – bearing with me, perhaps, a large basket of purple sprouting broccoli as a peace-offering?

So, at least, I analysed the situation. And since it was

all rather difficult, and since these emotional undercurrents were beginning to get me down, I changed the subject under discussion, and said, somewhat abruptly:

'I've just bought some Urns.'

'Urns!' Miss Kaye repeated the word in the gloomiest of tones, which seemed to carry the echo of a funeral cortège.

'Yes. Urns.'

'Urns?'

This was lunacy, I thought. 'Urns' is one of those words which, if repeated over and over again, ceases to exist. It becomes a sort of mad braying in space. Urns. Urns. Urns. Urns. Urns.

'I thought they would look pretty up there,' I said.

Miss Kaye, with the utmost reluctance, raised her heavy lids. And when her gaze lighted on the Urns she did a prize Flinch.

'Don't you like them?'

'I'm sure they're charming.' And now came the Brave Smile. 'I was only thinking of the boys,' she said.

'Which boys?'

'The Meadowstream boys. I'm afraid they may find them very tempting.'

'But if they're fastened with cement . . .'

'Oh, I didn't mean that they'd *steal* them; I meant that they'd use them as *targets*.'

'I hardly think . . .'

'Oh, but I assure you Mr. Nichols. You've no *idea* what the Meadowstream boys are like. None. They're not like ordinary boys at all. Not in the least. They're not *human*.'

She looked furtively over her shoulder into the coppice,

as though she expected to see some of these strange creatures lurking in the shadows.

'For instance,' she whispered, stepping very close to me as though she were imparting some deadly secret, 'look what they did to Mr. Stebbing's statue of Snow White!'

'Did he really have a statue of Snow White?' I asked. It seemed too good to be true.

'Indeed he did. He bought it after seeing the film. Most artistic it was, just like life, in white plaster. He had the sweet little thing set up on this wall, facing the lane, and people used to say she looked so natural that she quite gave them the creeps. And of course, he had intended to buy the seven dwarfs too, but after what happened to Snow White, he stopped at Grumpy.' (That must have been the plaster horror we found lurking in the nettle bed.)

'What did happen to Snow White?' I demanded.

I was never to know the answer. For at that moment Miss Emily gave a stifled scream and stepped back into the hedge.

'Oh dear!' she gasped. 'A cat!'

I looked round and saw that 'One' had jumped on to the wall.

'Yours?' She spoke as sharply as if 'One' had been an illegitimate baby.

'Very much mine.' I spoke somewhat sharply too, for I was beginning to resent her tone. 'He's supposed to be rather beautiful.' And indeed, 'One' did look very beautiful sitting there, gazing at her, with his blue eyes turning to green in the moonlight.

'Please don't think me foolish,' said Miss Emily, edging towards her car.

'He won't hurt you.'

'Mr. Stebbing was just the same. He always said . . .'

What Mr. Stebbing always said must remain for ever a mystery. For at that precise moment 'One' chose to indulge in one of his tragic wails. It is a way of Siamese cats. They may be sitting quite placidly, in the sunlight or the moonlight, making no complaints, offering no comments, and suddenly, for no apparent reason, they will lift their heads and from deep inside them will sound this strange, primitive lament . . . a cry that seems to echo back into the jungle, in the dawn of time. What it means, no man can guess, though I always think it sounds like a bitter criticism of the futility of all things created. We shall never know, for the thoughts of cats, like the thoughts of youth, are long, long thoughts which will never be interpreted on this side of the veil.

The effect on Miss Emily was electric. With three swift bounds she reached her car, leapt into it and slammed the door. As though 'a dreadful fiend did close behind her tread' she pressed the accelerator, shouted some phrase which I could not catch, and shot forward into the darkness of the lane.

So that was that. It was all very difficult and confusing and I could not imagine where it was all going to end. However, it was too late to worry about it tonight; besides, there were still several angles from which I had not seen the urns.

I walked back through the rough grass of the lawn for about ten paces, turned round, and saw to my delight that one of the urns had silhouetted itself against the harvest moon. It was the prettiest thing you ever saw, jet black against that great golden disc, and to make it even prettier there were the giant poplars in the field beyond, still and silver. Flowers in such a setting on such a night would take on a quality of magic.

Meanwhile, the urns were empty.

But no, they were not.

Out of one of them, very slowly, there rose a head. On top of the head was a pair of ears, standing up very straight, and out of the head sprouted a pair of whiskers, clear-cut against the moon. It was 'One' who had obligingly volunteered to climb into the urns and inspect them, and see if they were all right.

He turned, and once again the hush of the night was broken by the strange, seagull wail of the Siamese. Some people might have heard it as a lament; I knew that it was a cry of joy. The urns were all right.

CHAPTER IV

FALL OF THE ELMS

THE urns, as we have already observed, were really the beginning of the garden at Merry Hall; they were the first signs of order and elegance in the surrounding chaos; and as our story unfolds, and the years roll by, I hope that you will come to love them, and all the experiments we have made with them.

I think that they are at their loveliest on a summer evening, when the clematis Jackmanii – (which may be 'common' but is also ravishingly beautiful) – swirls up the pillars in a dark flurry of purple blossom to mingle with the Victorian pink of the 'apple-blossom' geraniums with which they are filled. It is an enchanting marriage of colour, a sort of floral love-affair; and if you walk down the lane so that you see this exquisite duel against the sombre background of the copper beech, you will feel that life is very much worth living, and that you really had a very bright idea when you decided to be born.

Or on a sharp March morning under the cold skies, when they are filled with tall white hyacinths. The best place to see them, then, is from the upper lawn. They look very formal and clear-cut and severe, and the white of the blossom shines like snow against the grey of the ploughed fields on the other side of the hedge.

Or in late September, when we do all sorts of cunning things with pots of grape vines, which twirl around and give the effect of Bacchanalian orgies, and put ideas into people's heads.

I need hardly say that there have been failures. There have been times when the urns have looked like the hats of angry old women at matinees. There have been other times when they have looked as though they had come straight from the crematorium at Golders Green, after the funeral of a very prosperous banker. There have even been times when they have looked cold and forlorn and empty and undecided. But those times have been very much in the minority. As a general rule they have been magic chalices, waiting for the gardener to come and weave his spells.

And it was through the urns that I first came to know Oldfield, and to realize what a remarkable old gentleman he was.

§ II

It was a curious situation.

A huge house, echoing to the battering rams of the builders and decorators. A huge flower garden – at least, five acres was quite enough for *me* – most of it knee-high in couch grass and nettles. And behind the old outbuildings, a spotless, immaculate kitchen garden, crammed with vegetables, tended by a hostile old man whom I hardly knew.

Hostile, did I say?

No . . . that is unfair. He was not hostile so much as suspicious. Oldfield had had a hard life. He had worked, as few men have worked, through his seventy years of life, for a wage which was ludicrously small, considering his capacities. When I knew him better I was to realize that there was no position in the world of gardening which he could not have filled. He ought to have been head man on some great estate, with a dozen men under him. There was absolutely nothing about gardening that he did not know; nor was it just a question of 'green fingers' or the knowledge that comes from experience; he kept himself up to the mark by an avid perusal of gardening literature, which he studied every night with his one good eye; whenever there was a good gardening talk on the wireless he would tune in to it, listening and making notes; and on the rare occasions when he took a holiday – (for his first three years in my service he refused to leave the garden even for a single afternoon) – it was of the busman's variety, and off he went to Kew, or Wisley, or the Royal Horticultural Society, whence he would return as from some great adventure, with his eye twinkling, and all sorts of stories about the marvels that he had seen.

One of the most remarkable things about him was the extraordinary delicacy of his fingers. I first realized this when I brought back a tangled old plant of the white scented jasmine, which I had rescued from the derelict greenhouse of a friend. Some of its trailers were at least twenty feet long, and when I gave it to Oldfield – it was late in the afternoon – I said to him that I was afraid there was nothing much he could do with it except cut it down and re-pot it and hope for the best.

His only comment was a sniff. But on the following morning when I went out to the greenhouse, there was the jasmine, with every tendril unloosed and retrained against the wall, looped against the wires by a multitude of tiny knots of bass. It reminded me of the finest sort of needlework.

''Tis a good jasmine, that,' said Oldfield. 'Man on wireless t'other day, he reckoned t'was finest smelling jasmine on market.'

'I think jasmine's almost my favourite scent.'

Oldfield gave one of his rare grins. 'There's one as wouldn't have agreed with you.'

'Who was that?'

'Francis Bacon.'

I was rather startled by this sudden reference to the classics.

'Francis Bacon, 'e reckoned that finest smell in t'world was smell of t'vine.'

'What – the smell of grapes?'

'No. He didn't reckon nothing of smell of t'grapes. 'Twas *flower* of vine he went by. That's the most beautiful smell you'll get up your nostrils this side of t'grave, that's what Francis Bacon used to say. And I'm not so sure as he wasn't right.'

Nor am I. For I remembered Oldfield's bit of Bacon, and a couple of years later, when I had planted a vine myself, and when it was beginning to flower, I went out to smell the tiny clusters of green blossom. Sure enough, it was ambrosia. Take the scent of a sunlit nectarine, add a pinch of lemon verbena, sweeten with a drop of the essence of a tuberose . . . and you have a faint idea of the fragrance of the flower of the vine.

There was more than a touch of poetry about the old man too, as you may have gathered. I remembered that when I bought some cineraria seed, and asked him if he would let me have an old box to sow it in, he gently but firmly took the packet from me. 'Better leave it to me,' he said. 'They're tricky things, cinerarias. When the little 'uns coom oop, they like morning dew on 'em. That's a wonderful thing, the dew. I reckon there's a power in dew. It's gentle like, but there's a power in it.'

I had never thought of it like that before. Dew is gentle, yes. A silver veil, laid on the lawns in the morning. But as Oldfield said, there was a power in it. And one of my happiest memories of him will always be the recollection of him bending over the various boxes of seedlings that he used to keep in the shadow of the old brick wall, away from the morning sun . . . lifting them up, and holding them close to him, and smiling at them . . . when he did not know that anybody was looking.

§ III

All this, however, was a long way ahead. I was still far from winning the old man's confidence, and until I did so I knew that I would never achieve my first ambition, which was to lure him out of the kitchen garden. That kitchen garden began to get on my nerves. There were battalions of leeks and cauliflowers and sprouts, and enough lettuces to supply a rabbit warren, and so many sorts of kale that it made one dizzy; there were no less than three large asparagus beds, and the most beautifully tended peaches on the walls, and espalier pears and plums; and raspberries and currants, and a herb garden; it was really enough to keep one awake at night.

'It's daft, all that stuff' said Gaskin. 'You ought to sell some of it.'

'You know perfectly well, Gaskin, that whenever we have tried to sell anything it has been fatal.'

It had. So he said no more.

'The only thing I can think of,' I added, 'is gradually to start planting flowers in the middle of the cabbages. Then he'll *have* to do something about it.'

(In actual fact, I did eventually resort to this subterfuge, appropriating a large rhubarb bed and turning it over to roses.)

It was all very difficult. Here was a gardening genius, and all I was getting was barrowloads of leeks, when what I really wanted was bunches of lilies. Nor was my task made any easier by the fact that I was perpetually haunted by the ghosts of Doovz and Mr. Stebbing. If it was not the one it was the other. Whenever I thought I had at last gained the old man's attention, whenever I was on the point of commanding his interest on some specific point, up would pop Doovz or Mr. Stebbing from the shades, jogging his memory, plucking at his sleeve, and dragging him off on irrelevant excursions into the past.

For instance, the main greenhouse was cluttered up with half a dozen giant plants of datura, which is a flower that leaves me less than cold. Even in its native habitat in the Mediterranean, where it can grow to its full height and send out a riot of white blossom, it always reminds me of a clump of laurels on which somebody has hung the weekly washing.

'Do you think we want all these daturas?' I asked him one morning.

A deep sigh. 'That's not for me to say.'

'I don't really care for them much, do you?'

He shook his head. 'No. Nor for all the white fly that's on 'em. I never see a plant like 'em, not for white fly.'

'Then don't you think we might get rid of them?'

At precisely this moment the door swung open, there was a chill draught, and in drifted the ghost of Mr. Stebbing. He *must* have been there, for Oldfield suddenly turned round and stared behind him, and when he spoke again it was in a quite different voice, as though somebody were dictating to him.

'Mr. Stebbing,' he said, 'set a great store on them daturas.'

The ghost nodded.

'There's nobody in Surrey, he used to say, with daturas like us.'

'But Mr. Stebbing . . .' I began, intending to say that Mr. Stebbing was dead. However, I did not say it because Mr. Stebbing was obviously not dead at all; the whole place radiated with his spectral presence. So I changed it to . . . 'Mr. Stebbing can't have liked the white fly.'

'There wasn't no white fly, not in Mr. Stebbing's days,' retorted Oldfield.

Whereupon the ghost chuckled, and rubbed its hands.

It was the same with the geraniums in the little conservatory. This conservatory, as you may remember, connected the music-room with the main body of the house, and since it was under Oldfield's personal charge, it was another centre of order and discipline in the general shambles.

Never had I seen such geraniums as Oldfield grew – (and still grows) – in that conservatory. There were four tightly packed shelves of them; many of them had stalks eighteen inches long; and they were almost as floriferous in the depths of winter as in the summer. Indeed, they are perhaps at their most sensational when there is snow on the glass roof, and you see them all hot and fiery with blossom against the icy white.

Well, I love geraniums, and anybody who does not love geraniums must obviously be a depraved and loathsome person. But I like my geraniums to fight, to clash in eternal contests of colour, to wage their petalled arguments in perpetual debate, and in order that they should do so there must be every sort of red, scarlet against magenta, cherry versus brick, crimson anti puce, etc.

Oldfield disagreed. Or rather, Doovz disagreed. The ghosts of Doovz, that is to say.

'Doovz couldn't abide scarlet,' said Oldfield, when I handed him an exceptionally outspoken red geranium which I picked up in the market. 'At least, Mrs. Doove couldn't abide it. She said it clashed.'

'I hope it does,' I replied, rather sharply. The idea of doing anything other than clash with Doovz would have been most distasteful.

'She liked pinks and salmons and blue lobelias with 'em.'

This did not surprise me at all. If Mrs. Dove had at that moment appeared in a pink and salmon nightdress, with a fringe of blue lobelias round the hem, it would have seemed just right.

'What did Mr. Dove say?'

'Mr. Doove didn't care overmuch, one way or t'other. He was all for a quiet life, was Mr. Doove. He always spoke soft, and walked soft; and he liked sitting in t'shadow.'

I could almost hear him cooing.

'And what do you think about it yourself?'

For answer he picked up the scarlet geranium and held it just where it was obviously longing to be put, against a plant of brilliant magenta. Instantly the two flowers flamed and fought; it was most exhilarating.

'I like it,' said the old man. ''Tis clear and fresh.' Then he glanced over his shoulder, as though he had heard somebody coming, and quickly put back the pot on the shelf. 'But 'tis not for me to say.'

Perhaps he had indeed heard something – the swish of a pink and salmon nightdress, or the stumbling steps of a wandering soul.

All the same, this was another little battle that I won from the ghosts. For as soon as he was able, Oldfield took cuttings of the scarlet geranium, and now they burn brightly in the red bonfire of blossom which flames in perpetual defiance of Doovz, and all the other things that go bump in the night.

§ IV

But it was still all a question of bits and pieces; the year was speeding by, the dark days were drawing near, and the garden was still much as it was when I arrived. A summary of our progress would have read like this:

Pond. Filled up, but replaced by a quagmire, from out of which there protruded a host of the speckled concrete rocks that we had thrown into it from the mound. They gave an effect of the heads of marine monsters with pebbly eyes, pushing their way out of the depths.

Lawns. Mostly still knee-deep in grass and nettles. Here and there, round a smothered border, we had cleared a space, and it was exciting to be able to go out and gather great clumps of Michaelmas daisies, and Japanese anemones, of whose very existence one had been unaware. But no sooner was a bed cleared than it began to fill up again.

Orchard. Untouched. The ground was littered with apples and pears and plums that nobody had any time to pick up. Nobody, that is to say, but Oldfield. For one morning, bright and early, I looked out and saw him staggering up to the orchard with a ladder. And there, for three days, he remained, flitting from branch to branch like a strange, ancient bird, gripping the sweetest, highest fruits with a home-made hook of wire, dropping them gently into an old sack that was hung round his neck, and then clambering down the ladder with astonishing speed to empty the fruit into a barrow, which he trundled off to the fruit room at the back of the tool shed. Not a bad performance for a man of seventy, with only one eye.

Field. Untouched.

Coppice. Untouched.

We will not continue the gloomy catalogue – though gloomy is not perhaps quite the right word. When I surveyed the apparently hopeless prospect, I had the same sort of feeling, in a minor way, that most of us had in Britain in 1940. The enemies, it seemed, were invincible, in the lowering clouds there was no rift of light, but we were not gloomy; rather were we excited, and eager to know what would happen next. We were in the mood which was expressed, on another occasion, in the immortal phrases of Queen Victoria during the Boer War. 'Please understand that there is no one depressed in this house. We are not interested in the possibilities of defeat; they do not exist.' Least depressed of all were 'One' and 'Four', who had a penchant for jungles, and did not always approve of my effort to clear them.

But cleared they must be.

And that brings us to the elms.

The battle of the elms was the first major engagement in the garden at Merry Hall; it was the sign that the 'phoney' war was at an end and that the gloves were off. They were giant trees that stretched right round the estate, even round the orchard, blocking out the light, robbing the soil of virtue and – worst of all – sending their suckers far and wide. Those suckers were so powerful and so predatory that they even wormed their way under the drive, burrowed through the wall into the kitchen garden, and reappeared in such unlikely places as the cucumber frames.

The battle of the elms was also my first direct challenge to the ghosts, for it need hardly be said that the elm had been Mr. Stebbing's favourite tree, and it was he who had planted them, nearly forty years ago. For this alone, he should have been cursed, and so should anybody else who ever plants an elm. They are useless, hulking brutes of trees, and as soon as Constable had finished painting them they should have been rooted out of the British Isles. It is true that their wood is still used for making wheelbarrows; otherwise its one function is to provide material for coffins. Sometimes they do this in more senses than one, for the elm is a deadly dangerous tree, which will come crashing down when you least expect it – maybe on the stillest night in summer – causing havoc and destruction and sometimes death.

So the assault on the elms began, and one fine October morning I went out to greet a little gang of foresters who arrived with an imposing array of tackle. Like all the best foresters, they looked rather like trees themselves, with long, branch-like arms and knotty trunks and flecks of green in their eyes. They were among the happiest and most natural human beings I ever knew, and to talk to them and to climb about the branches with them was to forget all the roars of the war-mongers and the cackle of the theorists, and to feel that men were, after all, noble and rational creatures, like monkeys.

There was only one mistake which I made in this matter. I omitted to tell Oldfield. It was a tactical error of the first magnitude for – as I was now to discover – if Oldfield was not informed about anything, if he was not consulted about it in advance, it did not exist for him. He made himself completely unaware of it. For him . . . it Was Not.

§ V

So the foresters arrived, and the keen, still Autumn air echoed to the sound of hatchets and saws and grinding ropes and falling branches, and the groaning of cables and the shouts of men swaying perilously against the clouds. It was quite impossible to concentrate on one's work while this was going on. During all this battle of the elms I was engaged in another battle, with a certain Member of Parliament called Mr. Gallacher, who was in those days Britain's leading Communist. I was writing a long dialogue between us, based on interviews I had had with him at the offices of the *Daily Worker*, and whenever I thought I had pinned him down to a heresy, and had my finger poised on the appropriate passage from Marx or Engels, there would be a crash from the garden and out I would have to run and see all the latest excitement, and climb over the recumbent giant, and rejoice at the light that had flooded in, and gloat over the thought of all the logs we should have for years to come. And when I got in again, Marx and Engels seemed even stuffier and more sullen than they had seemed before, which is saying a great deal. As a result, the dialogue was somewhat disjointed, though it did have the desired effect, when it was published, of raising the blood-pressure of the *Daily Worker's* editor to unaccustomed heights.

In the midst of all this uproar and confusion, Oldfield went his way, sternly and deliberately unaware that anything was happening at all – he, who in all other respects was so keen-eyed that you could hardly touch a Brussels sprout without his knowing that you had done so. He moved in a strange and uncanny aura of solitude.

If, in his passage across the lawn he had to pass a group of half a dozen large hairy men, gazing up into the branches of the elms, they were invisible to him. If they called out a greeting, he did not hear it. If, as the days went by, the drive was churned up by lorries, and the old barn of a garage was littered with more and more tackle, these things passed him by. They Were Not.

I had hoped that when the actual felling began, when the trees came crashing down and the lawns were trembling under their impact, he would relax, and admit that, at least, there might be some form of minor horticultural activity in his immediate entourage. After all, he *was* concerned. When a tree is felled, there are a number of valuable by-products to be picked up. For example, there are pea-sticks, and Oldfield was a great one for pea-sticks; he could never have enough of them. Again, there is wood ash from the bonfires of all the branches, and Oldfield had often sung the praises of wood-ash as a fertilizer. (I really needed no reminder, for I have always loved spreading wood-ash round young plants; there is a strange poetry in this silvery powder – in the thought that it still has a virtue and a potency.) And of course, there are logs . . . in this case there would be cartloads and cartloads of logs, of which I should be only too delighted that he took his share.

But no. Nobody had told him that the trees were to be cut down. Therefore they were *not* being cut down. It was all an illusion. 'Error', as Mrs. Eddy would have said. The trees were not falling; they were standing erect. The men were not climbing up them; there were no men. Men? They were ghosts . . . figments of the imagination.

It was impossible to tempt him into even the remotest reference to the (literally) earth-shaking events by which he was surrounded. On the evening of the first day, when the men had gone, leaving behind them a chaos of knotted trunks and leafy branches, I lay in wait for him as he left the kitchen garden and crossed the lawn for his tea. As he approached the house I hurried out to meet him, taking up a position by the side of a giant elm which barred his path. Surely he could not ignore *that*?

'Good evening, Oldfield.'

'Good evening, sir.' He touched his cap and waited, looking *through* the tree with such utter unawareness that if it had been human it would have slunk away and hidden its head in shame.

'Quite a day it's been,' I said, with a gesture towards the fallen leviathan. 'But I'm afraid it'll be worse tomorrow.'

Oldfield innocently raised his head and surveyed the sky. 'Wireless says there'll be rain. We could do with it.'

'I didn't mean the weather. I meant the trees.'

At the word 'trees', deafness assailed him. 'Yes,' he repeated. 'We could do with it. I never see it so dry by the celery.'

I tried another tack. I pointed to a deep rut which the van had made in the grass.

'It'll be a business getting these lawns back into shape,' I said.

'The lawns never has been right,' he retorted, still addressing the heavens, 'not for nigh on twenty years. Now if you could have seen 'em when Mr. Stebbing was here . . .' Forthwith he swung into his favourite theme; by sheer force of personality he evoked the ghost of his former master, and for five minutes I had to stand there, shifting impatiently from one foot to the other while he extolled the genius of Mr. Stebbing in all matters concerning lawns . . . how, under his patronage, they had been far greener, smoother and more luxuriant than in any other establishment. By the time he had finished he had made me feel, not for the first time, that there must have been a quality of magic even in the print of Mr. Stebbing's ghostly feet.

When he touched his cap to say good night there was a twinkle in his one good eye. The trees had not been mentioned. And I knew they never would be mentioned, not even if one were to fall on him.

§ VI

The climax of this remarkable performance came on the last day, which had been set aside for an assault on the largest tree of all, an immense elm that towered over the garage. It might easily smash the roof if it were not felled with the greatest skill. A high wind had risen during the night, and the little crew of foresters were not too happy about their job. They stood about, muttering among themselves, gazing up into the roaring branches; from time to time one of them would scramble half way up the trunk to tighten a joint or fix an extra rope; the lawn was littered with chains and blocks and saws and hatchets; and to give an extra touch of drama to the whole affair a group of villagers had gathered in the lane, and were standing on tiptoe, peering over the wall, prophesying all manner of disaster.

Surely Oldfield would finally be obliged to admit that *something* was going on? For now the battle of the trees had moved to the very heart of his territory. The old barn of a garage, which was itself in danger, was separated from his greenhouses by only a brick wall; all his cuttings – cinerarias, hydrangeas, plumbagos and the like – were neatly arranged in the shadow of this wall, under plates of glass; it was more than possible that when the tree came crashing down, some of the longer branches would smash them all to smithereens. Ought I not to warn him, to tell him to move them out of the way?

Even as I asked myself this question, his figure came pottering along in the shadow of the wall. Ah! At last he was going to capitulate! He was going to move the cuttings to a place of safety! He had held out till the very last moment; and though I could not help feeling a certain sense of triumph at his ultimate surrender, I had a sneaking admiration for his dogged independence.

And then it became only too obvious that I was congratulating myself too soon. He was not taking the cuttings away at all. On the contrary, he was removing the panes of glass, in order to give them an airing, so that now they were denied even this frail protection. It was too much. After all, they were my cuttings as well as his. I should run over and take them away myself.

But at that very moment the fall of the tree had begun. Warning voices shouted to me to keep back, and indeed there was no need of this counsel, for already it was leaning over at an angle of twenty degrees, swaying dangerously.

I stayed there, impotent. Higher and higher rose the screams of the protesting wood, swifter and swifter beat the rhythm of the saws, tenser and tenser stretched the groaning ropes . . . it could only be a matter of seconds now . . . the great giant was reeling like a drunken man. . . .

And then, at precisely the last earth-splitting, cloud-wracking second, the figure of Oldfield emerged once more, and shuffled, with the utmost indifference, towards his cuttings. In his hand he bore a small watering can. Good God . . . he would be killed! Through the general uproar of wind and wood and tortured branches I heard them shouting at him.

It was too late. With a final rush and roar the tree came down, seeming to drag the very clouds from the sky. It hit the earth with the force of a high explosive bomb, dead in the centre of the narrow line that the foresters had traced for it. In the hush that followed the downfall you could hear the dogs barking for miles around. And over the whole lawn came a sudden welcome flood of light.

But I was not looking at the tree nor listening to the excited comments of all around us. I was watching Oldfield. He was still watering his cuttings, and he had not even turned his head.

Later in the day, when a certain amount of order had been restored and when it was possible to get into the kitchen garden without climbing over a mountain of fallen branches, I went out to the greenhouses to see if the cyclamen seeds were beginning to come up. Oldfield was in the cold house, disbudding some winter geraniums. I was tired and rather irritable; a whole mass of gigantic new bills would soon be descending on me for the day's work, and the dialogue I was writing had got stuck in the middle. Rather tersely I said to him: 'I thought you might have moved those cuttings this morning, Oldfield.'

For a moment he did not reply. His wise old fingers . . . so gnarled and yet so unbelievably delicate . . . were gently nipping a bud from his favourite geranium, the double pink 'Apple Blossom', which nowadays one sees only in cottage porches.

'I did think of moving 'em this morning, sir,' he said at length.

I could hardly believe my ears. Was he at last going to admit that actually, without his permission, a tree had been cut down?

'You did think of it?'

'Yes, sir.' Another pause. Then he said: 'You see, there's a lot of insecks come out of that old wall. When you get an old wall you get insecks. That's what Mr. Stebbing always said. He said to me, Oldfield, he said, there's nothing you can do against that old wall, because of the insecks.'

He nipped off the last geranium bud, turned, and looked me straight in the eye. He did not actually say to me 'Have I won, or haven't I?' And I did not reply, in so many words, 'Yes, Oldfield, you have.' But that was the unspoken dialogue that echoed through the little fragrant house of glass.

For he *had* won. He . . . and, of course . . . Mr. Stebbing.

CHAPTER V

THE DIGNITY OF LABOUR

THE elms had gone. Now surely, at last we could begin to make a garden? And having begun, surely we could lure Oldfield out of his domain, and persuade him to come along and help us?

There were still plenty of fine trees dotted around the place. Beyond the main sweep of tangled lawns there was the old orchard, and then another field, and then a copse. There were all sorts of overgrown beds and borders which might, when uncovered, be worth keeping and incorporating into a design. But before we could even begin to think of a design, it would be necessary to scythe and hook and hack away at the ever thickening wilderness of weeds and brambles and suckers – as though we were cleaning a canvas on which we hoped to paint a picture.

And that meant . . . Labour.

About which we shall now say a few kind words.

Labour!

This grand and resounding expression has acquired in recent years a sort of halo. If a modern artist wishes to paint a mural depicting the Triumph of Labour – which unfortunately he only too often does – all the Labourers are painted with bright eyes, uplifted faces and gigantic muscles, marching towards a light on a hill, while in the background cower a number of frock-coated gentlemen, of sinister and Jewish appearance, among whom one can usually recognize several of one's most intimate friends. Accompanying the Labourers are a suitable number of

Labouresses, also very bright-eyed and uplifted, with immense bosoms, to which they clutch large, mottled, triangular babies.

But Labour, when you come to employ it, is not always quite like that.

The first Labourer I hired, in order to help Oldfield, was an elderly and cadaverous lunatic who stood in the middle of the lawn, sighing bitterly. I first noticed him from the study window. He was standing quite still, doing nothing at all but stare at the ground and sigh, so I naturally concluded that he was something to do with the rates (when strange men appear in your garden and stand quite still and sigh it is an almost certain sign that the rates are about to go up).

But when I went out to interview him it transpired that he had, in fact, come to work, and that the reason he was sighing so deeply was that Oldfield had told him to 'pick up' the old gravel path, but had neglected to give him a pickaxe with which to do so. I could not help thinking that a pickaxe was the very last thing which one should put into the hands of anyone so eccentric, but out of sheer pity I gave him one. After which I returned to the study to watch what happened.

For some time nothing happened at all; there was just the same silent figure, standing quite still, sighing, and leaning on the pickaxe. At three shillings an hour I reckoned that I had already paid approximately one and threepence for witnessing this tableau, and not unnaturally I was impatient to see the figure move. Suddenly it did. Gripping the extreme end of the handle of the pickaxe, it slowly lifted it, and let it drop, of its own weight. The pickaxe made a small dent in the gravel, which the figure bent down to examine with evident pride. After which it straightened itself, indulged in a little more meditation, and repeated the process . . . another slow raising of the pickaxe, another letting it fall, and another small dent in the gravel.

This, I thought, was fascinating, but from my point of view uneconomic. So I went out to ask Oldfield who the man was and what he was supposed to be doing.

Oldfield did not deign to glance at him.

'I reckon he cooms from institution.'

'What institution?'

'Institution on t'hill.'

'Do you mean the lunatic asylum?'

'Aye.'

'But . . . but what is he doing here?'

'You put in advert, didn't you? Well, he's t'answer.'

'But they *can't* send one people from lunatic asylums.'

Oldfield chuckled sardonically. 'Can't they? Reckon they can send out anybody, these days.'

It was evident that Oldfield was secretly delighted with the situation, so I went to seek advice from Gaskin. On the way I again had to pass the lunatic. He had made three more dents in the gravel, and one rather large gash in the turf; there was a very peculiar gleam in his eye and he was muttering to himself.

Gaskin, as usual, settled the matter with dispatch. In ten minutes the man had departed, no longer sighing, but whistling and looking quite jaunty, having been wisely assured by Gaskin that he had done a very good day's work. There was only one slight hitch; he returned five minutes later for the pickaxe; he had become attached to it and appeared to imagine that because he had used it he was therefore entitled to keep it. He became quite sullen when Gaskin told him that he could not have it, and muttered something about doing him out of his rights. He was, in short, a lunatic in quite the best modern tradition.

§ 11

The next representative of Labour seemed more promising – though he, too, bore small resemblance to the Workers of the murals. He was a wiry, wizened Irishman, with darting green eyes and long thin arms. He had a faintly fox-like expression and a more than faintly fox-like smell, but I liked him because he arrived bearing the tools of his trade, in which he evidently took a great deal of pride. I thought that was a good sign. There was a brightly shining scythe and a murderous looking hook, and a thing with three prongs which I always call a 'scrabbler', though it probably has a more dignified name.

'They call me the Wizard with the Knife,' he proclaimed, as soon as we had introduced ourselves. (I won't attempt to reproduce his brogue.)

Oldfield, unfortunately, was hovering in the background, and heard this somewhat challenging statement. He expressed his opinion of it with a portentous sniff. I knew what that sniff meant, and feared the worst.

'Yes,' repeated O'Casey, who had also heard the sniff and had evidently risen to it. 'That's what they call me,' he continued in a slightly louder voice. 'This'd chop off the leg of a man, it would, if I had ahold of it.'

A positively titanic sniff from Oldfield.

'I expect it would,' I said nervously, longing to steer him out of Oldfield's hearing, 'but . . .'

O'Casey interrupted me. He was not going to be sniffed at for nothing, not he. 'And do you know why this knife is so sharp?' Although he was peering close to my face, breathing astonishingly fox-like aromas at me, his remark was obviously addressed to Oldfield, glowering behind him.

'Not because it's grinded, nor because it's greased, nor because it's put away to sleep in a tool shed, nor any of that damn tomfoolery. No, sir!' He flourished the hook with a gesture that came perilously near to Oldfield's nose. '*This* knife is so sharp, *this* knife is so keen, because I leave it hanging in the boughs of a tree when the day's work is done, and when I come to fetch it in the morning there's a beautiful pale rust on it from the dews of the night, and when I cleans the rust off, it's so sharp it's a peril to be near it!'

A more awful challenge to Oldfield, and all that he stood for, could hardly be imagined; nothing was so calculated to upset him as any unorthodox treatment of garden tools, whether they belonged to him or to anybody else; if I myself were to use a spade and fail to clean it, dry it, wipe it with a greasy rag, and hang it in its proper place, I should be prepared for the blackest of looks. And black, at this moment, would be a mild way of describing the regard which he cast upon O'Casey.

Fortunately O'Casey was content with the effect which he had created. 'Now what was the little matter you'd like me to be seeing to?' he demanded.

I was only too pleased to show him.

§ III

In spite of the aforesaid Wizardry with the Knife, O'Casey's progress on the lawns was slow. They still looked like a series of small, irregular fields with a few scythed patches in them. I could not make this out, because whenever I wandered up the garden to see how he was getting on he appeared to be working quite hard. Perhaps it was because seven years of neglect had given the grass a toughness that defied even his skill.

'It's cruel it is,' he sighed to me one morning – a hot, sticky morning which was particularly favourable for the conduction of fox-like odours.

But he was not referring to the grass, he was speaking of his neighbours.

'Where I live,' he continued, 'there's nothing but Abyssinians.'

This information startled me. 'Abyssinians?'

'Every man of 'em. Every woman too. All Abyssinians. Hundreds of 'em.'

I was puzzled by the thought of so large a coloured colony in Meadowstream.

''Tis not their skins as is black,' he explained, ''tis their hearts.' And then – with a side-glance at the distant figure of Oldfield – who was weeding the herbaceous border – 'you'll find Abyssinians everywhere, these days. Where you least expect 'em.'

You certainly would, I thought, if Oldfield was to come into that category.

Meanwhile Oldfield was practising the technique which he invariably employed when confronted by anything in the garden of which he disapproved but over which he had no immediate control . . . he ignored it. He strongly disapproved of O'Casey and therefore, for him, O'Casey ceased to exist. He was not. He was a phantom, a figment of the imagination. Sometimes, even in so large a garden, it was inevitable that the two men should meet, and on these occasions one would have thought that Oldfield, to avoid embarrassment, would have halted, or made a detour, or pretended to busy himself with something. Not a bit of it. He plodded grimly on towards the hated figure, staring ahead of him with unseeing eyes, keeping so straight a course that at times I feared there would be a collision – for O'Casey had adopted the same procedure, and had banished Oldfield from *his* consciousness, except as a vague and Abyssinian menace, lurking in the background.

Nothing that I could say or do would induce either of them to pronounce each other's names. The nearest O'Casey would ever get to 'Oldfield' was 'Oldham' . . . and even then he gave it a faintly Abyssinian intonation. Oldfield did not even attempt to say 'O'Casey'; if he was obliged to refer to him at all he called him 'that old man', endowing him with a premature senility. O'Casey was at least twenty years younger than Oldfield, but Oldfield was not going to admit it.

'Have you seen O'Casey this morning?' I would ask him. 'Is there anything you would like him to do?'

Oldfield, thus attacked, was obliged to acknowledge the existence of O'Casey. But even so, he would not say his name.

'That old man?' he would retort. 'He's oop to something in t'orchard.'

'Oh yes. I see he's taken his scythe.'

'Scythe! Pshaw! Don't know one end o' scythe from t'other.' Oldfield's face flushed with righteous indignation. 'In fact, I reckon he don't know anything at all. Look at that!'

He pointed to the edge of the lawn, where a rake was lying.

'Did he leave that there?'

'He did. And look at it! Points upwards! If Mr. Stebbing'd seen fellows leave rakes on t'lawn, let alone *points upwards*, they'd have been out on their ears within t'hour!'

It was, of course, an impossible situation. After a few more weeks of increasing nervous tension, a few more weeks in which the grass continued to grow and the nettles to layer themselves and the thistles to dispatch their aery offspring far and wide, I told O'Casey that he would have to go. He did not seem either surprised or sorry. He was going back to Ireland, he said. He had had enough of England and the Abyssinians.

§ IV

After the departure of O'Casey we had a succession of Labourers, who had nothing in common except their total ignorance of anything connected with the art of gardening, and their iron resolution to avoid any form of physical fatigue.

There were old men like withered roots, who scuttled out of sight and spent most of the day lurking in hedges, eating things out of bundles. There were chronic hypochondriacs who, on being asked to tackle any job which required a certain amount of physical effort, immediately clutched their hearts or their groins or the smalls of their backs and launched into a description of their various diseases, which ranged from arterio-sclerosis to acute sciatica, in order to prove how impossible it was for them to bend down. There were village boys who giggled and threw stones at the birds and demanded star salaries for pulling up a basketful of groundsel. And there was a smart young man called Fortescue who arrived on a motor bicycle at nine o'clock, and sauntered out to work in chamois leather gloves in order that he should not dirty his hands. He was seldom without a cigarette, and at the first drizzle of rain he hurried indoors to shelter. Soon after four-thirty he would remove the gloves and stroll back to the motor bicycle, where he would be joined by a small, highly painted female who had been hovering in the lane.

There were also two female gardeners who insisted on being employed together. They had been comrades in the Women's Land Army during the war, where they had struck up a deathless friendship. One of them was square and tough, like a female blacksmith, with short-cropped hair and a rasping voice. The other was small and fair, with a rather sickly skin, pale blue eyes, and a habit of twittering. Their devotion was quite touching; they shared everything, even their names. The twittery one had been baptized Ninette, so the tough one – whose real name was Alice – assumed the name of Ninon.

It was very soon evident that Ninon's principal anxiety, during the brief period of her employment, was to see that no possible harm should come to Ninette. When, for instance, I supplied Ninette with a tin of weed-killer, and gave her some simple instructions as to how to water it into the paths, Ninon came lumbering up at the double.

'What's that you're giving her?'

'Weed-killer.'

'But it's poisonous!'

'On the contrary . . .'

'Here, let me see!'

She snatched the tin from my hand, and examined it, while Ninette swayed and giggled and lowered her eyes and traced patterns in the gravel with the toe of her idiotic shoe.

'Hmph!' grunted Ninon, when she had read the label, 'it mayn't be poisonous, but it's caustic.'

'Naturally it's caustic,' I replied. 'The object of a weed-killer is to kill weeds.' By now, it will be observed, I was beginning to feel slightly caustic myself.

'She might burn herself,' grunted Ninon.

This brought a girlish ripple from Ninette. 'Ninon *darleeng*!' she gurgled. 'Don't be so *seely*! Look! I've got these *beautiful* gloves!'

Ninon paused for a moment, to gaze in rapture at her adored one; then she scowled at me again.

'She might spill it on her legs.'

'She might indeed,' I replied, with mounting hysteria. 'She might suddenly decide to use it as a shampoo. . . .'

A positive gale of laughter from Ninette. 'A sham*pu*,' she panted, 'what a wonderful idea . . . a weed-killing sham*pu*!' *Ooh*, how comical I was. *Ooh*, I should put it in a book.

Well, *ooh*, I have put it in a book, and I hope she likes it.

It was not long before Ninon and Ninette went the way of the others. Even if they had been competent, it is doubtful whether it would have been practical to keep them, for the effect they had on Oldfield was positively explosive. When a writer observes of any character that he 'snorted', he may usually be taken to imply merely a vague sound of disapproval, but the effect of these ladies on Oldfield was to make him snort quite literally – although, needless to say, they were as 'invisible' to him as all the rest. I was afraid that he might do himself an injury, with so much snorting, and it was with a sigh of relief that I saw them go. The last I heard of them was that they had given up gardening and opened a snack-bar in Chelsea. That might be a good thing to put in a book, too, one day.

§ V

We will now indulge in some Gloomy Forebodings.

Having done so, we will follow them up with some Rays of Hope and – which is more important – some practical advice. But the gloom must come first.

I am still without any regular help in the garden, and though Oldfield looks like being good for another fifteen years, by that time he will be nearing ninety and will presumably be wishing to take things rather easier.

As things are, I see no prospect whatever of finding a successor to him. It is useless to advertise; nobody answers. It is almost as useless to make personal inquiries and solicitations; all that one ever gets is an 'odd man' at fabulous expense. These 'odd men' grow odder and odder as the years go by. Not only do they know nothing about gardening, but one would think that they had never been inside a garden at all. It was something of a shock to me when one of them – reputed to be 'experienced' – asked me if the seakale was white rhubarb. But I was soon to realize that such a question was comparatively erudite; for not long afterwards he was succeeded by a gentleman who gazed at the Brussels sprouts and asked if the funny little knobs on the stalks were a form of disease. I told him yes. Eczema.

Where are the Oldfields of the future?

Echo answers 'Where?' It is to be feared that Echo will continue to make the same answer indefinitely. The Oldfields of the future are beyond hearing; they are shut up in the factories and the workshops, leading a rackety and mechanical existence, to the damage of their bodies and the peril of their souls, for the sake of an extra pound or so a week, which they promptly spend on mental or physical narcotics. Not for them the slow miracle of nature unfolding; they don't believe in miracles. Not for them the patter of the rain and the whisper of the wind; they don't like getting wet; and if the wind has any message they wouldn't understand it.

Not for them, especially, the idea of working hard and faithfully in the service of a single individual. They would feel degraded. To slave at the behest of some anonymous corporation – that is quite all right; to lead an unhealthy life which they detest, in the bondage of the State . . . that is fine, that is dignified. But to work for, and with, a man who retains the technical title of 'master' . . . no. They would rather die; and die they do.

Here is a story to show what I mean.

Gaskin likes mowing the lawns. In spite of the fact that he has a large house to run and a great deal to do, he has usually 'finished' by about two-thirty. Whereupon a gleam comes into his eye; he darts upstairs, puts on an old pair of flannels, and goes out to the tool shed. A minute later comes the roar of the petrol mower, and off he charges, up and down, over the green, fragrant grass – as happy as a lark. I have never suggested to him, by the faintest hint, that he should do any mowing; if he took a hatred to it he could stop tomorrow. I sincerely hope he doesn't . . . but if he does, it is none of my business.

Well, here is the story. One lovely summer afternoon Gaskin, as usual, was roaring up and down the lawn. In the distance, fiddling about over a hole in the drive, was a young man employed by the Water Company – or maybe it was the Electricity Board; at any rate, he was in the Service of the State, and as such could be called a Representative of Labour. For once in a way he looked the part, like the young gentlemen in the murals, with knotted muscles and a heroic profile.

Five o'clock struck from the church clock. The Representative of Labour leapt away from the hole like a startled rabbit, appalled by the thought that he had inadvertently put in nearly thirty seconds more work than was strictly necessary. Then he noticed Gaskin, paused, and strolled over to him.

'Why you cutting that there grass?'

'Because it wants cutting,' retorted Gaskin, who is nothing if not direct.

'How much extra does your boss pay you for doing it?'

'Nothing.'

'Nothing?' The R of L stared at Gaskin as though he were some rare and exotic form of animal – which perhaps he is. 'Then all I can say is . . . you're a mug.'

Gaskin shrugged his shoulders and lit a cigarette, with some elegance. Meanwhile the motor mower purred happily beside him.

It was a cool, delicious evening; the scent of the freshly mown grass was delicate and fragrant. As the machine continued to purr, longing to be off on its business, the young man found it irresistible. After all, he was strong and ardent and . . . well, the grass did need cutting.

'Here,' he said, 'let's have a go.'

Whereupon he seized the handles and charged out over the lawn. For nearly an hour he carried on, in a sort of ecstasy, while the shadows lengthened, and the sweet, green heap grew higher and higher, and Gaskin sat on a log, watching him with a sardonic smile.

Dusk was deep when at last he finished. He stacked the final load of grass, took out a rag and wiped the moist blades, bundled the machine back to the tool shed. Then he lit a cigarette, and smiled with pride at the work he had done . . . for love.

But suddenly the smile faded and turned to a frown. He had remembered his philosophy. He took out his cigarette, spat on the ground, and turned to Gaskin.

'All I can say is,' he growled, 'you're a mug . . . doing all that for nothing.'

It is all rather sad. The gardens of Britain were once a long green gallery of masterpieces; they will soon be only a memory. For all gardens need gardeners, if they are not to suffer a swift and maybe irreparable degeneration – and so, I would suggest, do all nations. However, that is a topic too weighty for these flimsy pages.

§ VI

Now for the practical suggestions to meet this emergency – suggestions in which may perhaps be discerned the promised Rays of Hope.

Necessity being the mother of invention, my own garden is – among a great many other things – a sort of amateur research laboratory for experiments in labour-saving. That sounds rather awful, as though it were covered with sheds, and nasty machines making noises. There aren't any sheds or machines. My experiments are all green and growing, and they are all concerned with plants or shrubs which, as far as possible, look after themselves – and even, on occasions, help to look after their neighbours.

Consider the humble periwinkle.

Before I came to a belated appreciation of the periwinkle's virtues, my life was made a misery by something which should have been a joy – the large shrubbery which lies at the end of the lawn, in the shelter of the copper beech. It was in a very important strategic place, and it contained some of the choicest things in my possession. There were the seven camellia bushes, which I had planted myself, and the big double lilacs, violet and white, which were a legacy from Mr. Stebbing. (They were so beautiful that it is difficult to understand why he never rooted them out. Perhaps they had been so smothered by the speckled laurels, which I eradicated, that he never noticed them.) There were also several exquisite specimens of the rhus family – (the sort that cover themselves in a woolly fluff in August) – and a number of *daphne mezereum*, which are a mass of waxy pink flowers in February.

Planted among them were hosts of daffodils and jonquils and polyanthus and pale pink bluebells.

Well, one *should* have burst into song at the very thought of owning such a patch of miracles. But one didn't. One burst into dirges. For this shrubbery produced more weeds than one would have thought possible. There seemed to be almost every weed that has ever broken a gardener's heart, from bindweed to bird's-foot trefoil; in fact the only weed which was absent was ground-elder, and I went in constant dread of finding even this last calamity. If it had not been for all the shrubs and the bulbs, the whole thing might have been dug up, because with a pest like bindweed you have to go down very deep indeed, and remove the very last fragment of those unnaturally white roots.[1] I had not the heart to do anything so drastic. So it was just a question of an unending, unequal battle.

Then, one spring day when I was rummaging about in the orchard, I saw a gleam of yellow under the old chestnut tree. I realized that this must come from some of the daffodils that had been given to a friend to 'hide'.

(At the risk of seeming intolerably discursive, it must be explained that every autumn, when the new bulbs arrive, a proportion of them are handed out to any friends who may be around so that they may plant them in some secret place, where I can have the fun of discovering them in the spring. It is a sort of floral hide-and-seek which is vastly entertaining.)

These, then, must be some of the daffodils which had been hidden by a certain red-headed girl from Australia. They must be photographed, and we would send a copy out to Melbourne. But why – oh why – had she planted them in the middle of that mass of periwinkle? They would be smothered. Even as this reflection occurred to me I realized that it was nonsense, for they were *not* being smothered. They were flourishing abundantly, and as I walked closer to them I saw that they were as sturdy as any daffodils I had ever seen, with stems which

[1] Bindweed – *convolvulus sepium* – is one of the very rare examples of a plant that climbs round the supporting stem clockwise, i.e. in accordance with the course of the sun; and some old gardeners claim that if you disengage it from the stem, and make it turn round the other way, it will perish out of sheer disgust. I have never had the patience to test this theory, but it might be worth trying.

seemed longer and tougher for their struggle through the foliage.

That was the beginning of what may be called the periwinkle period. For periwinkle swiftly spreads a thick carpet under which absolutely no weed can survive, and yet, for some mysterious reason, it does not seem to throttle any bulbs that are planted beneath it. Moreover, it has an exceptional virtue in that it is a carpet that you can cut as easily as you can cut linoleum; if you see it encroaching too closely on some shrub which would obviously be weakened by the competition of the periwinkle's roots, all you have to do is to take a spade and cut a square round the shrub, and that is that.

It seemed then, and it has since proved in fact to be, the solution to the weeds in the big shrubbery. They are a thing of the past. Instead there is a glossy green carpet, which only needs a little trimming now and then – a carpet which in March is flecked all over with the curiously innocent blue of the periwinkle blossom.

I earnestly suggest that you become a periwinklist, without delay.

§ VII

More practical hints.

The problem, as we have observed, is to render ourselves as far as possible independent of 'Labour' – in other words to avoid paying vast sums to elderly invalids who demand a pound a day for sitting on the edge of the herbaceous border making a few petulant prods at a clump of groundsel. We also wish to rid ourselves of the co-operation of perky young men who demand a similar sum for arriving on motor bicycles half an hour late, and leaving half an hour early, and who have been known, on more than one occasion, to introduce trousered houris into the coppice, where they have been surprised in activities which were very far from horticultural.

We wish, perhaps most of all, to say goodbye to the politically minded young gardener, who looks at you as if you ought to be nationalized, and mutters dark things about what will happen when the 'workers' get hold of the gardens of England – a problem of which only one thing can be said with certainty, namely that the 'workers' will never work in them.

From all this crew we desire to escape. But how?

There seems to me to be only one answer; and it is so simple that I hesitate to give it.

Flowering shrubs.

More and more, as 'Labour' becomes scarcer and scarcer, the gardens of Britain are likely to rely upon flowering shrubs, and their owners to turn to them for solace and encouragement. (It really is quite pathetic, and makes one think of quantities of charming, reactionary old ladies cowering beneath vast umbrellas of buddleia, glaring out at a world which they find less and less to their taste.)

However, the expression 'flowering shrubs' implies infinitely more than most gardeners read into it. When they have ordered the customary assortment of forsythias, berberis *Darwinii*, philadelphus, syringas, buddleias – and if they are particularly enterprising, a rhus or two, they seem to think that they have done their duty, and that they can sit back and relax. Let me assure them that they have done nothing of the sort. They have most criminally failed in their duty . . . (for surely, if you are privileged to own a plot of earth, it is your *duty*, both to God and man, to make it beautiful?). And let me assure them that far from relaxing, they must now sit up and listen, and become very tense and rigid, with, if possible, slightly distended nostrils.

The first thing they have to be tense about is the berberis.

To most people the word 'berberis' means the orange-flowered berberis *Darwinii*, and nothing else. (They usually take remarkable pains to make it look quite hideous by planting it in the immediate proximity of something pink, such as an early pyrus. However, that is beside the point.)

It is not too much to say that if you were allowed no other shrub in your garden but the berberis, you could confidently expect to be in a state of mildly hysterical pleasure for nearly three-quarters of the year. There are over twenty varieties which give over twenty different performances, and they are all of them a delight. It begins in February with the *Bealei* – (the nurserymen insist on calling it *mahonia japonica*) – which has long, lilting racemes of lemon-yellow flowers which smell like lilies-of-the-valley. After that, through March and April, there is the *aquifolium* which has leaves like holly, and flowers of gold; and in the autumn it is covered with a mass of purple berries that look like tiny plums.

From April onwards the berberis parade is spectacular. The brightest yellow is perhaps the *canidula*, which flowers well into June, though it is run close by the *polyantha*, which follows it in July, and keeps on flowering till the autumn colours begin. Of these autumn colours it is difficult to write with restraint; they burn up in the most breath-taking bonfire of beauty that nature has yet devised; I will content myself by naming the three varieties which, in my own experience, glow most gloriously in this display:

Thunbergii This bursts into flame late into September; when the sun shines through it the illusion of fire is uncanny.

Koreana A steady glow from October onwards.

Rubrostilla Quantities of little tongues of flame, that seem to lick round the branches when the wind is blowing. These are formed by the profusion of its translucent coral berries, which are shaped like an inverted pear.

And do not forget that all these beautiful things can be relied upon to look after themselves. I have a big bank which is entirely given over to berberis of various sorts; they were planted about four feet apart, and for the first two years, naturally, it was necessary to weed the ground between them. After the third year they had flourished so luxuriantly that the few remaining weeds beneath them were pale and sickly; today there are no weeds at all. It is one unbroken display of berberis, with the bushes engaged in what is known as 'fighting it out'. It is a battle which they seem to enjoy, and they wage it, remember, alone. No representative of 'Labour' has ever approached them, or ever will.

But as usual, we have run on much too far ahead. We must leave the berberis and go back to the Battle of the Elms. For one fight always leads to another, as I was now to find out.

CHAPTER VI

VEGETABLE AND FEMALE

IT was soon after the Battle of the Elms that Miss Emily returned to the fray.

For some time I had forgotten all about her, and I had not answered the letter which she had written on the night following our meeting in the lane. It had been a very revealing letter, and though it is a few weeks old in our story I make no excuse for quoting it:

DEAR MR. NICHOLS,

Our meeting last night was so unexpected, and was brought to so abrupt a conclusion – (I do *hope* you will forgive my foolishness about your cat!) – that I had no opportunity to say how horrified I was to observe that by some *disaster* the beautiful holly hedge that shut off your front garden from the lane had been destroyed by fire. And not only that, but that two sections of the beautiful iron railings had fallen from the wall and were smashed almost beyond repair.

May I express my *deepest* sympathy for this most *unhappy* event? How can it possibly have occurred? I can only assume that one of your workmen – they are *all* Communists nowadays – must have thrown a match into the hedge. One would not be at all surprised to learn that it was deliberate.

I fear that it will be years before the hedge can be made to grow again, and I know how distressed you must feel, for it was one of Mr. Stebbing's special prides. Many is the time I have heard him speaking of it to poor Mrs. Stebbing – who did not really appreciate it, for towards the end of her life she suffered from delusions, and had an idea that it shut out the light. I am afraid that she was sometimes querulous about it, which was most upsetting to Mr. Stebbing, particularly when she was reading to him – he was *so* fond of being read to, and such an *eager* listener – and when she complained that she could not see.

However, time mends all things! And though holly is a slow grower, if you replant the hedge in the autumn it will be quite a respectable height in a few years' time. It may be more difficult to restore the railings, but perhaps you may be able to match them locally; if not, I know of a very good little man who does this sort of work – one of the real old school, who loves beautiful things, and is *not* a Communist.

Please forgive me for this intrusion. But one does so hate to see the destruction of such things, which are part of our national *heritage*, as I am sure you will agree. Yours sincerely,

EMILY KAYE.

Even if I had wished to answer this letter, it would have been difficult to do so, for the last of the holly roots had been torn up and thrown on to the bonfire. In their place I had planted a lavender hedge, which in time would just grow to the top of the low wall. As for the railings, they had been carted away, and by now they might well be at the bottom of the sea for all I knew or cared.

After this letter there was a brief interlude of peace. True, a visiting card had been pushed through the letter-box with her telephone number scribbled on it, which struck me as rather sinister, for I hate telephones anyway, and should hate them even more if I had to use them to explain why I was not selling my broccoli. And from time to time I had a strong suspicion that I saw her in the lane, strolling very close to the fence that shuts off the kitchen garden. There were a number of gaps in the fence, which I should have to close as soon as possible, for through them a passer-by could gain a very tempting vision of rows and rows of leeks and cauliflowers and winter spinach.

But there was no direct frontal assault until the second letter. We will let it speak for itself.

DEAR MR. NICHOLS,

It is some little time since I was bold enough to write to you about the possibility of purchasing some of your wonderful vegetables. It was so very unfortunate that we were unable to come to some arrangement for their delivery, owing to this tiresome lack of petrol, and I feel sure I am right in thinking *you* must have shared my disappointment, for I can imagine that you must feel as disturbed as I am, at the thought of so much valuable foodstuff running to waste. Every ounce of food is precious in these days, is it not? I always remember how Mr. Stebbing was only too *glad* to allow the village boys to pick up all the windfalls from the orchard, particularly as they harboured swarms of wasps which made it quite dangerous to approach his favourite plum tree.

However, where there's a will there's a way! So as soon as I had recovered from the shock of your letter I put on my thinking cap in order to try to find a solution to our little difficulty. And I believe that I have discovered a way that will make us *both* happy.

The name of Rose Fenton, the flower-specialist, needs no introduction to you. She is a near neighbour of mine, and she tells me that you have in fact met, though she regretted that the acquaintanceship had never developed; it seems that on all the occasions when she had written to you, suggesting a meeting, you were unfortunately just about to go abroad. Now that we are all so close, I am sure that you will wish to see a lot of her – such a charming woman, with whom you would be bound to have much in common.

Now for the point of these remarks. Miss Fenton, like myself, has a particular fondness for vegetables, and it is only the nature of her *work* that prevents her from growing them herself. As you know, she is a great expert on floral decoration – I believe she is paid quite *fantastic* sums for her arrangements at public banquets – and so her whole garden, which is quite extensive, is entirely devoted to flowers. She once said to me – she is so whimsical! – that she could not possibly give her mind to her work if she were surrounded by acres of spinach! Yet, as it so happens, spinach is one of the vegetables that are essential for her constitution, which is not robust (lack of iron).

So here is our little plan. Miss Fenton, happily, has almost unlimited petrol. (Essential work – earning dollars.) And she has told me that she would be only too pleased to collect the vegetables from Merry Hall for us both, at *your* convenience. The choice of the vegetables she would leave entirely to *you.* All she would ask, if it would not be too much trouble, is that perhaps it might be possible for them to be *washed* before they are put into the car. I hope you will not think this an unreasonable request?

I am so very glad that things seem to have worked out so pleasantly for all concerned. One might almost say, might one not, that one had killed three birds with one stone! The little remuneration for yourself, which I do hope will be welcome, is doubled; Miss Fenton and I are both accommodated; and last but not least, the country is saved the waste which we all deplore. I shall most eagerly await your reply.

With warmest good wishes. Sincerely yours,

EMILY KAYE.

If my lips were in the habit of setting in a grim, firm line, if I were given to iron frowns and mirthless laughs, this would have been my moment. As it was, I merely felt very confused, vaguely explosive, and rather red in the face.

For really . . . I mean to say . . . well, I *ask* you. . . .

For years, the very name of Rose Fenton had made me see red. To me, she was Floral Enemy Number One – just as Constance Spry was Floral Benefactor Number One. Maybe if there had never been a Spry there would never have been a Fenton, for Constance brought into being a whole host of imitators, who followed in her footsteps like a herd of female elephants. Constance, with her delicate genius, her impeccable sense of form and colour, could pick a bramble from the hedge and trail it across a table and make it look beautiful and seemly. Unfortunately, she could also make it look easy, which it is not.

Constance's star imitator was Our Rose. There are plenty of others, of course, most of them terrible, raging round the land lecturing and broadcasting and writing articles; but Our Rose has always seemed to me the worst, for she takes Constance's designs and makes a hideous sort of parody of them. Not that she would admit it, needless to say. If, in these days of her triumph, you mention Constance to her, she smiles sweetly and says: 'Oh yes – of course – yes, I remember – she's that nice little woman who does such amusing things with dead hydrangea heads.' Then, in an aside, she murmurs: 'I'm afraid they give *me* the creeps. *I* like natural beauty!'

Natural! Ye Gods! Need I remind you what Our Rose does to flowers? Must I recall, for example, those frightening arrangements of daffodils, mounting up like a sort of graph, with the heads of the lowest ones chopped off so that there is only an inch of stalk – and behind them, of all things, a stiff fan of iris leaves? But no! You have seen her 'creations' too often in florists' shops; you have also seen them at weddings, and in the halls of great hotels and restaurants. For Our Rose, let us face it, is a Success; she even threatens to put her ideas into a book, one of these days. If she ever does, it will certainly be a best seller. Which is a pretty poor reflection on British taste.

And now I, of all people, was being asked to supply vegetable sustenance to her in order that she might be strengthened to continue in her abominations! It was altogether too much.

I sat down to write my reply.

At that precise moment, unannounced, they walked into the room.

§11

For once in a way I was struck dumb, and could only stare at them as they came through the doorway, frozen, as it seemed, in a moment of time.

Miss Emily was wearing the same heather-mixture tweed as on our first meeting (I was to learn that this, with slight variations, was her invariable costume).

But it was the first time that I had met Our Rose, and I wondered why she had always been so careful to keep her photograph out of the papers. Perhaps it was because she wanted the public to form a mental picture of her as a flower. She was, indeed, rather like a large pink paeony. Not that she was plump; she was just pleasantly rounded, and the pale circle of her face was accentuated by the manner in which she did her dark hair, parted in the middle and drawn flat over her ears, like a madonna by Mabuse. She had brown eyes, which were sharp in spite of their roundness, and she wore absolutely no make-up. This, paradoxically, gave her a look of slight impropriety, as though she had omitted some essential article of clothing. She was dressed in what might be called vegetable hues, a lettuce-green coat and skirt, a sage-grey silk scarf, and grass-green gloves. Round her throat was a heavy necklace of moonstones.

I must admit – though it goes against the grain to say so – that she had her attraction. (Not that she was going to be allowed a single leek, nor even a sprig of parsley.)

The frozen moment of Time suddenly split and we found ourselves advancing towards each other.

Our first few sentences were so fluttery and inconsequent that it is difficult to recall them as dialogue; they were a vague hotch-potch of words.

This must be a terrible intrusion – not at all – did I know Miss Fenton – how d'you do, how d'you do – of course I've heard so much about you – and you too – and we do hope we're not disturbing you – not in the least – but I've so often walked through the door of this room – I'm sure you have – oh what a delicious bunch of love-lies-bleeding – look, Emily darling – yes dear, I am.

Miss Emily was indeed looking. She was one big Flinch. For a number of things had been done to the music-room since the days of dear Mr. Stebbing, and needless to say, they were all agony to her.

'All so fresh,' she hissed, looking around her as though

she had inadvertently strayed into a slaughter-house. 'So clean.'

However, she had not made this expedition in order to tell me that I was clean and fresh. After a few more flinches she steered rapidly to the point.

'It seemed so foolish,' she said, 'to write to each other when we're such near neighbours.'

'Yes, indeed.'

'So I thought that as we were passing, we might just look in to know if you've had time to consider my little letter?'

'Oh yes. Of course, your letter.' I did some lightning thinking, watched by two of the sharpest eyes that have ever glinted in a strictly vegetarian countenance. It was now or never. I took a deep breath.

'I'm terribly sorry. But I'm afraid it will be impossible.' An even deeper breath. 'You see, I'm giving up the kitchen garden.'

There was a moment's awful silence, while both ladies gazed at me in horror.

'Giving It Up?' gasped Miss Emily.

'Giving It Up?' echoed Our Rose.

'Absolutely. Or almost absolutely.'

'But . . . but . . . oh really . . . this is quite a shock.' Miss Emily sat down heavily on the arm of a sofa. 'You can't be serious?'

'You're surely not going to give up those wonderful asparagus beds?' pleaded Our Rose, with tears in her voice. (Somebody, I thought, has been looking through the fence.)

'No. I shall be keeping those.' For a fleeting second the eyes of the two ladies met. However, that did not worry me, because the asparagus season was still eight months away.

'And the raspberries and the blackcurrants and the gooseberries and all those *magnificent* beds of rhubarb and all that *superb* soil for onions and spinach and celery and heaven knows what? Are you giving them up too?'

'Most of them, though I expect I shall keep the raspberries, as they're so little trouble.' Once again, for a brief instant, the eyes of the two ladies met. Which was disturbing, as the raspberry season was still in full swing.

'But *why*?' demanded Miss Emily. 'Not of course that it's any concern of *ours*. . . .'

No truer word, madame, I thought, was ever spoken.

'But it does seem such a *pity*,' she continued, 'in times like these.' She turned to Our Rose with a tearful smile. 'Poor Mr. Stebbing must be turning in his grave.'

If by doing so, I thought, he was disturbing the earth sufficiently to bring down the exceptionally hideous marble angel which he caused to be erected in his memory, that would be a very good thing indeed.

Aloud I said: 'Yes, it certainly is a pity. It's just a question of labour. Poor Oldfield, you know. Getting on in years. Feeling the strain. . . .'

At that precise moment, through the window, I observed the figure of Oldfield walking across the lawn. He stepped as briskly as a guardsman, he was whistling to himself, and in the crook of his arm he bore a basket of vegetables of quite indecent luxuriance. The contents of that basket would have formed a very adequate foundation for a harvest festival.

The ladies heard the whistle; they turned their heads towards the window; their eyes lit on the basket; their necks slowly swivelled round, following Oldfield till he was out of sight. Then their eyes met. Slowly their mouths began to open, as though their lips were being lifted by invisible wires, and slowly they shut again, while a faint sound, as of steam, came from their nostrils. They were giving a classic example of the feminine art of Bottling Things Up.

It seemed a good moment to suggest that we might walk out into the garden. Perhaps they would excuse me for a minute while I went to put on my shoes?

It was five minutes before I thought it wise to return. By then it was evident that a great deal of Unbottling had been in progress. The ladies were comparatively calm, and were talking with assumed animation about my bowl of love-lies-bleeding, whose crimson tassels were nearly two feet long.

'I really must use those flowers some day,' said Our Rose, as we walked outside. I felt like asking her whether she proposed to tie knots in their tails. However, that would have been unkind. After all, for the moment she was defeated. But later? Time alone would show.

§ III

Since Our Rose, whether we like it or not, seems liable to stray through the pages of this chronicle, perhaps you will allow me to explain why she sometimes maddens me. I do not actively dislike her; indeed, as we have suggested, she has a soft, peculiar attraction – though admittedly it is the sort of attraction which makes one wonder if one is a secret sadist, with an unsatisfied itch for the whip. Not that I would wittingly do her any hurt. Or would I? Perhaps one had better not analyse one's motives too deeply.

But she has two habits which are enough to drive any man to the bottle.

One of them is to call inanimate objects 'he' or 'she'. She will pause in the hall, gaze at a Regency commode, put her head on one side, and then . . . with a gracious smile . . . turn round and say, 'I wonder if he's *quite* happy there?'

I ought to retort 'Who?' But I only grunt and shuffle.

'He's not *quite* sure of himself, do you think?' she continues. And then, with a quick clasp of the hands . . . 'Don't you think he'd be happier next to *her*?'

'Her', it should be explained, is in this case a small and slightly worm-eaten Louis Seize tripod table, which has been brought down from the attic in order to be palmed off on somebody as a wedding present.

Such archery dries one up and turns down the corners of one's mouth, as by suction. I cannot explain to Our Rose that 'he' would not be at all happy next to 'her', because she has the misfortune to be infested by worms. It would, and does, sound completely disgusting. Nor can I suggest that since 'he' is British and 'she' is French, and old enough to be his mother, they would make a very ill-assorted pair. It would all be too fatiguing. So I allow her to do her stuff, and fuss around, and drag things about, and make lines on the carpet, till she is quite happy and prepared to go out into the garden in a state of comparative satisfaction.

Our Rose's other little idiosyncrasy is even more worrying. When she is in a playful mood, and when she is addressing any friend with whom she can claim – or with whom she desires – to be on intimate terms, she says 'we' instead of 'you'.

You cannot believe how torturing this habit can be,

nor what murderous instincts it can evoke, unless you have actually experienced it.

Thus, Our Rose, if she encounters you when you are suffering from the results of a late night, will give you a look that is a subtle mixture of Gentle Reproof and Womanly Understanding and murmur 'I'm afraid we're not feeling *quite* on top of the world this morning, are we?'

It was this technique which she employed as we stepped into the garden, and walked, or rather waded, through the wilderness in the direction of the orchard.

'Oh dear,' she murmured, as she surveyed the gashes and furrows in the lawns, the piles of elm branches which had still to be removed, and the gaping holes in the hedges. 'Don't you think we have been a little rash?'

It is the sort of remark that the heroine of an early Pinero comedy might make as she emerged, all flushed and tumbled, from the summer-house at the end of Act One. But I took it at its face value.

'No,' I said firmly. 'They had to come down.'

'Are we *sure*?'

Before I could answer, Miss Emily had also advanced to the attack. 'So wonderful, they were,' she sighed. 'Be careful, Rose, there's quite a pit, just here. It used to be the begonia bed before Mr. Nichols had it removed. Quite a sight in July. Yes. The elms . . . oh dear, another pit – no, I'm quite all right, thank you . . . the elms were wonderful. To sit under them on a summer evening was such a joy.'

By now we had reached an oasis which had been scythed, so that we could pause to look around us.

'You don't mean to say,' I exclaimed, 'that you really sat *under* the elms?'

'But constantly. We would take out our deck chairs and stay for hours. Mr. Stebbing would have his crossword, and Mrs. Stebbing her *petit-point* – she was *ruining* her eyes by it, I always told her, which was so thoughtless of her when you think how much pleasure poor Mr. Stebbing used to get from being read to aloud – and I would just sit and dream.'

'It was lucky that you were not all killed,' I observed.

'Pray, why?'

'The elms might have come crashing down on you. They were all diseased.' Which was more than a slight exaggeration, but I was beginning to feel impatient.

'Surely *he* was not diseased?' demanded Our Rose. For a moment I thought she was referring to Mr. Stebbing, but 'he', in this case, was the torso of a recumbent elm that had not yet been removed.

'Yes he . . . it . . . was. Full of wasps' nests. Fungus. All sorts of horrors. A menace.'

By now the ladies were again showing very clear signs of Bottling Up, and so, after a few more sighs from Miss Emily, coupled with a few more artless warnings to her friend . . . ('be careful, dear, quite a marsh just here where all this rubbish has been dumped . . . oh but of course, this must have been the lily pond') . . . after a little more of that, they departed.

I walked into the house, kicking things *en route.* Women, I decided, were a mistake. A most lamentable error, both mentally and physically, whether viewed from the front, the back, or the sides. They should be abolished. No. Not abolished. They should be beaten with the utmost regularity – as Noel Coward once said – like gongs.

But women had one great quality. By their sheer

monstrosity they drove men to great decisions. They forced men to act. To take tremendous decisions. To rush out into deserts and make them blossom, to charge into mountains and blast them to the heavens.

Very well. If that was the mood of the moment, it must be obeyed. The whole place must be ploughed up. Men must arrive, almost instantly, with machines, and roar all over the estate, tearing it to pieces, rooting up rocks, hurling ancient stumps into the air, creating a blank canvas on which one might at last draw some sort of picture.

I called for Gaskin.

'We've got to start all over,' I said to him. 'We'll want ploughs and tractors and probably dynamite.'

'That's what I said from the beginning.'

'But how can we get such things, with all these restrictions?'

'I think it can be arranged.'

'Yes, but when?'

'Perhaps,' he observed calmly, 'you would leave that to me.'

I breathed a sigh of relief. When you leave anything to Gaskin it means that it is done, and done at once. I should not have been in the least surprised if the first tractors had begun to roll up the drive within the next ten minutes.

Gaskin departed, to spend a brisk half hour on the telephone, ringing up his astonishingly large circle of acquaintances, most of whom seemed to be called Bert.

I sat down and meditated on the general impossibility of women.

Into the room, with great dignity, stalked 'One' and

'Four'. They had mud on their paws, and they naturally decided to sit on my lap. They smelt of moss and loam, and they both set up a slow, tranquil purr.

'Cats,' I thought, 'are best.'

In the next chapter we will learn why.

CHAPTER VII

THE SCHOLAR AND THE CATS

THIS book – as you may by now have gathered – is not really a book at all; it is only a long walk round a garden, in winter and summer, in rain and in sunshine; and if it bores you to walk round gardens you will long ago have chucked it aside. So neither of us need worry.

But if you would like to go on walking, then this is a moment when we must stop and turn our heads. For we are being followed.

We are being followed by two creatures of the greatest elegance, one of them beige, with blue eyes, the other black with green eyes. Both their tails are sticking up as straight as masts, which is a sign that they are alert and happy. They choose their path very daintily, skirting puddles if it is wet, and occasionally giving a sharp shake to an uplifted paw. They keep behind us at a regular distance of about ten feet, until we reach the orchard and the long grass. Then they suddenly streak forward like cheetahs, and swarm up into the branches of an old apple tree, where they remain, with their arms stretched out on the trunk, watching and waiting for us to follow them, which, of course, we are compelled to do. For when they are ensconced in the apple tree, it signifies that they will condescend to play with us. And that, in its turn, obliges us to go over to the hedge, to strip off a suitable twig, with, if possible, some rustling leaves at the end, and then to return to the apple tree and do some serious work, darting the twig up and down the trunk while they make dabs at it with their paws.

Such are 'One' and 'Four', who have been with us since the opening chapters, though until this moment we have not had time to introduce them properly.

Before we go any further, I must explain their names. 'One' is a Siamese of distinguished pedigree. When he came into my life, about a year before I moved to Merry Hall, he had a brother who was called 'Two', and the reason I gave them numbers instead of names was because I wanted to have at least a hundred cats before I died, and the thought of finding for them a hundred names was really too fatiguing. It was bad enough to have to think of names for the people in one's books. (By the way, the best place to find names for fictional characters, if you are ever foolish enough to write a novel, is in a Bradshaw or an A.B.C. All the nicest people always sound like railway stations.)

So 'One' and 'Two' they were. In the first winter, 'Two' caught the damnable cat 'flu which was sweeping through London, and in spite of everything we could do he flickered out of life, a tiny bundle of fur in a basket, with blue eyes that slowly clouded and closed. Then, when we had buried him, and the danger of infection had gone, 'Three' arrived – another Siamese kitten, from an even more exalted family. A few weeks later there was the same heart-rending business all over again. We took it in turns to sit up with him at night, feeding him with glucose every two hours, and dabs of meat extract on the tips of our fingers, and Gaskin, who is a genius with animals, undertook the delicate and difficult job of giving him penicillin injections, which I was too clumsy – if not too cowardly – to do myself. It was all no use. 'Three' fought for life like a tiny panther; he would struggle to a sitting position, and stay there, with his head on the edge of the basket, swaying from side to side, staring out at the great world . . . the desert of the carpet and the mountains of the chairs – which he was never destined to explore. Then he would fall down from sheer weakness, and one day he too died, with a sort of choke, as I was stroking him, and he was trying to purr.

I said to myself: 'Never again. There is enough pain and misery in the world to distract one and break one's heart, without deliberately going in search of any more. So never another Siamese. They are among the most beautiful of God's creatures, and their minds are as fascinating as their bodies . . . but, well, I've had bad luck, and I'm not going to risk any more.'

So 'Four' was chosen – one might say – from the lower classes of the cat world, if there *are* any lower classes in feline society, which I am inclined to doubt, for even the lowest alley cat has a certain *hauteur*. 'Four' was strong, sleek and jet black, with enormous bright green eyes. He was a perfect foil for 'One', with whom he immediately struck up a deathless friendship. He has never had a day's illness.

§ 11

The comfort of 'One' and 'Four' was a first priority as soon as we arrived at Merry Hall, and I shall never forget the afternoon when I took them for their first really 'country' walk round the huge, deserted old garden. It was an experience so enchanting that it was almost worth buying the house, even for that. The first pause on the steps, with one front paw lifted up in a sort of curve of interrogation . . . the blinking around at the vast prospect before them . . . the venturing forth . . . the suspicious pause before the long grass . . . the glancing around over their shoulders at me, their master, to inquire if it was politic to enter this jungle . . . and then, the sudden dive into the grass, and the tails waving – one beige and one black, and the weavings and the scurryings and the tumblings and the chasings, and the sudden plaintive wails from 'Four' when he felt lost, and had to be lifted up, and have the grass seeds wiped from the corners of his eyes.

And then – the first dash up the trunk of the first apple tree in the orchard, and the quivering progress along the branches, with crossed feet and twitching tails, and the blue eyes and the green eyes staring up in amazement at this strange leafy paradise. And again the mews, because it was all a bit too much for them. And the liftings down, and the carryings back to the house, and the strokings and the reassurings, and the doing it all over again, and yet again, until one knew that they were all right, and could be left to go on their own happy ways, alone.

All that they now required was a cat door, or rather, two cat doors, which I proceeded to put *en train.*

Have you got a cat door? And if not, why not? It is an elementary necessity in every house that is illuminated by the presence of a cat, and the only reason why so many people do not instal one is because they do not trouble to put themselves in the cat's place, to see into its mind. If they did they would instal a cat door immediately. Supposing that you, as a householder, were obliged to scratch carpets and make wailing noises every time that you wished to go into the garden, you would undoubtedly feel that you had lost face. Supposing that you were compelled to dart hastily out of the front door through the postman's legs, you would feel humiliated and, quite possibly, you would gain a reputation for peculiarity.

If it were possible to give cats latchkeys, or devise some other means by which they could come and go as they pleased, responding to all their exquisite intuitions, answering all the strange calls of night and day to which our own clumsy ears are deaf, I would certainly do so. However, since none of the inventors of my acquaintance, with the exception of Professor A. M. Low, ever invent anything pleasant or useful, and since the whole question of feline latchkeys seems to have been neglected as a subject for research, one is obliged to fall back on the primitive device of the cat door, which is simply a square hole cut at a convenient level, with a wooden flap hanging on a hinge. To pass through this door all the cat has to do is to push the flap with its head.

'*Two* of them doors, sir?' inquired Mr. Gray, the carpenter, when I had explained what I wanted.

'Yes. One into the kitchen and one into the conservatory.'

'Wouldn't the one in the kitchen be enough? Not that they'll cost much, but it all mounts up.'

'I'm afraid we'll have to have the conservatory one as well.'

It would have sounded altogether too hideously whimsical to explain to Mr. Gray that there were moments when the cats felt like coming in through the kitchen and moments when they felt like coming in through the conservatory, and that I enjoyed indulging their moods.

As soon as the doors were completed, I introduced 'One' and 'Four' to them. The kitchen one was a great success, but the conservatory one was inclined to be stiff, and 'Four' looked extremely indignant when he got stuck half way through, with fierce whiskers on one side and a very angry behind on the other. So I ran out to get an oil-can to ease the hinges.

While I was fiddling about with the oil, a shadow fell across the path. I looked up and saw . . . well, we will call him Marius. Since he is to play some part in these pages I will endeavour to describe him.

§ III

In his late thirties. Pale and dark, with an unruly shock of black hair. When he holds himself straight he is very tall, but he usually has a pronounced stoop, which is accentuated whenever he is in the garden, because he is always bending down to peer at things. He has a sort of elegant untidiness, like the young Aldous Huxley in his Oxford days; and it was at Oxford, where he was one of the most brilliant scholars of his generation, that he earned the nickname of Marius, which has stuck to him ever since. Not that he was – or is – an aesthete, in the 'ninetyish sense of the word; it was simply that he so perfectly reflected the philosophy which Pater had proclaimed in his *Renaissance*, which is summed up in the celebrated passage which gave such offence to Jowett:

We are all *condamnés*, as Victor Hugo says . . . we have an interval, and then our place knows us no more. Some spend this interval in listlessness, some in high passion, the wisest in art and song. Of this wisdom, the poetic passion, the desire of beauty, the love of art for art's sake has most; for art comes to us professing frankly to give nothing but the highest quality to our moments as they pass, and simply for those moments' sake.

Like many other young Englishmen of equally anti-social tendencies – (though why it should be anti-social to love a picture because it is a picture instead of a piece of propaganda I have never been able to understand) – Marius played a quietly heroic part in the war. Today, very few people are quite sure what he is. I do not think he would care for me to enlighten them. It is enough to say that he is not exactly Foreign Office and not exactly secret service, but that he flits about in the shadowy but curiously British no-man's-land that lies between the two. In the intervals he lives a quiet and civilized existence in a converted gamekeeper's cottage on the edge of the woods above the village of H——, some five miles from my house. I should perhaps add that it is the cottage, rather than the gamekeeper, that is converted, and very charmingly converted too: in the Regency style.

So there was Marius standing over me, watching me fiddle with the cat door, and as usual his opening gambit made me feel an intellectual worm. Not that this was his intention, for he is the kindest and most courteous of creatures. It is rather that his mind has so wide a range, and so rich a retention, that he simply cannot understand that ordinary folk do not always follow him.

'I little imagined,' he said, 'that I should find you in the posture of Sir Isaac Newton.'

Oh dear, I thought, here it comes again. What on earth was the meaning of *that*?

So I just said No. Neither did I. And went on fiddling with the oil-squirter, trying to remember things about Newton.

> Nature and Nature's laws lay hid in Night
> God said, Let Newton be – and all was light.

That was Pope, and for a moment I thought of quoting it over my shoulder at Marius. But to quote Pope to Marius would be asking for trouble. Besides, what had it got to do with cats?

'However, you have only cut *one* hole,' continued Marius blandly. 'Whereas Newton, of course, would have cut two.' A slight pause. 'As I need hardly remind you.'

I put down the oil-can and turned to him. 'Odd as it may seem, Marius, you need.'

'But surely, you, a cat-lover, have not forgotten Newton's cat? And his kitten? And the two holes that he cut for them into his study door?'

'I'm afraid that I *had* forgotten.'

He sighed profoundly, and nodded. 'One does. It is fantastic, the things one forgets.'

'I should have thought you forgot very little.'

'I?' There was an echo of genuine astonishment in his voice. 'But my dear fellow, I assure you, my memory is a sieve. Only this very moment, when I was watching your two beautiful creatures, and smiling to myself at the thought of the curious names you had given them, I recalled the cats of Cardinal Richelieu. As one naturally would.'

'Naturally.'

'Cardinal Richelieu, as we all know, had fourteen cats.'

I nodded. 'Fourteen.'

Marius apparently misinterpreted my parrot-like interjection.

'Am I mistaken?' he inquired anxiously.

'Not at all. Fourteen cats. Cardinal Richelieu.'

'You sounded a little doubtful?'

'But no . . . I thought it was established.'

'So did I. But one can never be too sure. However, taking for granted that fourteen *was* the correct number, one would naturally expect to remember their names. *Can* I remember them?' He shook his head. 'Soumise – Serpolet – Gazette – Ludovic le Cruel – Félimare . . . And that is as far as I can go. Yet once I wrote a monograph on Richelieu, and those cats followed me about in imagination for weeks. My favourite, of course, was Soumise.'

Why Soumise should have been 'of course' his favourite is one of those mysteries that I never expect to solve. And fortunately there was no further immediate need to appear intelligent, for at that moment 'Four' appeared, sniffed at the cat door, registered approval, pushed it open with his head, and vanished into the house.

'Four,' said Marius, reflectively. 'Four. The name can be made to sound quite musical. Which is something one could never say about a name like Hodge.'

Here, at last, I was on firmer ground. For at least I

knew my Boswell; indeed, one of the qualities which had most endeared me to Doctor Johnson was his unfailing consideration for his cat Hodge, who would appear, from contemporary illustrations, to have been large, black and distinctly 'Alley'. ('He himself used to go out and buy oysters for Hodge,' wrote Boswell, 'lest the servants having that trouble should take a dislike to the poor creature.')

And so, with an artless interjection about the price of oysters, which, I hoped, would re-establish me in Marius's estimation, I ushered him into the house for a glass of sherry. I remember thinking how much pleasanter it would have been if we could have crawled in through the cat door.

§ IV

Sometimes when I am taking people over the garden, they turn round, observe that 'One' and 'Four' are close behind us, and exclaim, as though they were saying something very original: 'How extraordinary! Those cats are *following* us. Just like dogs!'

Which is enraging. It is not at all extraordinary that a cat should follow you; it merely means that you are worth following. In other words, that you can be relied upon, from time to time, to do some serious work, twiddling twigs up apple trees, with the accent on the word 'serious'; for if you twiddle twigs up apple trees in a careless, off-hand manner, no cat of intelligence is deceived for an instant; it will just sit in the long grass, staring at you with mingled pity and contempt.

Another infuriating comment which people are apt to

make about cats and gardens goes like this: 'I can't think how you can let those cats dart about in the borders; surely they must do a terrible lot of damage?'

When people talk nonsense of that sort I feel inclined to refer them to Gertrude Jekyll. More than any other woman she influenced the design of the English garden, and she did so with the earnest assistance and co-operation of an immense quantity of cats. Pinkieboy, Tittlebat, Toozle – Chloe, Tavy and Mittens . . . the list is far too long for anybody but a Marius to remember; and I was interested to learn, from the most delightful cat book ever written,[1] that Miss Jekyll had forestalled me in my idea of calling my cats by numbers, for one of them was christened 'Octavius'. All these cats skipped and romped and danced and purred around this wonderful old lady as she went her way, fashioning her delicate designs, and what was good enough for her is certainly good enough for me.

There are only a very few occasions when I am inclined, for a fleeting moment, to regret the gardening activities of 'One' and 'Four'. They may be briefly listed under the following heads:

DELPHINIUMS

On hot summer afternoons, if you happen to be strolling along the herbaceous border, you will probably notice that the largest clump of delphiniums is looking strangely fatigued. Instead of standing up straight, many of the tall spires are leaning out at a weary angle, and some of the bottom leaves are drooping. This phenomenon is due to the fact that 'One' has decided to honour the delphiniums by sleeping in the middle of them, because

[1] CHRISTABEL ABERCONWAY, *A Dictionary of Cat-Lovers.*

they are soft and cool and shadowy. But I am convinced that there is another reason for his choice of this couch. Cats have an infallible aesthetic sense which informs them where they will be seen to best advantage, and 'One' never loses an opportunity to place himself near something blue enough to show off his blue eyes; if there are half a dozen cushions on a sofa, he invariably seats himself on the blue one. So it is with the delphiniums. As you bend over him and speak to him, softly and tactfully, with a note, not of command, but of suggestion, inquiring whether there might not be some other clump of flowers which he might grace with equal comfort, he blinks and stares up at you with very wide eyes, and their blue is so beautiful, flecked with the reflected blue of the blossom, that you change the subject. After which, if you have any decency, you tiptoe away.

WATERING

Both 'One' and 'Four' are inveterate waterers; 'Four', in particular, will put aside all other work, such as mouse-watching and leaf-chasing, as soon as he hears the clank of a watering can, and come streaking across the lawn, like a black panther, in order to join in the fun. Unfortunately, their ideas of watering do not always coincide with mine; for instance, they like to spend an excessive time at the tap, having it squirted for them with one's thumb, so that they can dart off to chase the silver thread of water, and dab at the dust where it has fallen. They insist, too, that much of the water should fall on the leaves, where it makes pattering noises which excite them, and send them scurrying into the undergrowth. Indeed, I have sometimes been compelled to water by stealth, tiptoeing out in rubber shoes, and dipping the cans very softly in the old water tank. (What could be more beautiful than dark, cool water in an old tank under a fig tree, with the shadows of the heavy leaves upon it, and through the leaves the reflected gleam of the wild quinces?

THE GREENHOUSE

'One' and 'Four' are both keenly interested in the greenhouse, and have been intimately associated both with its design and its upkeep. Among their special responsibilities is a small family of frogs, who have established themselves under the water tank. They are such nice frogs that in case anybody should tread on them I have put 'Beware of the Frogs' on the glass door. This makes some people think that I am afraid of the frogs; the reverse is the case. 'One' and 'Four' sit and stare at the frogs, and the frogs stare back, and there seems to be no illwill on either side. Once 'Four' gave a baby frog a gentle box on the ears, but it fell on its back with such an outraged expression that 'Four' looked quite ashamed, and has never tried it again.

The only time that I am inclined, ever so faintly, to deplore the role which 'One' and 'Four' play in the greenhouse is in February, when the seedlings are coming up in their boxes. We all go outside for a brisk walk, we do a certain amount of twig work, we pay the necessary visits to snowdrops, aconites, early periwinkles and the like, and then we end up at the greenhouse – as a sort of climax. Needless to say, 'One' and 'Four' follow me inside; we could not conceivably leave them in the cold. In the greenhouse it is deliciously warm; the fragrance of the white jasmine is intoxicating; the little yellow balls of the mimosa are just beginning to fluff out; there is a pure white cyclamen which is just *au point* and must be carried indoors at once; and it is all so exhilarating that one wonders, not for the first time, why people do not live in greenhouses for ever. If everybody lived permanently in greenhouses, nobody – surely – would be foolish enough to start a war, for nobody would have enough Elastoplast.

Then I turn round, and note, to my sorrow, that 'One' is sitting firmly on the broad bean seedlings, and it depresses me, because I am very fond of broad beans, and their seedlings are especially appealing; they almost leap out of the earth, with tense stalks and heads that strain up to the light, as though they were 'rarin' to go' as the Americans would say. 'One' should really not sit on them. He must be lifted off. And as he is lifted off, I observe that 'Four' is not only sitting on the seedling peas, but casting a slanting green eye at the seedling verbenas.

It is evidently time to leave the greenhouse and to go outside.

Which we will now proceed to do.

CHAPTER VIII

THE PATH IN THE SNOW

FULL winter, and still no garden. Only a bleak, rolling field in front of us, stretching to an orchard in the far distance, and a bare, rambling old house behind us, with its walls stripped bare of the speckled ivies and diseased vines which had disfigured it. And above us the empty sky.

And we had to make a garden, and it was all somewhat intimidating.

It was not made any easier by the 'assistance' of one's friends. Bob paid occasional visits, stalked round the estate, rattled his chains, and prophesied ruin. Cyril arrived from time to time, accompanied by bright and hearty friends, who spent their whole time arguing about the best site for a hard tennis court – as if such a monstrous idea had ever entered one's head. Miss Emily drifted in and out, with the sole object of Flinching. And various well-intentioned females made bright suggestions, which all seemed to resolve themselves into endless arches covered with Dorothy Perkins roses. That was kind of them, but I do not like arches in gardens, and when they are covered with Dorothy Perkins roses I like them even less. I am not-at-home to the Misses Perkins, with their over-painted complexions and their common habits, and I am glad to learn that there is at least one great gardener who agrees with me – the poet Vita Sackville-West, who has less nonsense in her little finger than most women in their whole bodies, if you know what I mean.

Worst of all was Our Rose, for she now decided that she must give a Helping Hand. Though she had been thwarted in her quest for vegetables – not even a radish had she managed to extract from me – she yet soared nobly above the misunderstandings of the past in order to come to my rescue.

We have already noticed two of Our Rose's most irritating affectations – her trick of calling inanimate objects 'he' or 'she', and the way in which she says 'we' when she means 'you'. To these must now be added a third – her habit of looking rapturously into space and saying 'I see' this or that when, in fact, there is nothing there for her to see at all.

Thus, she would arrive unexpectedly, weave her way by various devices into the study, walk to the window, stare out on to the dark, empty earth, sigh deeply, and then, with a sudden clasp of her hands, exclaim:

'I see drifts of daffodils!'

The obvious retort would be that if this was indeed the case she should have taken more water with it on the night before. However, gentlemen are restrained from such comment.

'Yes . . . yes!' An eager nod of the head and a narrowing of the eyes, as though the vision were crystallizing before her. 'And beyond the daffodils a cluster of silver birches, dancing in the wind!' A moment's pause. 'And what is that . . . what *is* it? . . . curving towards us down the slope?'

I look over her shoulder. The only thing I can see curving towards us down the slope is the latest Odd Man, and Our Rose might well have some excuse for being puzzled as to what it was, for it is hardly human. But this is not what she meant.

'Why, of course . . . it's the garden path! And there are irises on either side of it . . . but I can't see what sort they are. Can *you* see?'

'No.' Very shortly.

'Blue flecked with yellow,' she muses, with her head on one side.

'If you were given your deserts,' I think, 'you'd end up by being blue flecked with yellow yourself.' It is awful, the sadistic instincts she arouses.

'And somewhere,' she goes on, '*somewhere* I can see a gleam of water . . . like the ghost of a water-garden.' And she holds out her hand, as though she were drawing a picture and measuring the perspective. Then she sighs, and drops her hand, and turns quickly, tosses her head and gives a smile to show what a brave little thing she is, in spite of the physical exhaustion which such visions must naturally entail.

It makes me happy to think that not one single suggestion of Our Rose's has ever been adopted. Needless to say, when the water garden was eventually made, she claimed that it was all her own idea, merely because of the 'gleam' which she had 'seen', out on the bare earth, that desolate day in January. She even suggested that she should be photographed with it, stretching out her hands for a lily. But if Our Rose is ever photographed with my pool, she will be well inside it, and she will be stretching out her hands for help.

§ II

Deeper and deeper into winter, and still no garden. The snow began to fall, and went on falling for day after bitter day, till the lane was white and hushed, and the old house seemed very still and deserted, with all one's friends and would-be helpers marooned in their various villages. Even the telephone wires were down; I was completely undisturbed; and outside there was nothing but a great white sheet of paper. Surely at last I should be able to trace on that paper some sort of design?

It was the nakedness of it all that was so alarming; I used to sit on the window ledge in the study, and stare out and shiver; it was as though the emptiness stretched to the end of the world.

There is a phrase from the jargon of psychoanalysis which at this period constantly occurred to me. It is a phrase that is rather disagreeable, but I will take the risk of quoting it because it expresses a profound truth, which is applicable to many people in these days.

It is called 'the desire to return to the womb'. Although it is a modern neurosis, it is as old as human nature. It means that there are times when the outside world seems so harsh and hostile, and the winds of circumstance so cruel and chill, that the victim feels like curling up in a shape that is literally embryonic, as though he or she would seek refuge in a strange, dark, pre-natal condition. In its extreme manifestations, this desire degenerates into lunacy; it has been said that Nijinski, for example, passed whole months curled up on his bed in a sort of tragic coma, in the wishful hallucination that he was as yet unborn. It is to be hoped that neither you nor I are ever likely to reach that stage.

As soon as one learns about this neurosis, one begins to recognize the germs of it in oneself. So, at least, it was with me. Was it not for this reason that I was so fond of caves . . . because they sheltered, and enveloped, and gave a momentary illusion of security? Once in a cave I was reluctant to emerge; I liked sitting in it and staring out to sea and listening to the wind roaring in the roof. I liked attics, too, with sloping roofs that could be touched with one's hands, and tiny windows that made the sunlight seem very gentle when it filtered through, and framed the vast night in a miniature that one could accept without being too intimidated, and just enough stars to brighten the horizon without dizzying the imagination.

And I liked – very much indeed I liked – curling up in bed on a cold morning, with the sheets completely over my head, in the happy knowledge that the morning papers with all their horrors were still an hour away, and that one was a sort of peculiar cocoon whom nobody, not even Stalin, could see or try to seek out.

This is not all so irrelevant as it sounds, for it was this neurosis – though I did not realize it at the time – that was responsible for the eventual design of the garden.

One day, when I was sitting alone in the study, hugging my neurosis, Our Rose arrived, and proceeded to go through her usual act. It was even more tiresome than usual, for she chose to be inspired by the snow, and 'saw' things all in white.

'A *sea* of white phloxes, don't you think?' she proclaimed, from her customary position at the window.

'Hmph.'

'And behind them, ranks and ranks of white foxgloves. Yes?'

'They don't come out at the same time.'

'But I can *see* them.'

'Then you must have very remarkable eyesight.'

A pursing of the lips, a raising of the eyebrows. 'Are we feeling a teeny bit scratchy this morning?'

'Not at all.' We are, in truth, feeling of a scratchiness that baffles description. 'It isn't a question of being scratchy, it's a question of being accurate. They don't.'

'Don't what?'

'Come out at the same time. Foxes and phloxgloves. I mean . . .'

A peal of girlish laughter greets this slip of the tongue. It enrages me to such an extent that I proceed to explain to Our Rose, with brutal frankness, the symptoms of my neurosis. There is no beating about the bush, whatsoever, and when I come to the word 'womb', I bring it out with a sort of whoop of defiance. The effect on Our Rose is just as I expected. She may be 'modern' – indeed she prides herself on being very modern indeed, and has several rather muddy reproductions of Picasso hung up on the walls of her cottage, because she says they 'do' something to her, which I can well believe – but she is not as modern as all that. Face up to the facts of life, by all means, she says, but arrange them prettily, like flowers. Don't go into horrid embryonic details.

So Rose departed in a huff, and if it had been the age of petticoats, she would certainly have given them an extra swish. As it was, it was to me that the extra swish had been given. She had goaded me into activity at last.

I seized a writing block and a pencil and went to the window. One had a neurosis, had one? Very well, face up to it. One wanted a garden in which to hide? Fine. Plant it. Draw a thick frame of trees right round. (Here I drew a bold curving line.) Dark and mysterious at the edges, with fir and cypress and box and yew and holly. (Here I scribbled feverishly, putting in the shading.) Bring it nearer and nearer to the house, with all the blossoming things, the laughing cherries and the foaming crabs. (Here a fusillade of dots and dashes.)

Even as I indulged in this display of temperament, I was making a few calculations; it needed only a glance from the paper to the garden outside to realize that I was letting myself in for several hundred trees, and I suspected that when we came to mark out the land, I should find that we needed a thousand. It couldn't be helped. If we must have a thousand trees we would have a thousand trees. Otherwise, it was only too likely that before the winter was out I should be found curled up in embryonic gloom in a dark corner of the tool shed.

So much for the frame. Now for the path. Caution whispered to me that surely I had done enough in the last quarter of an hour, deciding on a thousand trees. (For I *had* decided on them; there could be no thought of turning back.) I told caution to go to the devil. There had been enough delay. Whatever would be done would be done *now*. As G. K. Chesterton once said, a thing that is worth doing at all is worth doing badly. Which is the best possible translation of *le mieux est l'ennemi du bien.*

All the same, it was in a slightly more sober mood that I put on a coat, opened the door, sniffed the keen air, and indulged in a further mono-dialogue. 'A garden implies a garden path, doesn't it?'

'Yes, it does.'

'And if you walk down a garden path you walk *somewhere*, don't you?'

'You certainly do.'

'Very well. I shall walk *somewhere*. Quickly. Without forethought. In the snow. And where my footsteps fall, there shall be the path, for ever.' I am afraid that it sounds rather like the sort of thing that Our Rose would do, but that was how it was.

I looked out to the end of the garden. And at that moment the sun came out, and lit up the snow-laden branches of an old pear tree that stood all by itself on the outskirts of the orchard. It was an object of the greatest beauty, and I knew that in the spring its branches would again be white, laden with snows of blossom. That was where I should walk.

I stepped out on to the crisp snow. I have a feeling that I walked with my eyes half shut, twisting and turning ever so slightly, partly to keep with the lay of the land, partly to mark where I felt there might be a bed, or some shrubs, or a group of trees. As soon as I reached the pear tree I hurried off to the tool shed, and returned with an armful of canes to stake out the design. I not only traced the path, but appointed a place for a little flight of steps, and stuck in bamboos where I should plant paeonies and dig the iris bed. Finally, near the house, I made two very large, irregular beds for what is really my signature flower – the winter heather, *erica carnea* . . . the flower that brings the warm glow of

August into the depths of winter, and spreads its rosy carpet of blossom with sublime indifference to the frost and the snow.

That was five years ago. These words are being written in mid-January, at a window from which you can see the heather blooming, and the path stretching beyond it, up to the old pear tree. In the far distance, exactly as I designed them in that frenzied fifteen minutes, are the curving and intercurving lines of the evergreens, that are already tall enough to cast long shadows, and to drop dark hints of the mysteries which they will soon be hiding in their depths. There are other excitements, too, which have developed as we went along, and in due course we shall hear about them. But the main design remains as it was, stepped out in the snow.

If you were with me at this moment, I believe that you would agree that it looks inevitable, as though the path had led that way from the beginning of time. But even if you had doubts about that, you could have no reservations about the *erica carnea*, the sheets of heather in fullest flower, made all the lovelier because the rich hues of their blossom are powdered with the silver of the frost.

To this lovely thing we must now pause and pay tribute.

§ III

I called the *erica carnea* my 'signature flower', for it gives the clue to the whole garden.

It has the breath of the moorland, and yet it is neat

and elegant. It is, in a sense, a solitary, flaming away long before the crocuses have shown the smallest flicker of gold, and yet it is companionable, blending happily with all its neighbours.

The nurserymen do not make a tenth enough fuss about *erica carnea.* They should issue special catalogues about it. They should use their largest print and their most monstrous adjectives, like the film people, who say that it is 'stupendous' and 'gargantuan' when Jane Russell exposes an extra inch of her remarkable torso – which, indeed, it is.

For what other flower, within hundreds of miles of these misted isles, can be guaranteed – but *guaranteed* – in any soil whatsoever, to give a blaze of rosy blossom throughout December [*sic*], January [*sic*] and February [*sic*]? *And* March (. . . almost [*sic*])? What other flower will produce this blaze [*sic*] through the snow, so that after a storm you can have the sheer enchantment of seeing what seems to be an embroidery of brilliant pink on a coverlet of white satin?

Can you tell me?

What other flower has so sure and masterly a manner with weeds? The *erica carnea* treats these tiresome things with a most elegant disdain; like a rich and lovely woman at a matinee, spreading herself out, so that her cloak and her mink and her accessories gently smother her neighbours. The *erica carnea* is such a smotherer. She smothers with such grace that the weeds retire with hardly a murmur.

But please remember one thing about the *erica carnea.* By far the best variety of the pinks is the King George, which happens also to be the cheapest. The nurserymen will try to persuade you to buy all sort of other varieties, ruby and rose and crimson. Have nothing to do with them. They sulk and peek and straggle and go brown. The motto must be 'King George for Ever'.

Equally important it is to remember that supreme among the whites is Springwood. This is indeed the white of all whites; and when the snow falls around it the blossom disappears, gliding into the snow in an all-embracing whiteness. When the snow melts again, the blossom reappears, untarnished, immaculate, perpetuating the gleam of the snow. If you know your *Moby Dick*, and if you remember his 'white' chapter, which is one of the miracles of literature, you will not desire me to experiment in further expositions of the whiteness of Springwood. I will content myself by observing that if you have not grown it, you have never really lived.

§ IV

I tried to avoid it, but we seem to have drifted into a discussion of flowers in winter. I apologize, because it is more than possible that I may become a bore on this subject. Flowers in winter is another of my King Charles's heads, to give a comfortable name to an obsessional neurosis, and I find it difficult to write a book without mentioning them. Even when I was composing a long and factual study of modern India, there was a constant itch to describe Mr. Nehru as an embittered aconite, grown spotty in the shade, which of course he is. However, if you have an obsession it is better to yield to it, and though that sounds like a very tired echo of Wilde, we will let it pass.

Besides, as winter succeeds winter, I get madder and

madder at the thought of the multitudes of gardeners who absolutely *refuse* to grow flowers in winter. Particularly if they are women. Women are supposed to like flowers, but sometimes one really is tempted to doubt it, considering the number of months in the year in which they are content to do without them, for no reason whatsoever.

Only yesterday a women walked into the music-room, paused and gazed and gasped and said: 'But I've never seen anything so beautiful!'

'They are pretty, aren't they? I picked them this morning.'

'Out of doors? But there was snow on the ground!'

'Where these were growing there was a snowdrift. The buds were only just showing over the top.'

'You're joking? Why – they're like orchids.'

And they were. They were pale blue, flushed with mauve, striped with a deeper blue, lit in the centre with a tinge of gold. There were about fifty of them, in a big white basket under a lamp, and their petals were so frail and delicate that they trembled in the draught.

All out of a snowdrift only a few hours before.

'But what *are* they?'

'Common or garden *iris stylosa*.'

'But don't they cost a million?'

'You can get a nice clump for a bob or so.'

'But aren't they difficult to grow?'

'A half-witted child of four could grow them in a London slum.'

'Don't you want madly green fingers?'

'The colour of your fingers is no more important than the colour of your hair.'

She looked surprised. 'You sound quite cross?'

'I am. Furious. And with you.'

'But why? I told you I loved them.'

'That's precisely the reason. You're an intelligent, charming woman who likes pretty things. You've got a nice little garden . . .'

'In the suburbs.'

'They adore the suburbs. You're always moaning about the price of flowers. You spend ridiculous sums on mingy little bunches of daffodils and anemones, to say nothing of that absolutely repulsive rubber plant in the hall. When all the time . . .'

I was not allowed to finish the sentence. I was told that I was being rude.

Well, as I can't go on being rude to her, permit me to be rude to you. Permit me to ask you a few quite straight-from-the-shoulder questions on the assumptions. . .

(*a*) That you are female.

(*b*) That you are capable of bending gently from the waist in the direction of the earth.

(*c*) That you are not lying in your throat when you say you love flowers.

(*d*) That you are the owner of a shilling or two.

The possession of these four qualities is not unique; they do not add up to genius; there are numbers of women walking about with them who have never even been mentioned in the Press. To them I speak.

Why do you not DO – repeat DO – something about winter flowers?

Not only about *iris stylosa* but all the others?

What is the matter with you?

Perhaps you would *object* to filling your rooms with immense vases of pale waxy blossoms in mid-January . . .

blossoms that smell like lemon-peel with a faint tinge of apricot? Perhaps they would sicken you, or give you some sort of peculiar twitch? If so, of course, that is your affair.

And you must not order a *chimonanthus fragrans*.

Perhaps it would *irritate* you to be greeted, in the drawing-room, on New Year's Eve, by large branches of a shrub which appeared to be covered with a swarm of Chinese golden spiders? You might, conceivably, suspect that you were on the verge of delirium tremens? Too sad. I must leave you to go your own way.

And you must strictly avoid a *hammamelis mollis*.

Perhaps you would *protest*, and go into sulks, and pluck your blouse with nervous fingers, if you came home on a stormy night in January and found the hall fragrant with honeysuckle? 'These poltergeists,' you might mutter, 'are going too far.' Alas – if that is the sort of person you are, you must work out your own salvation.

And nothing must induce you to procure a *lonicera fragrantissima*.

But if, by some strange chance, you should happen to be the sort of eccentric who might like these things, who might actually enjoy the scents of summer in the dark of winter . . . if you should be such a person, then, I repeat, why don't you DO something about it?

For all these things are possible.

However, I know that one might as well talk to a lamp-post as to a woman who does not want to be convinced, so we will bring this chapter to a close. And you can put on your ridiculous hat and go out and spend ten shillings on a small bunch of imported mimosa which, I sincerely hope, will turn to bullets within ten minutes of being brought into the house.

CHAPTER IX

THE WOOD FOR THE TREES

IN the last chapter we looked out of the window and saw, in the distance, a wood containing about a thousand trees. Not, as yet, a very tall wood, though it is growing so fast that in May you would say that the trees were standing on tiptoe to reach nearer to the sun. Nor, for the moment, a wood in which you can actually lose yourself, though there are places where you can hide in it and sigh about the sad state of the world, notably in a little curve of the path where a group of mock-oranges has flourished beyond all reason.

Hiding and sighing in mock-oranges may not be among the more virile manly pursuits, but I like it, and shall continue to do it. It seems good for me, and judging by the results, it is also good for the mock-oranges.

Some of the trees in this wood have very romantic stories attached to them, which I shall shortly relate. But most of them, I must admit, came straight from the nursery gardens, in heights varying from three to six feet, and when they were planted they did not look romantic at all. They looked like quantities of clothes props stuck up on end in a rather dreary field. This might have depressed some people, but it did not depress me in the least; I have been planting woods since I was nineteen years old, and I knew that the clothes props were really magic wands, that would soon be bursting into pinks and whites and greens, and distilling delicious odours all around them.

However, in order to realize this you had to have not only imagination but experience. Our Rose, it would seem, had neither.

When I took her out to look at the wood, and showed her a line of lilacs that had been planted with a background of copper beech, she did her usual act of gazing and narrowing her eyes and clasping her hands; but then she shook her head.

'I'm terribly sorry. But I don't see them.'

'What do you mean – don't see them? They're there in front of you.'

'Yes, I'm sure they are. But I just don't *see* them.'

This was maddening. Our Rose, as we have observed, spent a large portion of her life 'seeing' things which weren't there at all, but now that she was confronted by nine glorious lilacs lurking in the shade of three majestic copper beeches, they were invisible to her. Admittedly, at the moment they looked like nine gooseberry bushes with three clothes props stuck at the back, but that was neither here nor there.

I snapped something silly about consulting an oculist.

She smiled, almost too sweetly. 'It isn't a question of my eyes,' she said. 'It's . . . ' a pause, and then a sweeping gesture to the bosom . . . 'it's *here*.'

'And what is wrong *there*?'

'I *feel* nothing. I *get* nothing. Or rather, what I get I can't accept. Mauve and brown . . . oh no!'

'Nobody has ever suggested mauve and brown,' I replied, with mounting fury. 'Five of the lilacs are deep purple, two are almost red, and two are white. And if you had ever *seen* a copper beech' – (at which she emitted a faint, treble snort) – 'you would realize that whatever else it may be it is not *brown*. It is sepia with red in it, it is chocolate with green in it, and at dusk it can be black with blue in it. Anybody who dismisses it as brown must be colour-blind.'

'Thank you,' she hissed.

'Not at all.'

After which we walked, with some stiffness, to the greenhouse. And thereby hangs a story. It is called 'The Tale of the Thirty Cypresses', and I shall proceed to tell it, if only because it gives me an excellent chance of getting rid of Our Rose, of whom, for the moment, we have had more than enough.

§ II

It all happened in the second year at Merry Hall – the year, that is to say, after the main body of the wood had been planted. A thousand trees were settled in their places, and were flourishing exceedingly. But as the seasons went by, I found it necessary to make considerable additions to the wood, on paper, for I was constantly being reminded of things which had been forgotten. Thus, when I was out for a walk in the village, I would

AIR

peer over a hedge into somebody else's garden and see a flash of pink in the distance, and realize with a sudden pang that it came from a Judas tree, and that I had been idiotic enough to forget about Judas trees. And as soon as I reached home, I would hurry out to the wood and stick in three Judas trees – that is to say, three bamboo canes to mark the places where the Judas trees would be planted in the autumn.

Among the additions to the wood which had to be ordered were thirty cypresses. They were to be of the ordinary Lawson variety, of no special interest, and their only purpose was to fill in an empty corner with a dark mass of branches as a background to a big group of snowball trees. Well, on the morning that I went out to stick in the bamboos to mark their places, I happened to pause at an old fig tree, to see if there was any fruit on it. Needless to say, there was not; there never is, on any fig tree with which I have been even remotely connected. However, I did not curse it, for near by the fig tree was an old Lawson cypress, and I noticed something about it which I had never noticed before; all the ends of the branches were fringed with a glowing red. It was quite beautiful, a sort of Van Dyck red against the dark green. And I realized that this red was caused by the seeds, hundreds of thousands of little cypress seeds.

I was seized by a wild idea, of revolutionary import.

Trees grew from seeds, did they not?

They did.

Seeds, if sown, might come up?

They might.

This was a tree, this tree had seeds, if these seeds were sown other trees might, in due course, occur?

They might.

Such a mental dialogue, to anybody but a gardener, must sound like lunacy; indeed, it sounded rather like lunacy to me. For though trees might grow from seeds, and though vast oaks might spring from acorns, there was such a thing as the time element; I was no longer nineteen; I was in a tearing hurry; and I wanted that dark background for the snowball trees right now.

Nevertheless, the prospect of growing my own trees from seed, of producing, as though by magic, a baby forest, was so compelling that I could not resist it. Without a moment's delay I hurried back to the house and crossed off the cypresses from my order list. Why spend twenty pounds on thirty of somebody else's trees when you could have ten thousand of your own trees for nothing?

Then I went out, shook about a tablespoonful of the seed into my hand, and sowed it in a box in the greenhouse.

Just as I had finished, Oldfield appeared.

'Morning, sir.' He touched his cap, and his one eye fixed itself on the seed-box. I felt like a very small boy detected by the headmaster in the act of writing rude remarks on the blackboard.

'I was just sowing some seeds, Oldfield.'

'Hmph.' The one eye remained fixed on the box.

'Cypress seeds. Off the old tree by the fig.'

'Hmph.' He bent over the box and touched the soil with his finger. That finger may be hard and horny, but it is so sensitive that I swear Oldfield could analyse the nature of a compost merely by touching its surface.

'T'soil seems all right,' he admitted grudgingly. He gave a long sigh, and straightened himself.

'D'you think they'll come up?'

A sigh from the very depths. Then he said: 'They *might* coom oop.'

This, from Oldfield, had I only known it, was equivalent to an accolade. To say that a thing *might* coom oop, meant that it almost certainly *would* coom oop, because it was his invariable policy to be on his guard against anything cooming oop at all. It was just his way, and it took me a long time to realize that this pessimism was purely verbal, and that behind it was a shining light of faith. It took me even longer to understand the reason for it. It was because he had been fighting a sixty year battle against all those forces, whether animal, vegetable or mineral, which conspire against things cooming oop, and though in this long, leafy contest he had emerged, time and again, triumphant, he – like the wise old strategist he was – was taking no chances. He was making no facile promises. He would do his best – yes – but as far as cooming oop was concerned, he would give no guarantees.

So when Oldfield said that the seeds *might* coom oop, I ought to have been delighted.

As it was I felt faintly depressed. If I had only been able to interpret the gleam in his old eye, I should have known that he was quite as excited about the cypresses as I was myself, that henceforth he would adopt them, and take them under his wing, and make sure that I did not commit any major follies with them.

The cypresses, as usual, led to a reminiscence.

'Last time I planted cypresses,' he said, 't'was for Doovz aunt.'

'Oh!' I could not think of any very helpful comment on this news item. 'Was she very fond of them?'

'She couldn't abide 'em. But when she died, Doovz

planted 'em by 'er grave. You can go and look at 'em in t'churchyard.'

'I will.' And I would. For I was beginning to have a fondness for anything connected with Doovz. And it was pleasant to think of their having a nice, real aunt.

'T'usband was buried in same grave,' continued Oldfield, 'so Doovz put up inscription on t'gravestone. Like this it went . . . "*In Memory's Garden we Meet Ev'ry Day*". Mrs. Doov thought that one oop on her own. "*In Memory's Garden we Meet Ev'ry Day.*"'

The old man seemed so attached to the line that I murmured something about its being very suitable.

'Hmph!' snorted Oldfield. 'They was never very pally at t'best o'times. I remember. . .

I began to make plans to drift away, for I now knew Oldfield well enough to realize that though he was a rich and spicy raconteur, he liked to take his time, and I happened to be in a hurry. I had also learned that a very special technique was necessary if one was to terminate a conversation without offending him. It was no use looking at one's watch and saying . . . 'Oh dear, I shall miss my train' . . . for that meant that one had to hurry out of the drive, and charge down the lane in the direction of the station, and spend hours lurking in the village. Nor did it help very much to say . . . 'Well, I must be getting on with my work.' He did not seem to hear it. Or if he did, he dismissed it with the lofty contempt of the man who really *does* work . . . the man who sweats over a patch of earth versus the man who fiddles over a piece of paper.

No . . . there was only one sure way of bringing the conversation to a close, and that was to drift backwards, slowly, artfully, step by step. You had to do a sort of involved, crab-like slither over the lawn, always keeping your face towards him, and always maintaining your end of the dialogue. Thus . . .

'Mr. Stebbing always said as broad beans weren't fit to eat. Feed 'em to the pigs, that's what he used to say.'

'Well, fancy that' . . . (two steps backward) . . . 'I can't say I really agree . . . (a long swift glide of nearly four paces) . . . 'I'm rather fond of broad beans myself.'

'Trouble about broad beans,' continues Oldfield, raising his voice, because we are now at some distance, 'is that either you have too much of 'em or too little of 'em.' (While he is delivering himself of this aphorism I glide, as though propelled by invisible wires, some six feet further away.)

'Now Doovz was great ones for broad beans . . .' Here he has almost to shout. And I feel that without ill grace I can smile and wave and toss off some light and airy broad-beanesque remark, and make an exit. All the same, I never feel very happy about it. I would rather linger. Not only to avoid hurting his feelings but because . . . well . . . there are so many things in life less interesting than Doovz and broad beans.

§ III

No – we have not forgotten the Tale of the Thirty Cypresses.

The clock must now be switched forward some six months. During all this period I had been so busy in the house that the garden had been comparatively neglected – by which I mean that there were occasional moments when the hedges did not shake to the sound of falling trees and the lawns roar beneath the assault of motor ploughs.

Then came the spring, and the almost unbearable excitement – which can only be enjoyed in an ancient garden – of discovering where the previous owners had planted their bulbs. Of all the treasure hunts in which men have ever engaged, this must surely be the most enthralling . . . to wander out on a February morning, in an old garden which is all your own and yet is still a mystery, and to prowl about under the beech trees, gently raking away a layer of frozen leaves in the hope of finding a cluster of snowdrops . . . to scan the cold hard lawns in March for the first signs of the fresh green blades of the crocuses . . . to go through the orchard with a thin comb, putting a bamboo to mark every fresh discovery of daffodils.

I need hardly say that when I embarked on this fresh treasure hunt I was very soon to discover that Mr. Stebbing, in his planting of bulbs, had employed to the full his extraordinary genius for putting everything in the wrong place. For example, the obvious place for snowdrops – a site which positively screamed for them – was under the old copper beech. It was perfect soil for them; they would be visible from all the chief windows in the house; and they would catch enough of the winter sunlight. Mr. Stebbing, of course, had firmly turned his back on such a site, and after days of fruitless search I came to the conclusion that he had not planted any snowdrops at all. Then, one day I was going out to fetch some kindling from the woodshed, and was crossing a small concrete courtyard, when I observed to my astonishment that in the four corners of this courtyard, set in rigid squares, were four beds brimming with snowdrops. It was really one of Mr. Stebbing's master-strokes, and for a moment I could not help giving him a grudging admiration. With one decisive stroke he had achieved the acme of the inapposite. Not only had he managed to make the snowdrops look quite hideous – like squares of wet, white paint – but he had placed them in a spot where they could only be observed by the tradesmen and the chimney sweep.

There and then I got a spade and transplanted the snowdrops to the copper beech. (In case you did not know it, snowdrops 'lift' best when they are in full flower, providing that you dig them up in a solid chunk of soil.) It would be too whimsical to suggest that when I set them in their new quarters, they gently bowed their heads and thanked me, like ladies of quality who have been rescued from vulgar circumstances. Still, I like to play with such thoughts, and if you cannot bear them you can always turn the page . . . where you will probably find a great many more.

It was the same with all the other bulbs. As we all know, the only way to plant daffodils is to pile them on to a tray, and then to run out into the orchard and hurl the tray into the air, planting them exactly where they fall. There may be other, less orthodox methods; if so they should be spurned. The tray, the ecstatic gesture . . . that is the only sure road to success.

Mr. Stebbing had thought otherwise. He had planted his daffodils in triangles. After the word 'triangles' I feel impelled to write the word '*sic*', particularly as the triangles were of the variety known to schoolboys as Isosceles. There they were, on those first March days, greeting me in the orchard, as though disposed for battle.

They were fine daffodils, they gleamed and sparkled and held themselves very erect, like soldiers on parade. But they did not dance, nor did my heart dance with them.

Not that it mattered very much. For a great deal of dancing of the heart was about to be experienced.

Which brings us back to the cypress seeds.

§ IV

On a certain lemon-coloured morning in the last week of April, I was wandering among the cold frames, peering at the little shoots and leaves in the boxes, when in the corner of the furthest frame I saw an old box that seemed to be falling to pieces. I was in a cleaning-up mood, so I bent down to pick it up and throw it on the rubbish heap. Then I paused, for I noticed that the surface of the earth with which it was filled was covered with a thin film of very fine grass – or so it seemed – grass so pale and delicate that as I peered more closely it rippled in the puff of my breath. 'This must be some special sort of grass' I was thinking, trying to remember if there was any major madness I had committed in the shape of ordering ornamental grasses. It seemed unlikely, because I very much dislike ornamental grasses. Then, all of a sudden, I realized what they were. They were the cypress seeds.

The shock was so great that I almost dropped the box. You see, I had forgotten all about them. It had been a momentary autumnal folly, which had been swept out of my mind by all the other follies that had succeeded it. But now I saw that it was no folly at all.

For in my hands I held a forest.

Very slowly, very gingerly – for the wood was half rotted – I lifted the box and rested it on the wall, so that the sunlight caught the tiny green blades. Of all the thrills of my gardening life I do not think that any exceeded the thrill of that moment.

Every one of those pale threads of green – (in a few seconds you could have snipped off the whole lot with a pair of nail scissors) – was a potential giant. Each of them – (and you could have crushed them all into a salt spoon) – might one day grow higher than the house, and take in its branches the songs of the wind, and thrust its muscled roots deep into the earth. On its strong shoulders the snows would press in vain, and its shade would be too deep for the summer suns to penetrate; it would be a shelter and a home and a fortress, throughout the years, for countless birds and tiny creatures who would come to it for protection.

My mind leapt ahead. I saw myself at the age of sixty or so – no, it would have to be later than that, more like seventy – tottering through a forest, down dark mysterious paths, with only weary gleams of sunlight to mark the way. And then I should lean against a gnarled old trunk and turn to some senile companion, and say:

'I've always had a particular affection for this forest.'

'I'm not surprised,' he would reply, in a quavering voice. 'Fine lot of timber, you've got here.'

'Thank you.' Here I would bow, if rheumatism would permit. Then . . . stifling my bronchitis, I should continue, in the most casual voice: 'It always amuses me to remember that I once held the entire forest in the palm of my hand.'

'Eh? What's that?' croaks my old friend, who, like most old friends, will presumably be hard of hearing. 'You did *what*?'

'Held the entire forest in the palm of my hand.' Here I shall wave my stick towards some giant. 'I seem to remember that *that* tree was once stuck to a piece of caramel in my pocket.'

To which my aged crony would reply that caramels are not what they were.

Then he would prick up his ears, wondering if he has heard aright. 'What d'you say? Tree stuck to a caramel? What?'

Whereupon, with many coughs and wheezes, and a great deal of sucking of aniseed lozenges, I will tell him the Tale of the Thirty Cypresses, as I have told it to you.

Not that the story, even yet, is quite finished. When I had done gloating over the filmy grasses, I fetched Oldfield to see them. For once in a way he seemed almost enthusiastic, and a broad grin lit up his face.

'Reckon there's five hundred pounds' worth of trees in that theer box,' he observed. 'We'll have to take good care of 'em.'

'What shall we do with them? How shall we treat them?'

'We'll put box in t'shadow of wall, and I'll rig up special frame over it. Coom a thunderstorm and they'd be washed away.'

'When can we transplant them?'

'November maybe. You'll be needing some extra fine soil.'

So it was. In November we planted six long rows of tiny cypresses, about the size of matches. It seemed impossible that they would root, but nearly all of them did. Throughout the following year they put on about five inches of sturdy growth. We left them in their bed that winter, but potted thirty of them the following spring, distributing over a hundred others to various friends. A year later, when they were eighteen inches high, they were reverently placed in their appointed positions. At the moment of writing they reach to my shoulder; by the time these words are printed I shall be looking up to them. Indeed, I look up to them already, in another sense. For though it is true that only God can make a tree, they are to me an eternal reminder that man, if he wishes, can often lend God a helping hand.

So ends the Tale of the Thirty Cypresses. I apologize for taking so long to tell it.

§ v

There are many other stories about the trees in my wood, but I will not bore you with them, because they would probably mean little unless you were standing by my side.

Unless, for instance, you could actually see my eucalyptus – twenty feet tall and climbing skywards all the time, with its frail, aristocratic limbs – you would not appreciate the drama of the night when there was a hurricane, and the whole household rushed out to take turns in holding it up, until it could be properly staked.

Unless you could actually smell my scented poplars – yes, there is a poplar of such fragrance that on a May evening it makes you wonder if you have strayed into a lemon grove – you would not get the comedy of the occasion when we tried to make scent out of it from a recipe invented by Our Rose.

We will therefore conclude these random observations with a few hints on planting woods, in general.

But first, a word to those who do *not* plant woods.

If you are in a position to plant a wood, and if you refrain from doing so, you must be, *ipso facto*, of a bleak and sullen disposition. You are to be shunned. It is arguable that your very existence should be made an offence in law. To own a plot of land – to have enough money to plant that land with lilacs and maples and pines and pears, and not to do so, but to spend that money on something horrible like a mink coat . . . it is indecent. Who wants to see you in a mink coat? Nobody. You look repulsive in it, and if you had ever met a mink – which I have – you would be ashamed to be seen in such a garment, for minks are the most amiable and intelligent little creatures, whose morals compare very favourably with those of the women for whom they are slaughtered. Women who wear mink coats are only one degree better than the fiendish Frau Koch, who made lampshades out of the skins of the Nazi's victims.

However, that bit was really meant for another book; it 'crept in'. All the same, it shall stay, because it happens to be bitterly true.

To return to the wood.

If your 'expectation of life' is, say, thirty-five years, you will have a chance of planting at least three more woods before you die, which is perhaps one of the most consoling thoughts that can occur to mankind.

And by 'woods' I do not mean just six-foot trees stuck in a field, with labels hanging from them and circles of earth dug round them. I mean real woods, with solid trunks, and overlacing branches and dark rich leaf mould and gnarled roots and birds making nests and peculiar animals scurrying about. All these things really will be happening at the end of a single decade, though for the first three years you will be inclined to doubt it. The more trees you put in, and the further you spread afield, the more barren it will all look. The trunks remain, spindly, the branches refuse to overlace, and if any bird comes to perch on a twig you feel like shooing it off in case it should break it. As for shelter or shadow or hiding from the world or crouching in bushes when the news is very bad – or when anybody comes to call – not a hope. You will feel more naked and exposed in the centre of your wood than if you were standing in the middle of a ploughed field.

But do not give up. At the end of the third year something happens, and it happens with a bang. I do not know why it should have to be the third year, but it always is. One day you discover that the weeping cherries that have stood stock still ever since you planted them are reaching out long green arms that sway and tremble in the breeze, as though they were trying to touch one another – one foot, two feet, three feet, four feet in a single year. When you walk over to the silver poplars you realize that instead of looking down at them you are actually beginning to look up, and as the weeks go by you hurry out every few days with a tape-measure to register their quite astonishing growth. The mays bush out and burst into such an orgy of blossom that it is really quite shameless, and the maples and the mountain ashes and the spindles and all the lovely autumn things swell and burgeon and expand, making the most alluring promises of what they will be doing when the frosts come, and dropping, from time to time, a little hint in the shape of a single scarlet leaf that has dressed up too soon, having made a mistake in the date of the party.

Moreover, as soon as you have a wood that is even the shadow of a wood, you will find, to your increasing delight, that guests begin to arrive, in the shape of all sorts of charming wild flowers, and shy, shrinking little plants that would never flourish in the open fields. These guests, though uninvited, are more than welcome, and I have often wondered how they find their way into my wood. They may have floated on the breeze, perhaps, or the birds may have brought them, but surely there is more to it than that? It is as though the flowers *knew* that here was a place where they would find shelter, and shadow, and somebody who was waiting for them . . . as though there were a whispering among the wild white violets in the distant valley, and a rustling through the spindles on the hill, and a gentle dropping of hints by the primroses on the river bank.

CHAPTER X

CONSIDER THE LILIES

SUPPOSING that you were allowed only *one* something or other for the rest of your life, which would you choose?

That is an irritating question which some people never tire of propounding, in one form or another. Supposing, they suggest, you were allowed only one composer, who would it be?

You fall into their trap and begin to rack your brains. Mozart? That would seem to be the obvious choice, but then, what would happen to a man's immortal soul without Bach and Beethoven? But if it were all Bach and Beethoven and no Chopin, might not he grow into rather a prig? And if there was no Brahms to counteract the Chopin, would he not soon be moonstruck? And though he might live with Handel for quite a while, might there not come a day, or more probably a night, when the thirst for Wagner was an agony?

It is not fair to put such questions about the arts.

They should be confined to the subject of food. If anybody ever asks you to choose one dish which you must eat for the rest of your life, and if you fail to reply 'eggs and bacon', you are obviously certifiable.

The favourite form of this question is 'supposing you were allowed only one sort of flower . . .' It has been asked so often that I have my own answer ready. It is 'lilies' – with a rider to the effect that by 'lilies' are meant *all* lilies, not only of the garden but of the fields and the woods, for that is where we shall soon be going out to find them.

There is scarcely a month in the year when you need be without some form of lily in your rooms, if you can manage to provide just a little heat for them. (You could, you know, if you would only stop roasting yourself in front of enormous fires, and carry the coal to the conservatory, where it would be much better employed.)

You begin with the arums, which, for some reason best known to themselves, the botanists have insisted on renaming *Richardias.* (In America they are called *Zantedeschias aethiopica*, which is really an insult.) If you can keep the conservatory ten degrees above freezing point, you can pick arums soon after Christmas, with great benefit to your spiritual life. With even one arum in the room it is impossible to think wicked thoughts; it would be like swearing in front of a nun; and if you do have a wicked thought, in spite of the arum, you must go out and have it in the hall, closing the door gently behind you.

After the arums come the exciting varieties of amaryllis, which are not so good for your spiritual side; indeed, with their flaming hues of orange and tango they might well put ideas into your head if you sat with them too long.

However, since they come on in March, when it is beginning to get pleasant out of doors, you can always hurry away from them and go for a brisk walk round the crocuses, which are a cure for most mental distempers.

In April, the long and lustrous pageant of the lilies begins to muster in the open garden, headed by the lilies-of-the-valley, who play the role of heralds in their dainty coats of green. I often think that lilies-of-the-valley were specially designed for a bachelor; he cannot hold a bunch in his hand without feeling paternal and protective.

My own lilies-of-the-valley were the result of a country walk with Marius – and so were my martagon lilies, but that is another story. Marius is an ideal companion for a walk; he scatters scraps of erudition in his wake as though he were in a sort of mental paperchase; and when he has nothing to say he does not say it, which is original of him. Sometimes, as he limps along with his hands behind his back, he hums snatches of Bach fugues, starting with the main treble theme and then, when he comes to the counter-melody, putting in little grunts in the bass. ('It is tragic,' he said to me once, 'that we are only born with one voice. Imagine how delicious it would be to be able to sing contrapuntally. One would be torn with delight.') Usually he holds his head very high, as though he were scanning the skies, but he never seems to trip over anything; nor does the smallest detail escape him.

It was he, as I said, who found the wild lilies-of-the-valley. We had wandered rather far from our favourite route, turning aside from the heath and dipping down over the hill into some thick woods. As we were scrambling over the edge of a steep ditch, he panted to me:

'If we should meet a dragon at this moment I should feel singularly ill-prepared for the encounter.'

'So should I. But is it likely?'

'One never knows. It was in a wood not far from here that St. Leonard had his unfortunate experience.'

'St. Leonard? What makes you think of him?'

'My dear fellow, look where you are treading!' I looked down expecting to see some sort of pitfall. Instead I saw the lilies-of-the-valley. There were only a few tiny clumps, but to find them at all, in their wild condition, was exciting enough, and it was the work of the moment to kneel down and take up one of the clumps with a trowel. (It should be a crime in law to dig up more wild flowers than is necessary, or to dig them up at all if you cannot give a reasonable guarantee of their survival.)

As we walked on Marius told me the old Sussex legend of St. Leonard and the dragon, how he had fought it in the woods near Horsham, in mortal combat lasting for many hours, and how, when he had died, the lilies-of-the-valley had sprung up wherever his blood had fallen.[1]

Once embarked on the subject of lilies, there was no stopping him.

'Consider the lilies,' he mused. 'It is most admirable advice, but it is very seldom needed, particularly by men of letters. Take Browning, for example.'

'Well?'

'Has *anybody* any idea what he meant in *Saul*?'

Not I, certainly. I had never even heard of *Saul*, let alone read it.

[1] These woods still bear the name of St. Leonard's Forest, and the wild lilies still grow there.

Marius recited the passage in question:

. . . And those lilies
Still living and blue,
As thou break'st them to twine round thy heart-
strings.

'It is one of the mysteries of literature,' he observed. 'Blue lilies! Twining lilies! Some people have tried to excuse Browning by suggesting that he was really meaning to refer to the "Lilies of the Field", under the delusion that this was originally some form of convolvulus. But surely he should have known better than *that*?'

§ II

I want to hurry on to July, for that is the crowning hour of the lilies, though you must not forget that the procession marches on for many weeks, ever raising fresh flags of colour to the slowly darkening skies. Even in November, if the frosts have not been too cruel, you may gather big bunches of the nerines from a southern wall, which are of a pink as delicate and feminine as the satin of one of Boucher's ladies.

But it is in the beginning of July that we are *en fête* with the lilies, and in particular on the first Sunday of the month. That was the day when I first came to Merry Hall, and had my first glimpse of the regales, and therefore it may be regarded as the most important of all the anniversaries. (Though every garden, when you come to think of it, is a bundle of anniversaries. You cannot look into a certain cherry tree without remembering the day that 'Four' got stuck in it and had to be fetched down with a ladder. You cannot pick a paeony without recalling that the first time you took paeonies into the house was the night of the burglary – which I really must tell about one day. And how the burglars knocked over the flowers and trampled on them, which somehow seemed to add insult to injury.)

I shall never forget the first Sunday in July which began my second year at Merry Hall. I had been obliged to go to London for several days, and during the whole time I had been up there the sun had blazed down pitilessly. Sunshine in a city is always something of a mockery, but it becomes a positive torture when one knows that far away, in the country, it is pouring down on a bed of lilies from which one has been unnaturally torn away, coaxing them into a premature display.

Every night I would ring up Gaskin for the latest bulletin.

'Have any more come out, Gaskin?'

'Yes; they're coming out beautifully.'

'That's not what I meant. Are they coming out too fast? Will there be any left?'

'There'll be masses left. Most of them are still only buds.'

'But in this heat . . .'

'Would you like me to cut some of them and put them in a bucket in the larder till you come back?'

'Yes, I think that would be a very good idea.'

I rang off, feeling a little better.

Ten minutes later, in great haste, I ring up again, to remind Gaskin not to cut the stalks right down to the ground, because otherwise the bulbs will be starved for the rest of the summer. He replies, somewhat shortly, that he was well aware of that already.

When at last I got down, and hurried out to the kitchen garden, there they were . . . and all I can say is that I am glad that nobody else was present, for it was eminently an occasion for secret prowling and gloating and muttering to oneself, and squinting with one's head on one side, and taking long, deep, ecstatic inhalations. And if you feel impelled to do these things, at an age of comparative discretion, it is preferable to have the stage to yourself.

After some twenty minutes of these shaming activities, there was a step behind me. It was Oldfield.

He touched his cap and grinned. 'I was afraid you was going to miss 'em,' he said.

My mind leapt back a year. I remembered the first time I had seen him – the cold, almost hostile stare he had given me – the sense of being not wanted. Well, we had come a long way since then. Not far enough, maybe, but still, a decent stretch. At least, I was 'accepted'.

'It would take a lot to make me miss them.'

'Aye. Miss Emily dropped in to see 'em this morning on her way to church. Said she could smell 'em from the lane. But I didn't give her any; I said you'd be needing 'em for t'house.'

What poor Miss Emily's thoughts must have been on hearing this I dared not think.

'So I shall. But I really feel I ought to take some up to London to give to people.'

'Aye. You'd be popular with t'young ladies.'

I certainly should. They would go mad. They would swoon. An awful thought occurred to me.

'I suppose we couldn't get any more?'

As soon as I had spoken I realized that I had said the wrong thing.

Oldfield's face darkened. 'Get any more?' he repeated,

with the accent on the 'get'. 'Were you thinking of buying boolbs?'

I had, very definitely, been thinking of buying boolbs. But I realized my mistake just in time.

'Oh no. . . .' I stammered.

'Hmph!' His one eye pierced me through and through. 'Because if you *had* been thinking of buying boolbs . . .'

I shook my head.

'T'would seem to me to be a pity,' he observed.

There was a long pause.

'Seeing as 'ow all these was grown from seed,' he added.

(I should explain that this episode occurred some time *before* the sowing of the cypress seeds, which we described in the last chapter. Perhaps it may have been indirectly responsible for that experiment.)

'You mean, we could grow some more from seed?'

For answer he took a step forward, and put his fingers round the pod of a lily that had already shed its petals.

'Coom September,' he said, 'these'll be ripe for sowing. We'll keep 'em in frames next year. T'year after, we'll plant 'em and a few of 'em will flower, but we won't cut 'em. T'year after that, they'll be as tall as yourself.'

Three years! It would be bitter to have to wait so long, but I realized that there was no alternative, so I said 'yes', and left him with mixed emotions. I was longing to buy boolbs, I was itching to send telegrams for boolbs, but it was obvious that if I were to retain even a shadow of Oldfield's respect, boolbs were 'out'. He would regard them not only as a wanton extravagance but as a personal affront.

Seeds it must be. And as I walked slowly back to the house, over the shadowed lawn, I began to have a curious feeling of relief that it was to be seeds. They would give me yet another reason for wishing the calendar to speed forward, and this, I think, is a healthy desire. It is only to the gardener that Time is a friend, giving each year more than he steals. In the thirty-six months that lay ahead, those seeds would provide endless excitements, from the first day that they were shaken out of their pods. For in each of them one would be confronted by a miracle – the miracle that so tiny a thing should hold in its core a whole chalice of perfume, not yet distilled, and wings of white and gold that were floating about somewhere in infinity, or sleeping far below in the cool earth.

Ladies, no doubt, have similar reflections when they are preparing to have babies. But I cannot see how you can regard the birth of a baby with such awe as you regard the birth of a flower. That is one of the drawbacks – or maybe the consolations – of being a bachelor.

§ III

But there are also drawbacks, strange as it may seem, to having an excess of lilies. In case you have been feeling envious, I will mention some of them.

The first drawback is that all through July one is disturbed by a phenomenal number of trunk calls from London. 'Such a lovely day . . . we thought we would go down to the country . . . passing very close to you . . . might we look in on the way back for a few minutes . . . so kind . . . about six?'

In due course the ladies arrive, and from the moment they set foot in the house there are high bird-like noises, claspings of hands, gasps, and – quite obviously – frenzied plots to get hold of lilies.

'*Never* have I seen. . .'

'The *scent*. . .'

'They're almost *too* much. . .'

'I *can't* believe they're real. . .'

'*What* wouldn't one give. . .'

Sometimes one of the ladies, in an excess of candour, will observe that a single bunch of the lilies would cost several pounds if one were to attempt to buy it in London; this is a sure signal for sharp and darting looks at her from the others, to remind her that she has said quite the wrong thing; when you are angling for a present it is unwise to emphasize its value in cash.

We go out and sit on the lawn, the cocktails arrive, and the olives, and I spend an enjoyable half hour watching the various techniques employed by the ladies in the disposal of the olive stones, from quick heel-grindings into the grass to airy, absent-minded droppings underneath the chairs. One can learn a great deal about feminine psychology by watching women deal with olive stones. But all the time it is the lilies that they are thinking of, and in the end the pressure of mass suggestion is too strong to resist; I have to get up and lead the way to the lily beds, and once again there are gasps and bird-like noises, slightly higher in pitch than before. At last the gasps and bird-sounds stop, and they just stand and gaze, in silence.

And then I tell them that there is a nice bunch waiting for each of them in the cool of the larder. Whereupon, with whoops of delight, they return to the house, and we send them off into the night, looking as though they were about to attend a carnival in Nice.

It is all great fun, and though I sometimes pretend it is a bore, I should be unhappy if these visitations were to cease. As one grows older a number of platitudes begin to shine out like new-found stars of truth, and one of them is that there are times when it really is more blessed to give than to receive.

There is one bunch of my lilies – the first to be cut – which has a special significance, for it always goes to the same person, to Madame Massigli, the wife of the French Ambassador. One day in June I was at the French Embassy, and she was arranging a few white roses in a bowl, and talking over her shoulder at the same time to the poet Louis Aragon, saying how much she loved white flowers and telling him that he must write some verses about them. As I watched her, delighting in her grace and her charm, I made a plot. Here was a great lady of France; she loved white flowers; she herself was like a lily, and the lily was the national flower of France; she should have a bunch of my lilies. A bunch *de grande luxe*, tall and stately, of truly ambassadorial elegance. And she did, and does, on the first Sunday of every July. I believe she looks forward to the little anniversary; I certainly do myself.

So why did I complain that there were 'drawbacks' to having an excess of lilies?

If you could bear to come with me while they are being picked, perhaps I could make you understand.

We will assume that the lilies are *au point*, that we have decided to give away as many as the car will hold, and that we have sent warning messages to the metropolis, telling various charming people that showers of lilies will be descending on them in the morning, and that they must be ready to receive them.

This is what happens. On the night before I set out, in this role of floral Maecenas, I go out to the lily beds in the cool of the evening, carrying two big buckets of rain water. As I walk across the lawn, followed inevitably by 'One' and 'Four', I try to convey to them, by facial expression, or by mystic twitches of the dorsal muscles, that there is no time for play, that there is work to be done, and that they must not expect any attention. They will almost certainly ignore these warnings, so that I must set down the buckets and speak to them in plain English:

(To 'One') I am *not* going to play with twigs.

(To 'Four') There is *not* going to be any watering.

(To Both) I am going to pick *lilies*.

The effect on them is very depressing. 'One' sits down and stares at the ground; and if there is a leaf in the neighbourhood perhaps he will give it a half-hearted push with a crooked paw. 'Four' does not sit down; he 'weaves', first pushing against my legs, and then scraping his back against a bucket, regarding me, meanwhile, from over his shoulder with enormous green eyes, which would melt a heart of stone.

So that is the first drawback. It is necessary to offend 'One' and 'Four', to ignore them completely for a whole summer evening, while making endless journeys backwards and forwards over the darkening lawns – journeys which must seem to them to be singularly pointless. If you value the goodwill of your cats you will realize that this is a very real drawback indeed.

The second drawback is the whole business of transporting the lilies to the city. The car is filled to bursting point, the boot is crammed with sheaves of them wrapped in tissue paper, all the seats are loaded, and there are also two large bucketsfull on the floor. I clamber in with difficulty; the back view is totally obscured by a solid phalanx of white blossom, and the scent is so agonizingly sweet that there are times, on a hot day, when it seems to be having the effect of a powerful anaesthetic, so that the road quivers and wavers as it winds ahead. However, I trundle along; and while I am still in the country, curling through lanes or bowling over commons, it is not too embarrassing; but when I approach the suburbs I begin to feel somewhat self-conscious, and by the time the heart of the city is reached, it is painfully obvious that a considerable sensation is being created. When the signals turn red at the traffic lights, girls dart out from the pavement and stare into the car as though I were some peculiar sort of fish; people stand up in buses; policemen glare; occupants of other cars nudge each other and forget to put on the brakes. And there is a constant stream of comment from all around.

'Coo! Look at 'em!'

'Whatever can they *be*?'

'Don't be *sillay* – they're *lillays*!'

'No they aren't. Are they Mum?'

'I never seen *lillays* like 'em.'

'Bet you they are. Arsk the gentleman.'

By this time, the lights have usually gone back to green, and the gentleman is away again, without having been called upon to make any tiresome explanations. By this time, too, the lilies have begun to open in the heat with astonishing rapidity, shedding their tawny, cloying pollen far and wide. There are stains all over the gentleman's neck, patches of the gentleman's hair look as if they had been dyed a glowing orange, and a glance at the gentleman's fingers would suggest that he smoked a least a thousand cigarettes a day.

The gentleman is also feeling more than faintly sick, and by the time he reaches his various destinations he is looking such a tramp that it is a wonder the servants do not say 'Nothing today, thank you,' and slam the door in his face.

The third drawback to having too many lilies is that they insist on a party being given for them, and since they are so grand and elegant you have to try to be grand and elegant too, and that means dinner jackets, and hiring masses of very ugly silver, and it is all inclined to be rather expensive.

But what can one do? With all those lilies one cannot shut oneself up in a sort of tower and slowly suffocate; the world must be brought in to share them.

Don't you find yourself in the same predicament, when your garden is excelling itself in some way? However solitary you may be by nature, however averse to entertaining and giving parties, don't you find that there are times when the sweet peas, as it were, send out their own invitations to tea, or when the irises inform you, in no uncertain voice, that they will be 'at home' next Sunday afternoon? You simply cannot keep these things to yourself; it would be as wicked as allowing a banquet to go to waste. Besides, the flowers like it. That may be a 'whimsical' idea, and whimsy may be the unforgivable sin, but the flowers do like it; when there is a party in the air they perk up. There is a great deal of truth in the old saying that in a garden the best fertilizer is 'the shadow of the owner'; it is equally true of the shadow of the owner's friends. Even flowers need love.

So out go the invitations, and the candles are set in the music-room, and an extra sparkle is given to the old blue chandelier, and there are fierce arguments as to whether the buffet shall be placed in the little conservatory where people will see the geraniums, or whether it will be placed in the hall where they will see the smoked salmon. I am always in favour of the conservatory, and I always lose, because in times like these it is Gaskin who has the last word.

But whatever else people may see, they cannot help seeing the lilies. They are all over the house, like groups of dancers, poised and waiting; those that stand near mirrors seem to take on a silver sheen, and those that catch the glow of the candles are lit with gold; in the full light they sparkle like sunlit snow, in the shadows they are luminous . . . and always, upstairs, downstairs, in every nook and cranny, there is fragrance.

CHAPTER XI

HARVEST FESTIVAL

FLOWERS make friends – and enemies too.

What is politely called a 'coolness' is at this very moment stunting my friendship with a very charming woman who has an almost morbid passion for camellias. I told her that she could not grow them if she had not got an acid soil; she said she could.

'I shall deluge the ground with peat,' she said, 'and dig in barrowfuls of leaf-mould.'

'No use whatever; the lime will trickle through.'

'It will not. And if it does, I shall put in more peat.'

'It will still trickle through. All the leaves will go yellow and all the buds will drop off. If there *are* any buds, which I doubt.'

'You are absolutely hateful. I don't believe you want me to grow camellias at all.'

Which, of course, was quite true. I should have been livid if she had succeeded, for I had been through all this agonizing process myself.

In due course, the leaves of her camellias went yellow, and the buds dropped off; and it was impossible to avoid referring to her as 'La Dame Sans Camellias'. And now, though there is still no acid in her soil, there is a great deal of acid in her conversation, whenever my name is mentioned.

Vegetables, too, càn lead to estrangements. A really prize dish of asparagus, if offered to a neighbour who has neglected his own asparagus bed, will arouse such murderous instincts that he finds it difficult to eat it without choking. A dish of very early peas once so inflamed a lady who shall be nameless, that she observed, in stifled accents, that no doubt they 'had come off the ice'. They had not come off the ice; nor has our subsequent relationship.

The mention of vegetables reminds me, inevitably, of Miss Emily, who has not strayed through these pages for quite a while, though she has been constantly in and out of the garden. Here is a letter from her, which arrived on a certain glorious summer morning.

DEAR MR. NICHOLS,

I feel very diffident about writing this letter, because once again it is concerned with *vegetables* . . . a subject which I am afraid must be unwelcome to you in view of our past correspondence!

However, this time I am pleading for a very special cause, the Harvest Festival at our little church of St. Luke's, which I believe you have visited on several occasions. As you know, the Festival falls on Sunday week, and I am to be responsible for the decorations – a task which I should not have presumed to undertake were it not for the fact that Rose Fenton has kindly promised to help me. So good of her, with all her commitments.

Do you think you might find it possible to spare just a teeny basket of vegetables from your wonderful garden? (I am so thankful to see that, after all, you have not given it up!) With so many marrows I expect that you will find you have quantities that are too large to eat, and I imagine that your man will not be able to bottle even a fraction of such a bumper crop of tomatoes. A few of them would be of the *greatest* assistance in decorating the windows.

If you do find yourself able to grant this request, I wonder if you would also be able to include a small bunch of your exquisite lilies? So suitable, for such a celebration. They would be treated with the utmost care, and only Miss Fenton would be allowed to touch them. I am sure that we could rely on her to do something quite remarkable with them. Yours sincerely,

EMILY KAYE.

It was the last sentence of this letter that captured my attention, though I had not missed the dainty irony of the preceding paragraphs. I too was sure that we could rely on Our Rose to do something quite remarkable with the lilies, if she ever got her hands on them. We could rely on her to chop their stalks off, or dip them in red ink, or hang them upside down on a monkey puzzle. But she should *not* get her hands on them. If Miss Emily wanted a few tomatoes to balance on the end of the pews she could have them. But the lilies . . . no.

Then I reproached myself for these unworthy sentiments. After all, St. Luke's was a dear little church, and if you like churches – as I happen to do, though I greatly prefer them when they are empty, and when I can sit in them and make up my own services – then you like to help them, and give them things, and make them feel that somebody loves them. It would be shameful to be niggardly on an occasion like the Harvest Festival. Miss Emily should have her basket of vegetables, and a great deal more. She should have such an avalanche of vegetables that the congregation would be dazzled by the bounty of nature, and sing the Magnificat with a fervour that they had never shown before.

But the lilies?

I thought of a compromise. The little church should have its lilies, but I would arrange them myself. If Our Rose was offended, well – she was offended, and that was that. So I wrote:

DEAR MISS KAYE,

Of course I shall be delighted to let you have some vegetables for the Harvest Festival. Perhaps it would be best if I brought them straight to the church on the Saturday morning? I shall also be happy to bring along some lilies. But please do not dream of troubling to ask Miss Fenton to arrange them; I will see to it myself if you tell me what part of the church they are for. In any case, they are not flowers that demand any special treatment; indeed, they have a habit of arranging themselves. Yours etc.,

Miss Emily replied in suitable terms, informing me that the lilies were to go along the altar railings. She added that 'should anything happen' or should I feel 'in need of any help', Miss Fenton would be only too glad to come to the rescue.

Saturday week duly dawned, and I rose at six to pick the lilies while the dew was still on them. I gathered three big armfuls and took them back to rest in buckets of cool water in the larder, which was already brimming with a quite vulgar display of vegetables. I wondered how they would all get into the car, particularly as I was also taking some branches of copper beech to go with the lilies.

After breakfast I went along to the music-room, to spend half an hour on the waterfalls. By spending half an hour on the waterfalls I mean practising the double descending cadenzas in Chopin's Third Scherzo. It is perhaps the most superbly 'pianistic' piece of music ever written; to be able to play it properly must give to any pianist a sense of almost god-like power . . . a feeling of floating on wings over a sea of roses. I do not feel at all like that when I play it; I feel as if I were stumbling, with bare feet and with considerable pain, over the sharpest pebbles of Brighton beach. So, no doubt, do my listeners. But I have been practising it for nearly ten years, and I shall go on practising it, flat by flat and sharp by sharp and natural by natural, with an increasing hatred against the fourth finger of my left hand, which has Communist tendencies.

Then the telephone rang. It was Miss Emily, who appeared to be in a state of considerable agitation for reasons which I could not understand, as the line was indistinct and she was speaking very quickly. It was like trying to decipher a mutilated telegram. 'If you would come early . . . Avoid misunderstanding . . . So strange about Miss Fenton . . . Quite a different person . . . if you come immediately so much simpler . . . not mention it to Miss Fenton . . . Such a pity . . . could be so charming when she wanted . . . would be waiting for vegetables in an hour's time . . . expect it will blow over . . . goodbye.'

What was expected to blow over? And why was it a

pity about Miss Fenton? Had she met with some painful accident? Or had she been up to something extra dreadful, such as filling the font with pink watercress? These were questions which demanded an immediate answer. Twenty minutes later, with the car loaded to the hilt, I was speeding down the lanes on my way to St. Luke's.

§ II

Miss Emily was waiting for me in the porch. Apart from an extra glint in her eyes, and a slight trembling of her hands, she appeared to be in full possession of her faculties. Indeed, the only thing which would have struck an outsider as at all abnormal was the frenzied haste with which she proceeded to unload the vegetables from the car; one would have said that she was rushing them to the inhabitants of some beleaguered city. She darted backwards and forwards, from car to vestry, using her skirt as a sort of basket; and she returned only the most evasive answers to my inquiries about Our Rose.

'An accident? Not that I am aware of. In blooming health, I believe. What superb tomatoes! Oh, and a melon! I'm sure I couldn't say whether she will be here or not. Cucumbers too! All very foolish . . . so petty . . . shouldn't really have mentioned it.' These confidences were accompanied by constant nervous glances over her shoulder, as though she were dreading the advent of some spectral visitant.

There seemed no point in making further inquiries, and so, after unloading the rest of the vegetables, I set about my own task of decorating the altar rails.

It was a pleasant interlude of peace and quiet. There was no sound in the church save the rapid breathing of Miss Emily, who was building what appeared to be a solid phalanx of tomatoes and cucumbers up the steps of the pulpit. How the preacher would manage to surmount them was a problem which would doubtless be solved when the time came; at the moment he would appear to have no alternative but to grasp the rails, tread lightly on a melon, land on a marrow, and hope for the best.

My own task was easier. The railings were charming; they were eighteenth-century iron work, covered with faded gilding, and the branches of the copper beech twined in and out among them like a design in bronze. They had the added merit of concealing the jam-jars in which I placed the stalks of the lilies. When I stepped back to look at my handiwork I felt that it was a success. It had a pleasingly pre-Raphaelite flavour, and if a Rossetti angel with a swan-like neck had drifted down the aisle it would have been quite in keeping.

This peace was suddenly broken by the sound of voices in the porch. Miss Emily, cucumber in hand, became rigid, and then, murmuring something about 'being back in a few minutes', darted off in the direction of the vestry. A moment later the door creaked open, to admit Our Rose.

On seeing her my first sensation was one of relief; she had evidently met with no mischance; she looked in the full tide of health and vigour. She was hatless, and her cheeks were flushed, as though for some forthcoming battle. I noticed that her hair had been freshly done, more *à la Madonna* than ever; indeed, her whole costume had a distinctly religious note, with its long trailing sleeves and its full black skirt. It was the sort of dress which was much affected by the late Queen Marie of Roumania.

Our Rose had not yet seen me, for she was turning to her Czechoslovakian maid, who had followed behind her, and was staggering under the weight of two immense baskets, one loaded with several varieties of convolvulus and the other piled high with grapefruit.

'Be careful, Frieda dear,' she was crooning. 'We should hate to snap the convolvulus, shouldn't we?'

To which Frieda responded with a look of such malevolence that one would have been justified in supposing that nothing would have given her greater pleasure than to snap very large quantities of convolvulus.

'And we must mind the step, Frieda dear, or we shall spill the grapefruit, and bruise it, which would be such a pity for the poor people in the hospitals. Oh dear! One has fallen and rolled down the steps. Never mind. Perhaps if you would put the baskets down you would like to fetch it. Ah! Mr. Nichols . . . how nice to find you here. I am longing to see what you are going to do with your lilies.'

To which I replied that I was longing to see what she was going to do with her convolvulus.

'My convolvulus? That is for the lovely old pulpit.' A saintly sigh. 'I have quite a feeling about the lovely old pulpit.'

So had I.

Till then, Our Rose had been blissfully unaware of the lovely old pulpit – or so it seemed. Her back had been firmly turned to it, and when she had been obliged to turn round to pick up a piece of convolvulus that had fallen out of the basket, she had kept her eyes to the ground.

But now, still smiling with fierce determination, she moved towards it. And as soon as she saw what Miss Emily had done, the smile vanished like a piece of snapped elastic.

'Oh dear!' she exclaimed.

She took another step forward, and heaved a dramatic sigh. 'Oh dear!' she repeated. Then she turned to me. 'I don't think we care for *that* very much, do we?'

I murmured something non-committal about not having really noticed it.

'Not noticed it?' She gave a not-so-silvery laugh. 'You *must* be absent-minded this morning. Not to notice that an entire greengrocer's shop has been emptied higgledy-piggledy into the pulpit which I am supposed to decorate.'

This was terrible. At any moment Miss Emily would be back, and then there would be fireworks.

Putting her hand to her cheek and speaking in a most sinister tone, she said: 'I wonder who could possibly have been reponsible for anything so very unpleasant?'

It seemed better to tell her, though I was quite certain that she already knew. 'Well,' I began, 'a few minutes ago I seem to remember seeing Miss Emily . . .'

'Oh no,' she interrupted. 'Not Emily. Quite impossible.'

'But indeed . . .'

'Out of the question,' she snapped. 'You must have been mistaken. Dear Emily has such taste. Such judgment. Such restraint.' The hissing intonation in which these tributes were delivered somewhat detracted from their value as compliments. 'If you think you saw Miss Emily anywhere near this pulpit, I'm quite certain that she was as horrified as we are.'

At which precise moment Miss Emily emerged from the vestry, bearing yet another basket of tomatoes, and walked briskly towards us.

'Good morning dear,' said Our Rose.

'Good morning darling,' said Miss Emily. 'Delicious convolvulus.'

'Not so delicious as your tomatoes. Are they for bottling?'

'No dear. For my pulpit.'

'*Your* pulpit?'

'Yes dear. My pulpit.'

'I think there must be some mistake. *I* promised to do the pulpit.' She spoke with great calmness, but I noticed that she was twisting a piece of convolvulus as though she were wringing somebody's neck.

'No dear. I think not.' Miss Emily was equally calm, but she was clutching a tomato so tightly that the skin had broken and was oozing juice through her fingers. 'I seem to remember that there was some talk about it, but you were so vague . . .'

'Vague!'

'And so full of engagements, and business, and affairs . . .'

'*That*, at least, is true. I sacrificed a wedding at Claridge's to come down here this morning.'

'In that case, my dear, I can only say I'm exceedingly sorry.' She held out the basket in my direction, as though to indicate that the discussion was closed. 'Would you mind holding these for a minute, and hand-ing them to me when I ask for them? My pulpit is not quite finished yet.'

'No dear. So I see.' Rose nodded with great energy. 'Evidently.'

'Why – evidently?'

'Because you still just have room to balance a very small tomato on top of the reading lamp.'

Miss Emily flinched, but made no reply.

'Not that the reading lamp will be needed,' continued Our Rose, stalking towards the pulpit with a great fluttering of her religious garments. 'Because it is obvious that no preacher could possibly get into the pulpit at all, over all these vegetables. Unless, of course, you have made arrangements for him to be let down from the roof on wires.'

'No dear,' countered Miss Emily. 'This is Church of England. Nothing of that sort. All quite simple. Oh, be careful! You will upset your maid's basket.'

But Rose, in her agitation, had already kicked over the basket of grapefruit which her Czechoslovakian maid had placed in the shadow of one of the pews, and the aisle was alive with yellow, rolling balls. As I hurried to pick them up, the dialogue of the two ladies continued.

MISS EMILY Whatever are these?

ROSE Grapefruit, dear. You must try them one day. So good for acid.

MISS EMILY But what are they doing here? Had you intended to use them in the church?

ROSE I *do* intend to use them in the church.

MISS EMILY This is Surrey, dear. Not exactly a grape-fruit country. A harvest festival is supposed to be a thanksgiving for the fruits of the earth.

ROSE It is also supposed to be beautiful.

MISS EMILY Since each of the fruits is plainly marked 'Produce of Israel', in large black letters, you may find that a little difficult.

ROSE I hope that none of the congregation will be so vulgar as to start fingering the decorations.

MISS EMILY Perhaps if they are placed high up on some window . . .

ROSE They will not be placed high up on any window. Particularly as the photographers will wish to have a good view of them.

MISS EMILY Photographers? You don't mean to say that you have arranged for photographers to come here? For the Press?

ROSE Certainly, dear. When *I* do a floral decoration it is apt to be news.

MISS EMILY (*choking*) I hardly think it is legal to have photographers in a church.

ROSE (*also choking*) In that case dear, the Archbishop of Canterbury ought now to be in gaol. To say nothing of the King and the entire Royal Family. You must tell them one day. Nice for them to know.

The two ladies stood there, glaring at each other, the one as rigid as the cucumber which she was clutching, the other as sour as the grapefruit which she held to her breast. And there, for all one knows, they might be standing yet, had not Providence tripped through the door in the ample shape of Mrs. Pattern.

§III

Mrs. Pattern is the vicar's wife, and we must pause to introduce her, for she is one of my favourite women.

'Pattern' is not her real name – (we really must keep a few veils thinly draped round this chronicle of fact) – but it suits her very well, not so much because she is a model of rectitude but because she has the right platitude ready for every occasion. At luncheon, for example, it is impossible to take up a chicken bone in one's fingers without hearing, from the other end of the table . . . 'I always say that fingers were made before forks!' Mrs. Pattern begins most of her sentences with 'I always say', which suggests that she is apparently unaware that other people have been saying the same thing for many centuries. She has never in my presence gone so far as 'I always say that a stitch in time saves nine'; but she has done nearly as well with 'I always say that handsome is as handsome does.'

When Mrs. Pattern first came into my life, she was gossiping in the lane with a nursemaid who was wheeling a perambulator containing a baby of exceptional repulsiveness. Babies, as all bachelors will agree, should not be allowed at large unless they are heavily draped, and fitted with various appliances for absorbing sound and moisture. If young married persons persist in their selfish pursuit of populating the planet, they should be compelled to bear the consequences. They should be shut behind high walls, clutching the terrible bundles which they have brought into the world, and when they emerge into society, if they insist on bringing these bundles with them, they should see that they are properly cloaked, muted, sealed up and, above all, *dry*. They should not wave them about in the streets to the alarm of sensitive persons who are used to the company of Siamese cats.

However, that is by the way. I only wanted to tell

you that Mrs. Pattern, as she had leant over this hideous infant, had crooned, '*She'll* be a great breaker of hearts one day, *I'll* be bound.' Which was an inaccurate statement in more senses than one, as the infant happened to be a boy, who had been put down for Eton that very morning.

To return to the church.

As Mrs. Pattern tripped down the aisle, it was evident that she was in a state of considerable excitement. This was indeed fortunate, for otherwise she might have noticed the fierce tension of the group which she was approaching. As it was, she merely smiled and fluttered and murmured how nice it all was, and then, clasping her hands and turning to Our Rose, she exclaimed:

'*What* a stroke of luck to find you here! I always *did* say that two heads were better than one!'

This was too much for Miss Emily. 'There are times when one is inclined to doubt it,' she snapped.

Mrs. Pattern did not hear her rightly. 'I beg your pardon?'

'If you will excuse me,' murmured Miss Emily. With which she turned on her heel, and stalked towards the pulpit.

Mrs. Pattern stared after her, with an expression of bewilderment on her kindly face. 'Is there . . . is there anything – not quite right?'

'I think poor Emily must have a bad headache,' observed Rose. 'All those vegetables in this heat. So heavy to move.'

'Oh dear! Poor thing! I wonder if I have an aspirin.' Mrs. Pattern began to fumble in her bag. 'I *always* say that aspirin. . .

But I could not wait to hear what Mrs. Pattern

always said about aspirin; besides, I did not like to think of Miss Emily being left all alone. So I too began to drift away. But not too far to miss the sensational import of the news which Mrs. Pattern was pouring into Our Rose's eager ears. I heard something like this:

'The Princesses . . . mumble mumble . . . yes, staying there for the week-end, only three miles away . . . mumble mumble . . . lady-in-waiting this morning, so gracious . . . mumble mumble . . . she couldn't promise for both but *certainly* Margaret . . . mumble mumble . . . so exciting, such an honour, vicar quite beside himself . . . mumble mumble . . . I beg your pardon?'

A hissing query from Rose, which I could not catch.

'Yes, they will be sitting in *this* pew.'

Another hiss from Rose.

'Oh, *would* you? That would be too wonderful . . . mumble mumble . . . an arch of convolvulus? . . . most interesting . . . and the grapefruit too . . . so original . . . if you would not mind leaving room for the prayer books. . . .'

I did not stay to listen to any more. The whole atmosphere was too explosive. I tip-toed gently out of the side door, ran the car down the lane, and hurried home for another go at the waterfalls. But that evening I could not resist the temptation to return to the church to see what had happened. It was, to say the least of it, startling. Our Rose had transformed the front pew into something which looked like a cross between Cinderella's coach and a prize-winning stall at the Horticultural Exhibition, with a triumphal arch of convolvulus at the entrance, finished at the top with immense bows of ribbon in red, white and blue. Miss Emily, not to be outdone, had transferred most of her vegetables from the pulpit to the opposite pew, which was for the ladies-in-waiting, and had used my vegetable marrows as pin-cushions for quantities of miniature Union Jacks. It would be difficult to say which display was the more distracting, and one could only hope that the princesses would find room to sit down.

I wish that this chronicle, with its high passions and frenzied hopes, could be given a suitably dramatic conclusion. Alas – since this is a true story, it must be admitted that it ended very tamely. The Princesses, through no fault of their own, were unable to come. The congregation, in consequence, consisted of the usual handful of villagers, who were so intimidated by the floral and vegetable displays of the two front pews that they huddled together at the back.

There was only one moment of tension. Just before the service, at the end of the voluntary, the two side doors opened; through the one swept Our Rose, through the other swept Miss Emily. They had each agreed, at the vicar's suggestion, to sit in the pews they had decorated themselves, and they were both so determined to be invisible to one another that they did not quite see where they were going. As a result, Our Rose, as she sailed through her triumphal arch, caught a piece of convolvulus in her veil, where it remained trailing down her neck throughout her devotions, giving her a curiously raffish appearance. And Miss Emily, equally aloof and unaware, dislodged a large tomato from the ledge, which rolled down on to the seat behind her. When she arose from prayer, and sat down on the tomato, she gave a superb exhibition of lady-like composure. By not a single twitch or flinch did she betray the disaster. She merely moved slightly to the left, and reached for her light summer coat, which she wore for the rest of the service. It was only during the singing of the Benedicite that an outsider might have suspected that anything was amiss. There was a distinct shudder down her back when she sang, 'Oh all ye green things upon the earth, bless ye the Lord!'

CHAPTER XII

EXOTICS

WE have been so busy in the garden that ever since we stepped into it the outside world seems to have drifted far away; when you are concerned with really important things, such as the dew on a spider's web, or the first fragrance of a freesia on a shelf – when you are dealing with such matters, which are infinite and everlasting, it is difficult to look over one's shoulder, as it were, and remind yourself of such shadowy and transient details as the Red Army. In the scale of eternal values, a hundred military divisions are outweighed by a single pinch of thistledown.

Lest that sound like some tiresome pronouncement from a tower of ivory, I must be permitted to say, in self-defence, that there have been many occasions, during the slow unfolding of this chronicle, when life has taken me far from the garden. In addition to scribbling notes, such as these, about the things I really love, I happen to be a professional journalist; and if that is your job you cannot spend your entire existence pursing your lips at clumps of Christmas roses – though, should you happen to go in for Christmas roses, you will probably find yourself doing a lot of lip-pursing, because they are such dirty little things. (Unless, of course, you are Mr. Ernest Hemingway, who has never pursed his lips at anybody but himself.) What I am trying to say – though it really doesn't signify much – is that these quiet hours, these days of dreaming, had to be paid for by a good deal of quite strenuous work outside; by getting 'stories' out of hard-bitten senators in Washington, by tracking down negroes in the swamps of Mississippi, by crashing about Africa in very rickety aeroplanes. Such pastimes can be exhilarating, and I expect to pursue them for some years to come, but you cannot persuade me that they are important in the sense that the first bud of a daphne is important.

Moreover, the fact that I had to go abroad so often on business prevented me from going abroad on pleasure; after three months of compulsory absence from the garden it was inconceivable that I should root myself up again and go swooping off to the Mediterranean, as in the past; there were too many things to do in the borders, too many things to do in the wood, too many things coming up and too many things *not* coming up. Apart from that, it would have been impossible to go to the Mediterranean even if I had wanted to do so, on account of a series of extraordinarily ugly men who suddenly became Chancellors of the British Exchequer, and refused to allow me to go anywhere at all unless I promised to bring them back bags of dollars. Nobody remembers the names of these persons, but everybody – alas – remembers their faces, which were at once grim and flabby, like blanc-manges that had not quite set.

These dreadful men said to me – not personally, but as a British citizen, and as such, a member of a seafaring, wanderlusting race of pirates – 'You shall not go abroad. It is un-British and anti-social to go abroad. You shall stay at home. For preference, in Ealing.'

It was all very frustrating. For though I did not want to leave the garden for long, I craved for just a little while on the Mediterranean, not only for the sunshine but for the flowers that sunshine brings. The third winter at Merry Hall was the coldest, so the papers said, for sixty years; and for the first time since I became a gardener the winter flowers seemed to find the climate too much for them. True, there were patches of pink from the indomitable *erica carnea*, but you had to dig through the snow to find them; and round the beds of *iris stylosa* the drifts were so deep that they could not be found at all. As the grey and bitter days dragged by, I could not help remembering that already the hills around Mougins would be strewn with the pink and white petals of the almonds and the cherries, and that the flower market at Cannes would be as gay as a painting by Dufy. I found myself recalling and desiring, with an almost physical hunger, those flowers which, by their brilliance, had remained with me from former travels; I had only to close my eyes to see, once again, the great clumps of blood-red poinsettas that had glowed against the grey walls of Malta, the rose and ivory oleanders that had piled up in the valleys of Cyprus in the spring, like drifts of sunlit snow; the golden mohurs of Bombay, the waves of blue gentians, fringed with wild narcissi, that had surged and frothed around the lower slopes of the Pyrenees.

But most clearly of all I remembered, and most bitterly I craved . . . the bougainvillaea. What would I not have given for a single spray of this flaming, flaunting, adorable plant?

The memory of the bougainvillaea became an obsession; it nearly made me break the law; there were times when I was on the point of stuffing my socks with pound notes and slinking across the Channel in the hope of reaching the Côte d'Azur before those strangely hideous Chancellors of the Exchequer got on my tracks. Fortunately I was not compelled to such extremities. For though I could not go to see the bougainvillaea, I found a way of making it come to me. This is the story of how I did it.

But first, in case your life has not been lit by the fires of this miracle plant, let me explain why it means so much.

§ II

The bougainvillaea is, *par excellence*, the flower of the Mediterranean; it hangs, like a purple fringe, all round those glittering coasts; and more than any other flower I know it arouses the emotion of nostalgia, at least for those of us who were lucky enough to go sunwards in the golden days before the war. It is a 'thanks-for-the-memory' flower. To hold a spray of it in your hand is to hold a lamp of Aladdin, so many enchanted souvenirs does it conjure up . . . the echo of a concertina, mingling with the laughter of the matelots, outside the door of the Welcome in Villefranche – the scent of the jasmine fields over the hills of Grasse in September – the sigh and surge of the long rollers at Hammamet, on an early April morning when the sun still slants gently on the white roofs of the Arab village; and more material things as well – wild strawberries and sour cream in a garden of Vicenza, white resinous wine in a sweltering café overlooking the Piraeus, the scent of sun-tan oil on the rocks at Taormina, and crystallized tangerines under striped parasols at Juan-les-Pins. To all these scenes the bougainvillaea has signed its name, in long, sweeping, purple characters.

These delights, as we have already suggested, were not part of the pattern of life in Britain's Welfare State in the winter of 1947. No doubt some people would claim that one had no cause of complaint . . . one had enjoyed these things in the past, and so one should be grateful. This, needless to say, was the view of Mrs. Pattern, the vicar's wife, who came bobbing down the lane one Siberian morning when I had gone out early to shake the snow off the trees in the new plantation. I was in none too good a humour; my boots were full of snow, my hands were numb, and during the night there had been many casualties among the trees – tall silver birches snapped at their stakes like matchsticks, golden cypresses with their main branches lacerated, weeping cherries that were weeping all too literally. And the snow was still falling so quickly that hardly had one cleared the loaded boughs before they began to droop again.

Into this white and desolate world Mrs. Pattern tramped like a Breughel peasant, with a blob of red paint for a face, three blobs of black paint for a mackintosh, and a delicately painted mist hovering around her large, kindly mouth.

'Saving lives?' she cried heartily, tramping across the lawn.

It should have been a pleasant thought – 'saving lives'; it ought to have made one feel like a nice sort of floral St. Bernard; instead it put me in mind of air-raid shelters. So I merely grunted and said something about wishing the snow would stop.

'Mustn't grumble,' she cried, even more heartily. 'I always say that snow is really healthier than the rain.'

'The silver birches wouldn't agree with you.'

'Never mind, spring will soon be here. The evenings are beginning to draw out already. I always say that when the evenings are drawing out, it's a sign of spring.'

'Some of the silver birches won't be here to see it.'

'Then you must give them stronger stakes. Better to be sure than sorry. That's what I always say.'

'You can't be sure of anything in this weather.'

'Never mind. You should follow my example and pretend that you're at St. Moritz. Then it all becomes quite exciting. And in any case, I *always* say that what can't be cured must be endured.'

With which she left me, in an even deeper state of gloom than before. For the thought of St. Moritz brought with it the memory of hot sweet glu-wein in huts like eagles' nests, with the whole world a miracle of white below and blue above; it evoked the picture of tiny trains panting up the mountain slopes towards Semmering, leaving behind them trails of golden sparks to mingle with the stars. And it vividly recalled the greatest sensuous pleasure which I have ever known in my life . . . the pleasure of stripping to the waist on the uplands of Villars, straddling a toboggan, and plunging down the dazzling slopes, tingling to the whip of the snow and the kiss of the sun.

However, it was impossible to explain these longings to Mrs. Pattern. She would have called them anti-social. She would even call 'One' anti-social because 'One' is beautiful, expensive and 'arranged'. And if you are beautiful, expensive *and* 'arranged', there is obviously no place for you in modern Britain.

So I just went on shaking the snow off the cypress trees, while Mrs. Pattern marched off down the lane with a look in her eyes that told me she was on her way to the British Restaurant, in order to eat something sinister. But the skies were already darkening for another storm, so I left the trees to fend for themselves, squelched indoors, dragged off my gumboots and sank into a chair by the fire.

The second post had just come. Should I open it? For a moment I thought not; apart from a couple of bills and a circular there were only two letters, which were both from lunatics. (One can always tell lunatics by their handwriting, as most authors with a large correspondence will agree. And if an author, in the course of his career, does not amass a large assortment of lunatics, who write to him as regularly as the waxing and waning of the moon, he can consider himself a failure. I have a very representative collection, which I am prepared to swop with any other author of a similar standing. It includes a large set of Jehovah's Witnesses, in practically mint condition, some very rare and early Social Creditors, and one triangular female astrologist, unused. I know she is triangular because she once sent me a picture of herself, standing by a bicycle, which she was clutching with an expression of extraordinary malevolence.)

I threw the lunatic letters into the fire – (after opening them to make sure that they did not contain a cheque, though nobody has yet been so mad as to send me *that*) – and glanced at the circular. Then I sat up, feeling very much brighter. It happened to be *The Planter's Handbook*, published by my favourite nurserymen, Messrs. Jackman's of Woking. This paper-bound booklet must be unique among horticultural publications, for it is written in a prose as vigorous and as healthy as the shrubs it advertises. For example:

Symphoricarpus Chenaultii. A broad spreading, twiggy shrub with oval fresh green leaves. Its suckers can easily be removed with a spade. *The small, pink, bell-shaped blooms make this shrub throb with bees.* 3/- each

What could be nicer than this conceit . . . to 'throb with bees'? It would not have come amiss from the pen of Francis Bacon.

However, we cannot linger over the symphoricarpus, bees or no bees. The bougainvillaea awaits us. I need hardly say that it was listed in Messrs. Jackman's catalogue. The price was 3s. 6d.

§ III

It arrived early in March, together with a number of other things which, at the moment, seemed of greater importance . . . such as brooms, white, yellow and chocolate, for planting on the slope that led to the orchard, and quantities of hibiscus, for massing at the sunny end of the herbaceous border, and so many varieties of clematis that I could not imagine where they could all be put. Indeed, while I was unpacking them, slashing at the coarse string with a razor blade, and dragging them out of their cones of straw, I sincerely hoped that Oldfield would not appear, to reproach me for such ridiculous extravagance. So as soon as they were undone I bundled them, as rapidly as possible, into a wheelbarrow, with the idea of trundling them round to the back of the woodshed and hiding them till after lunch, when I could come out and dart from place to place, sticking them in somewhere, and hoping for the best.

Alas – the wheelbarrow was made of iron, which clattered with a deafening noise over the cobbles, and before I knew what was happening, there was Oldfield walking towards me. (Sometimes I feel that he must be permanently suspended in the heavens on a wire, watching and waiting to pounce.) With a less powerful personality it might have been possible to steer the wheelbarrow straight past him, whistling in an offhand manner, or – at most – just making some casual remark about 'putting these in later on'. But his hypnotic gaze stopped me in my tracks.

'The clematis have just come,' I said, rather lamely.

'Are *all* them clematis?'

'Yes. It's . . . it's a collection.'

' '*Tis* a collection,' he agreed, with some acidity, bending over the barrow. One could have sworn that the wretched plants wilted under his scrutiny.

For a few moments he busied himself with the pots,

doing the most discouraging things, such as lifting them up to show how pot-bound they were, with all the roots struggling through the hole in the bottom.

Then he straightened himself up with a long sigh, put his hands on his hips, and demanded:

'Where we going to put 'em?'

I racked my brains for a suitable answer. There must be *somewhere* in five acres of woods and gardens . . . but where? There seemed to be hardly a square inch that was not accounted for. Then I remembered.

'I thought they might look nice by the urns.'

No sooner had I said this than I regretted it. 'T'urns?' echoed Oldfield. 'T'urns? What about t'wistaria?'

'They might be trained together . . .' I began.

'And t'honeysuckle?' he interrupted. 'And t'Japanese vine? And t'jasmine?' All this on a tone of rising indignation, like an Old Testament prophet when the Amalekites had been up to something extra nasty.

I was silenced; it was too true; already, round the base of the urns, there was a wistaria and a honeysuckle and a Japanese vine, and a jasmine was on the way. (So, for that matter, was a pair of Lemon Pillar roses, but Oldfield was fortunately unaware of this latest folly.) That is the trouble about having one particularly attractive or outstanding feature in a garden; you want to use it all the time. In the long winter months, while I had been poring over the nurserymen's catalogues, I had constantly been enticed by descriptions of things that twined and draped and wept and curled and twisted, and always I had said to myself 'How lovely those would look around the urns', forgetting that the urns would already be completely smothered if half the things around them were, in Oldfield's phrase, to 'coom oop'.

However, Oldfield's wrath never lasts for long. As soon as he has asserted himself, and put his master in his proper place – which is just above the bottom of the class in the third form – he is kindness itself. So it was on this occasion.

'Well,' he grunted, 'we'll have to see what we can do.' Which, being interpreted, meant that he would make himself personally responsible for them – that somehow or other the old miracle man would find the right place, with the roots in the shade and the flowers in the sun, that he would prune them and stake them and top-dress them, and that when they began to grow, his gnarled fingers would be waiting to guide them on their way, coaxing the fragile tendrils into a design as delicate as a master jeweller's.

§ IV

The bougainvillaea was still waiting for us, together with the brooms and the hibiscus, which had so far escaped Oldfield's attention. And since I was feeling quite sick at the thought of what he might say when he saw them all, it was with a sigh of relief that I observed, coming towards us, the familiar figure of Marius, bearing the bougainvillaea in his arms. For Marius is a great favourite with Oldfield. He recognizes him as a 'proper gentleman', and he likes to hear him talk, even when – like myself – he is taken far out of his depth.

'This wonderful flower!' exclaimed Marius, as soon as he had greeted Oldfield. 'Not, of course, that it *is* a flower.'

That, I thought, was a very good beginning.

'What's that you've got there, sir?' demanded Oldfield.

'But a bougainvillaea!' he cried, tapping the pot delightedly . . . only to add, in the same breath . . . 'Not, I need hardly say, that it *should* be called a bougainvillaea.'

Better and better. Out of the corner of my eye I watched Oldfield; I had a suspicion that for once in a way he was horticulturally at a loss, and that the bougainvillaea was not a flower with which he was very familiar. Particularly as Marius had just informed us that it was neither a flower nor a bougainvillaea at all.

Marius turned sharply in my direction. 'What do *you* think?'

'I feel too cold to think at all. I expect the bougainvillaea does too. Supposing we all go into the greenhouse?'

So we all went into the greenhouse, which was warm and deliciously fragrant.

'I always think,' said Marius, placing the bougainvillaea, or whatever it might be, on the staging, 'that this should be called a Commersonia.'

'Hmph,' from Oldfield.

'Or even a Baretia.'

Another 'hmph' from Oldfield.

'Because Monsieur Baret might well have been the one who found it. Not – of course – that Monsieur Baret *was* Monsieur Baret.'

This was too much for me. '*Not* Monsieur Baret?'

Marius, with his usual tact, covered up my confusion and ignored my mark of interrogation.

'Perhaps the story might amuse Mr. Oldfield?' he suggested. 'If it would not bore you to hear it again?'

As I had never heard it at all, I assured Marius that it

would not bore me at all. So Marius swung himself on to the staging, and told us the strange story of the bougainvillaea, still holding the pot in his hands.

§ V

'When Admiral Bougainville set out from France,' he said, 'to sail round the world in the eighteenth century – I have no memory for dates but I *think* it was the sixth of December, 1766 – he took with him, as one of his staff, a certain Monsieur Philip Commerson, who had attained a considerable reputation, not only as a botanist, but as a man of almost saintly disposition. So strict were his morals, and so upright his conduct, that he had set aside a large part of his fortune to provide funds for an annual prize to be given to the Frenchman who should prove himself most chaste and most immaculate . . . though how such proof was to be rendered I have never been able to ascertain.

'This saintly Monsieur Commerson was valeted, on the journey, by an exceptionally handsome youth, whose name was Baret. And it was very soon evident that Baret's character was as charming as his appearance; throughout the voyage he showed the utmost devotion to his master, fetching and carrying for him, attending to his every need, solacing him during long bouts of *mal de mer* . . . to which Commerson was a martyr . . . and even sharing his cabin, where he slept on a narrow mattress at the foot of his master's bed.

'As the days went by,' continued Marius, 'as the sun grew brighter and the first hot breath of the tropics stirred the sails, it was inevitable that so fair and graceful a figure as young Monsieur Baret should excite the attention of the sailors. They would have liked more of his company. But, for some strange reason that they could not understand, he never gave it to them. He kept himself withdrawn, aloof . . . appearing only for the briefest intervals, a slim, sun-gilt figure on his way to – or from – the beloved Monsieur Commerson. . . .'

Marius suddenly interrupted his narration with a boyish chuckle.

Turning to Oldfield . . . 'Am I boring you?'

Oldfield, with some emphasis, assured him that he was not.

'You've guessed, of course?'

'Well, sir . . . this young man Barry was . . .'

'Well?'

Oldfield cleared his throat. 'A young lady?'

Marius nodded.

'I thought as much.' There was, I suspected, an echo of relief in the old man's voice.

'And in the end, of course, he . . . or rather she . . . was unmasked, in circumstances which it would perhaps be better not to explore too fully.'

'What happened in the end?' I asked.

'Well, at last they reached Tahiti. If my appalling memory is not at fault, it was the second of April 1768, as dawn was breaking. There is a charming description of their arrival in the book which Bougainville afterwards wrote about it . . . he tells of the first rays of the sun lighting up the distant mountains, and white cascades tumbling down the cliffs, which were a riot of scarlet and purple flowers among which, no doubt, the bougainvillaea was predominant. But it was the fauna rather than the flora of the island that claimed the attention of the sailors; out of the mists that still shrouded the beach glided troupes of exquisite girls, clad only in the most airy of garments which, as they entered the water, they cast aside, leaving them to float on the waves. It was like some fantastic dream – the laughing girls in the half-light, the surge of the surf, the ardent young men crowded to the edge of the ship. A situation which one might perhaps describe as almost excessively French.'

'And Baret?'

'Ah – Baret! Even in the face of such overwhelming competition the charms of the young valet held their own. For as he stepped out of his cabin, where Monsieur Commerson was sleeping off the effects of his latest bout of *mal de mer*, a certain young sailor, whose name completely escapes me, stepped roughly up to him, breathing a suggestion so completely at variance with Monsieur Commerson's philosophy, that the startled boy – or should I say the outraged girl? – darted with a shrill cry to the edge of the ship, and plunged in desperation into the scented surf. There ensued a chase, which led up the cliff, past the thundering cascades, into the heart of the purple flowers that Bougainville had noted in his book. And there, perhaps, we had better leave them.'

Marius sighed, and turned to Oldfield. 'It is a pleasing picture, you agree? The mountain side? The damsel in distress . . . the ardent sailor . . . the ship in the distance . . . and all around them the brilliant curtains of this enchanting flower . . . not that it *is* a flower?'

Oldfield straightened his shoulders, cleared his throat, removed the pot from Marius's hands, and stared fixedly at the little barren twigs which had evoked this recital. For a moment I feared that he, too, might be tempted to reminisce. I need not have worried. He gave the side of the pot a sharp tap, as though to remind it that he was having no nonsense with it, however glamorous its origin.

'T'will need a good top dressing,' he said.

§ VI

'Not that it *is* a flower,' Marius had said.

By which, of course, he meant that the long sprays of purple 'petals' are really coloured leaves; the actual 'flower' is only a tiny speck of white in the centre of this glowing frame.

To watch the growth of these leaves, to follow their early, tentative coloration, and to be present at their sudden, spectacular flamboyance, is one of the greatest thrills in the life of a gardener – a thrill, moreover, which can be shared by anybody with enough glass to keep the frost out.

The first faint flames of colour begin to flicker around the stems towards the end of April; then there is a pause, in which the green leaves at the bottom of the branches seem to grow deeper and more glossy, as though they were building up a fitting background for the conflagration that is on its way.

This period of pause is agonizing; one goes out to the greenhouse before lunch, before tea, and before dinner to see what is happening; one even goes out with a torch, after dinner, and climbs up on to the staging and flashes the light over the branches, catching, here and there, the gleam of a purple leaf, and trying to decide whether it is more, or less, purple than it was at noon.

There is only one thing to do, when the bougainvillaea is smouldering in this manner, and that is to go away. To take a train to London, or to ring up friends and propose oneself, and remain firmly ensconced, much against one's will – and probably against theirs – till it is safe to assume that the bougainvillaea has really caught fire.

And then – to go home again. And not to tell anybody that one is coming, but to slink up the drive and skirt round the bushes, and glide unseen into the greenhouse . . . and stand back and gloat.

For really, it is something to gloat about. The back wall of my greenhouse is about fifteen feet high, and from the end of April till late in the autumn it is solid purple with bougainvillaea, with a plentiful lacing of the scarlet variety, which is not so floriferous as the purple, but forms a sharp and exciting foil to it. To stand in front of it makes you feel like a Rothschild; in fact, it looks so beautifully opulent that sometimes it quite alarms me; I feel that I must be on the verge of ruin, with all this grandeur, and I hurry out of the greenhouse and go indoors and start to write like mad in order to pay for it.

But really one need not be frightened by it. My original bougainvillaea, as we saw, cost 3s. 6d., the scarlet sort 5s., and the whole display comes from cuttings of these two plants. The only real expense lies in the upkeep – (a generalization which applies not only to plants but to people, to friends and to lovers). Even then the cost is not so appalling. If you can keep the frost out in the winter, the bougainvillaea will at least survive; if you can manage a temperature that does not sink below forty it will not only survive but flourish and flaunt itself and make you feel that after all there is some colour left in life, and some folly, and some sense in being senseless.

As an indoor decoration it is unique.[1] Against a white wall the long branches dispose themselves with the harmony of a Japanese print, and the coloured leaves are lambent; they seem to glow with an inner fire. And do not forget that all this splendour can be yours for nearly two-thirds of the year. As late as December I have slushed across a snow-covered lawn, between the hours of one and two, when Oldfield is having his lunch, clutching a pair of secateurs and glancing to left and right to make sure that the old man is not going to bounce out of a bush and stop me picking a really exciting bunch – which means, in his opinion, a bunch which destroys all the growth for the following year. (It never really does.) And I have thrown open the door, and sniffed that unforgettable smell of an English greenhouse in winter – which is a compound of lemon verbena and warm moist earth and early freesias, with a tang of the last chrysanthemums and a spice of tarred twine. . . .

We will leave it at that. You may have gathered by now that I am very pro-bougainvillaea. I hope that I have made you 'pro' it too.

§ VII

We must still linger for a while among the exotics. Let us hope that you are reading this on a day as cold and cheerless as the day on which I am writing it, so

[1] But you must always remember to plunge the stems into boiling water for at least five minutes after you have cut them.

that you will welcome the gleams of sunshine which I am trying to tempt on to the paper.

Some of those gleams are shining in the greenhouse at this moment; they come from a flower which rivals even the bougainvillaea in what may be called 'nostalgic value' – the mimosa. Right up to the roof its feathery, golden blossom laughs through the glass at the frozen skies. My own mimosas have a rather romantic story, which shall be told in a moment. But first, a word about this flower's nostalgic associations.

Mimosa, or *acacia dealbata* to give it the correct botanical name, means many different things to many different people. To working girls in big cities it means a flash of yellow on a barrow, a sudden pang – like a pain in the heart – at the sight of anything so quintessentially delicate and feminine, a fumbling in the bag for half a crown, and an exciting journey home in the bus, peering from time to time through the folds of the paper in which the flower is wrapped and bending down to catch its scent, which is not really like the scent of a flower, but has the tang of sweet, cool moss.

Mimosa, to the exile from the Mediterranean, means yellow shadows on the dark waters of a Venetian lagoon; and foaming cascades over the cliffs of Capri, like golden spray dashed against the rocks; it means ethereal avenues at dusk on some island in the Aegean Sea, with Lombardy cypresses in the background, standing stiff and straight and sombre, like disapproving elders. It means carnival in Nice, and shimmering groves in Sicily, and flashes of gold through the mists of the lower Pyrenees.

To me, mimosa means a song – a song in Melba's garden, on an evening in spring, with the Blue Mountains of Australia in the distance. Even to recognize the name of Melba, in these days, is a confession of middle age; to have heard her sing at her best would be an admission of senility. But though she was old when I knew her, there was still a magic in her voice that has had no echo since; it was like a light that has faded from the world. It was not a question of being 'better' than other sopranos; it was no matter for comparisons; it was simply that the voice was of another world. There is a language of gods, and there is a language of men, and when Melba sang, the divine language poured from her throat.

One evening we were sitting in her Australian garden in the shadows of a mimosa. It was an immense tree, as tall as a fair-size English oak; it was in full bloom; and it was of such breath-taking loveliness that we spoke in whispers. It seemed almost to sigh under its golden burden, and yet, when there was a little wind, it danced, and through the changing, flickering patterns of the blossom you could see the silver stars, like diamonds on a yellow dress.

It was then that Melba sang. Leaning back in her chair, with eyes closed, unaccompanied. Only once again was I to hear her voice in such beauty . . . in Venice, a year later. That is another story. This time the song that she sang was short and simple. It was the Aubade from *Le Roi d'Ys*, and maybe she should not have sung it at all, since it was not written for a soprano but for a tenor. What did it matter? When Melba sang, sex seemed to be forgotten, sublimated into a cool, strange, silver sweetness. The voice drifted up, like a moonbeam, stealing through the golden flowers, hanging there, echoing and re-echoing. . . .

But one should not attempt to describe such miracles.

It is better to be terse and simple, and to leave it at that . . . to me, mimosa means a song.

But not only a song.

Let us come down to earth, return to the greenhouse, and take a look at the plants which evoked these reminiscences. To call them 'plants' is perhaps misleading, for they are really small trees, reaching to the summit of the greenhouse and arching over on wires, with trunks as thick as your wrist. And yet, five years ago, they were seeds in my waistcoat pocket.

I was walking down a dusty road in Cyprus, after a very dusty day, arguing with a lot of very dusty people – in particular, with a collection of Communist officials who had been propounding the doctrine of *enosis* . . . i.e. union with Greece. By uniting with Greece they implied, of course, that they desired to escape from the brutal tyranny of the British Crown in order to nestle in the velvet folds of the Iron Curtain. It had all been very heating; my head was buzzing with facts and figures which would have to be transformed, before nightfall, into what a certain American editor described as 'the crisp, nervous prose to which you have accustomed our readers'. And though I felt faintly nervous, I felt far, but far, from crisp.

Overhead, the trees were white with dust. What trees were they? Why – of course, they were mimosas. They must be lovely in the spring. Today, they were only dust traps, hung with rows and rows of brown pods. The pods were bursting with seeds. I reached up and plucked a pod and stuck it in my pocket . . . thinking vaguely of things 'coming up'. After that, I forgot all about them till I had returned to England, and till one day when Gaskin had been pressing my clothes he came down with the seeds in the palm of his hand and asked me if I still wanted them.

From that idle gesture has come an endless cycle of delight.

§ VIII

We have almost done with the exotics. But it would not be fair to finish this chapter without mentioning what may be called the Absurdities. Everyone who owns a greenhouse, everyone who likes popping odd seeds and pips into the earth to see if they will 'coom oop', probably has one or two Absurdities on his shelves, which mean a great deal to him but not much to anybody else.

I shall confine myself to one Absurdity – for there is no time to tell you of the banana tree that was not a banana tree, nor the strange sequence of the grapefruit pips, nor the long and frustrating drama of the date stone. But I insist on taking time to tell you about the Absurdity of the Avocado Pear.

Do you know this epicure's delight? It is the size and shape of a large pear, the flesh has the flavour of a walnut and the consistency of ice-cream, you eat it with oil and vinegar, and anything that sounds more revolting, as I have described it, can hardly be imagined. It is, none the less, delicious.

One day I went to a dinner in London of quite exceptional dreariness; it was something to do with Planning for the Welfare State; and from the moment the *hors d'œuvres* were put before us it was apparent that whatever else the Planners might be able to do they could not plan a dinner. It was all quite terrible until the savoury, which, to my delight, took the form of an avocado pear. Most of the company regarded it as though they had been presented with a hand grenade.

While I was still eating, the speeches began, and my thoughts strayed to the huge stone in the middle of the pear. If one were to plant it, would it 'coom oop'? There seemed no reason to suppose otherwise. Although it was a tropical fruit, one could give it enough heat to ensure that at least it made an effort. It would be most exciting, and would almost compensate one for such a nasty evening.

But how was one to steal this great, sticky stone without being noticed? If one had been surrounded by normal people it would have been easy, but these were not normal people . . . at least, not in my opinion. Immediately opposite me was a huge female Planner, laced with mauve, who, after my derogatory remarks about the Ministry of Supply had kept me under a constant glare of suspicion as though she expected me to pinch the silver.

Meanwhile the speeches were going on. A cabinet minister was on his feet.

'We must have a Plan,' he stated solemnly.

'We must indeed,' I thought, 'because this stone is so enormous, and that mauve woman is glaring worse than ever.'

'We must *stick* to that Plan,' he proclaimed, in rising tones.

'Too true,' I agreed, 'or the stone, which is somewhat glutinous, will stick to *us*.'

'We must act with courage,' he cried, 'and above all, we must act with *speed*.'

This clarion call so excited the mauve woman that she turned her head in order to cheer. I took the minister's advice. I acted with courage, and I acted with speed. I deftly enveloped the stone in a napkin and transferred it to my pocket. The rest of the evening was more than ever of a torture, because I expected at any moment to feel the hand of the hotel detective on my shoulder, and to be marched off to gaol for stealing hotel property. However, nothing happened, and twenty-four hours later the stone was reverently planted in rich Surrey loam (yes, I did send back the napkin).

Today it is a tree four feet high, with rich glossy leaves and a tropical swagger. It shows not the faintest sign of flowering, to say nothing of fruiting, and I don't suppose it ever will. But I could never bring myself to throw it out of the greenhouse, for it is an eternal reminder of a modern principle which I am often inclined to forget – the Importance of Planning.

CHAPTER XIII

ENCORES

ALL the time that these dramas have been unfolding themselves the garden has been growing up around us. This has been happening so fast that sometimes it seems like a transformation scene in a pantomime, where giant forests are whisked away at the turn of a wheel, and out of the stage rise bowers of roses, which open to disclose houris in open-work tights. If you substitute earwigs for houris – which I would greatly prefer to do – it has been like that with me. Far away, a solid screen of pine and larch and golden cypress . . . rising, rising, year by year, painting a dark background for the cherries and the almonds and the crabs which dance ever nearer to the house. Close at hand a long, broad border which is already so crowded that every autumn it has to be drastically trimmed. And up the walls of the house a swift climbing and clambering, hand over hand, branch over branch, as though rose and clematis and wistaria were racing each other to see who would be the first to look in at the upstairs windows.

All of which is very soothing if you suffer from the return-to-the-womb complex which we mentioned on an earlier page. Each of these things helps to protect you from the outer world. Every leaf that taps against the attic window, every thorn that nestles against the bricks, is part of a barrier that keeps the twentieth century at bay. I have always taken a dim view of the twentieth century, so that I consider this to be a laudable ambition.

There is only one thing that cannot be kept out, and that is noise. Most country noises I welcome – the shrill arguments of blackbirds in the shrubbery, the patter of big raindrops on the copper beech on a summer afternoon when thunder is abroad, the creaking branches of the chestnuts in the wind, and indeed all the tunes that the wind may play, from the Wagnerian passages that whistle in every window when the south-wester sweeps across the meadows, to the low drum-like roar that resounds down the great chimney of the music-room when there is a gale from the north.

But there are other noises which cannot be fitted into any romantic pattern. Since this is a factual chronicle, perhaps we should pause for a moment to listen to them, for I am trying to show you a garden not as it might be, but as it is.

The nearest human habitation to Merry Hall is a farm. It lies just across the road, and it is owned by a lady of grace and intelligence, whom we will call Mrs. X. No man could ask for a more charming neighbour. Alas – the lady is sometimes abroad for long periods. And, again alas, the lady has a cowman who, though replete with all the manly virtues, though a faithful husband, an honest worker, and a stalwart citizen, suffers from one minor peculiarity . . . he appears to enjoy the sound of cows that shriek their heads off and cockerels that almost strangle themselves in an effort to give the world some message which the Creator presumably considers of importance.

It does not happen often, and it does not go on for long, but it *does* happen. And lest you should suspect that this is a book in which I have put in all the sweet and left out all the bitter, I think it should be mentioned.

Every year this little comedy is played.

SCENE. *The kitchen at Merry Hall. A large airy room looking out on to a country lane. Over the lane is a hedge, and behind the hedge is a cow of quite exceptional vocal capacity, roaring away like a foghorn on four legs.*

(*Enter a distracted author*)

SELF It's too much.

(GASKIN shrugs his shoulders. Cow roars again, and continues to roar throughout dialogue)

SELF It's even worse than last year.

GASKIN No, it was just the same last year.

SELF *Much* worse. Last year it never began till five. Today it began just after breakfast.

GASKIN You only notice it because you've taken to working in the drawing-room. If you went back to the music-room on the other side of the house . . .

SELF Worse still. There's a sort of echo and it seems to roar down the chimney.

GASKIN You surely can't notice it when you're playing the piano.

SELF That's worst of all. It roars in C. I can't transpose everything into C.

GASKIN Well, I don't know what *I* can do about it.

SELF You should speak to Marshall (*Marshall is the aforesaid cowman*).

GASKIN I had to speak to him last week about the cockerels. He thinks we're a funny lot if we can't stand a few cockerels.

SELF It isn't a *few* cockerels. It's only one. That one that starts at midnight. It isn't natural for a cockerel to start at midnight. It must be ill.

GASKIN Anyway, they're killing it next month.

SELF That's a long way off. They should tie something round it and stop it. *Listen* to that cow! It must be ill too . . .

GASKIN There's nothing the matter with it. It's just lonely.

SELF Then they should get something to play with it. How in the name of, etc.

Off stalks the author, and sits down at his desk, muttering, thinking how much easier it would be to write in a telephone booth at Waterloo Station. The cow continues to roar. Suddenly it stops. There is a golden, exquisite silence. The sun comes out, the world is at peace, and faintly there echoes – (cue for song) – the trill of a lark. The author tiptoes to the window, and sees Marshall leading the cow down to the bottom of the field, past the haystack, past the three tall poplars, into the lush distance of the water meadows.

Gaskin has done it again.

And now we can get on with the story.

§ II

I scribbled the word 'Encores' at the top of this chapter because it seemed to express an important truth about the gardener's life as opposed to the lives of other people – the fact that each new year is, *ipso facto*, more startling and more rich in beauty that the one that preceded it. In another book about another garden, I wrote a rather obvious little sentence which people sometimes put on calendars . . . '*A garden is the only mistress who never fades, who never fails*'. It is of course an understatement, for a garden is a mistress whose beauty, far from fading or failing, increases every year. With every passing season she reveals some fresh charm, some new allurement, and one of the greatest delights of gardening – particularly if you keep a diary – is to set down a record of the latest loveliness that time has written on her face.

Consider, for instance, my climbing roses. I have six on the walls of the house – two Etoiles de Hollande, one Gloire de Dijon, one Lemon Pillar, one Paul's Scarlet and one Reve d'Or. They are listed in alphabetical order because it is impossible to decide which is the best. For single blossoms, perhaps, you cannot beat the Etoile de Hollande, which produces flowers of such fantastic beauty that you feel that the only thing to do is to lay them on the altar of a church. But then the Lemon Pillar catches your attention and you realize the odiousness of comparisons, for this is a rose that is moonlit even in the blaze of noon. Stand over it, shade it from the sunlight, and it shines with a secret phosphorescence. And what about the Reve d'Or, which is most worthy of its pretty name, for its life is spent in dreams of gold? And Paul's Scarlet, which is so prolific that you can see its floral bonfire half a mile away? And finally, how can one ignore the claims of the Gloire de Dijon? There are roses more elegant in design, more glorious in colour, more delicate in perfume, but there is no rose so rich in memory. It is the rose of everybody's childhood – of everybody, that is to say, who ever played in a garden. For me it recalls the little white cottages of Devonshire, and when I look into its petals I can see once again the bowls of clotted cream which were cooling in everybody's larder.

However, I was talking of the yearly increase in the

beauty of the garden, and the reason I stepped aside to consider the climbing roses was because after three or four years they were peeping into the upper windows, pressing their heads against the panes as though they were trying to see what was going on inside, and I cannot think of a more graceful compliment that a flower could pay to a man than to seem to seek entrance into his house. The first rose to 'get away' was the Gloire de Dijon; it sent a single shoot racing up the wall, and one bright morning as I was coming down the staircase, on which there is a tall window, half way up, I saw a small, creamy bud pushing its head over the ledge. It might have been standing on tiptoe with the express object of peering inside. I got the ladder and trained it over the edge, and a fortnight later it had been joined by two others, and the three of them leaned in at the window, which was always kept open, so that one could bend over and sniff them as one went up to bed.

It was five years before the first plumes of the wistaria reached my bedroom window, but they made so brave a display that I was able to train them all round; when one drew up the blind in the morning one saw the world through a frame of blossom, and when one turned over to sleep at night the scent was what some people would call 'overpowering'. So much the better, as far as I was concerned. To be 'overpowered' by the fragrance of flowers is a most delectable form of defeat.

§ III

An 'encore' in a garden, unlike an 'encore' in a concert hall, is almost always more exciting than the original performance; to do something for the second time in a garden is always better than doing it for the first, and the third time is better still, and the fourth and fifth, ad infinitum. Every time you push aside the damp, frosty chestnut leaves at the beginning of January, to greet the first snowdrops, the flowers seem to gleam with a purer white; and time cannot wither, nor custom stale, the beauty of Coventry Patmore's line about the snow-drop which always rings in my memory at these times. . . .

And hails far summer with a lifted spear.

That is the attar of poetry.

It is the same with what one might describe as the rites and ceremonies which every gardener creates for himself in his perpetual pilgrimage round his estate, be it large or small. Every May for instance, when the old crab apple on the lawn – (*pyrus malus floribunda*) – is draped from head to foot in a rosy lace of blossom, I wait till a warm moonlit evening in order to do something so simple that it will probably make you laugh . . . to feel the branches with my hands. However, before you begin to make rude noises about such conduct, let me explain that this ritual is not so precious as it sounds. For in an old tree there is always a certain amount of dead wood, and one night by pure chance I discovered that the dead wood is warm while the live wood is icy cold, even on the hottest night. Why this should be, I do not know, still less why it should fascinate me. But it does. I love standing there, in a sort of pink and silver tent, with maybe a nightingale singing in the copse, exploring by touch this strange paradox – the warm wood that is dead, and the ice-cold wood that is filled with the sap of spring.

That happens year by year.

So does the first search for the Indian boy in the chestnut tree.

In case that sounds somewhat obscure, I should explain that the Indian boy is the result of a curious convolution of branches in an old chestnut; there are two perfectly formed legs, a long slim body, a small knotted head, and two branching arms uplifted to the sky. Usually, when people ask me to see pictures in natural objects I am a dismal failure, which annoys them very much indeed.

'But you *must* be able to see the face of that old man in the cloud,' they exclaim. 'Look! There's the nose, and there's the eye, and there's his long white beard.'

'So it is,' I murmur, blinking up and seeing nothing at all.

'No, *no* . . . you're looking the wrong *way* . . . over *there* . . . it's too fantastic . . . you can't possibly *not* see it . . . and heavens, now he's got an arm and he's holding a scythe!'

With a great effort I peer up and gaze at a cloud which looks to me extraordinarily like a cloud. And then out of sheer politeness I pretend to see the picture, the beard and the eye and the scythe and the whole boring business, only to be informed, in the coldest of tones, that I can't possibly be seeing it because, by now, it has gone away.

However, you really cannot fail to see the little Indian boy. The only drawback is that in order to do so you have to be lying in the bath. Unless you are in a prone position, gazing out of one particular window, he refuses to materialize. When he does, he springs to life with startling clarity, his brown body dances in the wind, and his uplifted arms hold up a white parasol of blossom. He reminds me of a figure I once saw in Benares. Twilight was falling on that melancholy city, and the grey waters of the Ganges were veiled with the blue smoke of burning ghats. I was standing by the river, wondering how so dirty and desolate a flood could ever have attained its reputation for sanctity, when out of the mist floated a barge, containing the recumbent figures of three rich Hindus. At the end of the barge stood this slim, almost naked youth, holding aloft a white parasol against a sun that had already burned its way through the horizon. I remember thinking how inconsiderate it was of the Hindus to keep him standing like that. A girl was sitting cross-legged at his feet, singing a sad, monotonous song . . . and that was all there was to it, a fragment of melody and a glimpse of beauty against a sombre background. But it was a picture I have never forgotten, and every spring it is painted for me again, in fresh English colours of white and green.

But very few other people have seen him. You cannot ask people to come up to the bathroom and lie flat on their backs in order to see a little Indian boy. It would make them gloomy and suspicious, particularly if they were females.

'If you come up and lie down in the bathroom I will show you my little Indian boy. . . .'

No. Definitely not. Out.

All the same, it would be nice to think of some way of saying it which did not sound improper. For I like sharing things.

§ IV

Of all the 'encores' that seem, year by year, to increase in satisfaction, none can compare with the bonfires. If it is true that we all contain in us the seeds of every vice in the catalogue of human sin – and it probably is – then I have more than my share of arsonomania, to coin a word which has escaped the attention of the *Oxford Dictionary*. I have never yet met a boring bonfire, nor failed to find some plausible excuse for making one.

Not that there was any need, in those first two or three years, to find excuses. It was a long time before we had burned away the mountains of twigs and debris that had been left in the wake of the fallen elms. (The main trunks and larger branches had been dragged by chains to the side of the field, to 'weather' and mature.) But even after the elms had gone there was plenty of felling to be done; at least a third of the old plums and apples in the orchard were so root-bound and decayed that I decided to do away with them, so they were grubbed out and dragged over to join the elms, to be sawn up later for the house. That meant another bonfire of the debris which smelt so sweet that it was a pleasure to be choked by it.

The sweetest bonfire fragrance of all came from the smoke of the laurel. There were dozens of clumps of speckled laurel all over the estate, which I hacked down with the smallest compunction, for speckled laurels are surely almost the ugliest form of vegetation known to man; they make one think of suburban railings and municipal gardens; they conjure up all the horrors of the 'English Riviera'. But when you burn their branches, that is another matter; the perfume is exquisite, bittersweet, like honey with a tang in it; and it has a strange quality of travelling for immense distances – indeed, I have savoured the first fragrance of my own laurel fires when I have still been half a mile away from the house. Again the ash left by the laurel is of a very special beauty, as white as snow, but with a faint and curious tinge of green, as though the ghost of the sap were still hovering round its own grave.

Did you know that wood ash was luminous? Did you know that long after the flames were quenched, long after you have raked the whole heap over and trudged back over the dew-laden lawns, and turned out the lights and gone to sleep . . . it stays up there in the orchard, glowing with a strange secret beauty? The first time I discovered this was on a dark October night when I could not sleep. It was in the early hours of the morning, and I thought a walk round the garden would do me good. There was a good deal of stumbling and barking of shins, for it was pitch black, and there were only three matches in the box which I had put in my pocket. But it was worth it; for when I neared the orchard I saw this strange silver glow, like a patch of moonlight. As I stood over it, warming my hands, the silver was so bright that you could have read a paper by it. Then I struck a match – and the illusion vanished, it was just a grey pile, without life or lustre. But when the match flickered out, the ash shone again, as brightly as a host of fireflies. There is doubtless some simple scientific explanation of this, but I have no particular wish to learn it. I prefer to regard it as a piece of magic, which I can reproduce at will, as the years go by.

Yes, the bonfires are certainly among the most excellent of encores. How, for example, could anybody ever have too much smoke? There are endless shapes and colours and fragrances and variants of smoke, all of them beautiful, and it is difficult to decide which is most desirable. Of the infinite variety of designs these are my two favourites; firstly, the thin, tenuous column that climbs straight upwards from a slow-burning fire on a windless day, like a white finger pointing the way to heaven; secondly, the great billows and bolsters of smoke that come creaming and cavorting out of a big pile that you are trying to damp down with clods of grass and bundles of wet leaves. The smoke, on such occasions, has an almost solid quality; it is like living sculpture; you feel you could sit on it, float up with it in an ever-changing whirl of white limbs and curling branches and monstrous, ghostly blossoms.

§ V

Nor is it only in bonfires proper that the lure of the fire exists. Burning the grass itself is almost as good. My terrain for this 'encore' is the field next to the orchard, and there are two seasons in the year when it can be achieved with the greatest delight, in February and in August. It is hard to say which is the more pleasing; in February the grass is tougher and often it is fringed with frost, so that the pale blue smoke curls up through a veil of silver. On a cold day, as you run round the field, lighting new patches all over the place and piling on extra clumps so as to make a dozen little individual bonfires, you constantly encounter blasts of hot air which are more than welcome. But maybe August is even better, for then, if the summer has been dry, there is an element

FIRE

of danger; before you know where you are a hungry tongue of flame is gliding towards a sapling, and before you have beaten this out with a broom you have to rush over to the other edge of the field, where the flames are threatening one of the old apples. By the end of the afternoon you are as black as a sweep and it takes twenty minutes to clean the bath, and it is all quite delightful.

Besides – think of all the labour you are saving! Think of the elderly hypochondriacs who do *not* have to be paid to scythe and the nasty youths who do *not* have to be bribed to hook. Instead of that the swift, consuming flames do it all for you, leaving the earth clean and open, and in a condition to welcome all sorts of charming little wild flowers that soon come sprouting up and shining in the sunshine against the charred soil, like patterns painted on a black enamel tray.

Think, too, of the insects you destroy! And that is where I pause. For I do think about them, a great deal too much, and instead of being filled with satisfaction, it greatly worries me. I think of the ladybirds scurrying away, and the startled grasshoppers, and even the slugs, for slugs cannot help being slugs, and all the ruin and destruction one is causing. And life suddenly seems so messed up and tangled that no philosophy can straighten it out.

Therefore . . . as we are really thinking aloud . . . I am going to write a chapter called 'Not for the Tough', and all tough-minded persons had better skip it, because they will find it very sickening indeed. But before I do that, I want to finish the present chapter with a foot-note about Miss Emily, who, as you may have gathered, is one of the most persistent 'encores' in my gardening life.

§ VI

You will not be surprised to learn that Miss Emily, who is nothing if not a bargain hunter, has cast a great many longing glances at my stores of timber. She has never asked me in so many words if she can purchase it, but she has asked Gaskin and Oldfield, with no effect, for I have told them that I will not sell a log of it – not a single twig. Why should I? Wood is 'going up', like everything else. But I would not sell it even if it were 'going down'. Burning your own wood is quite different from burning wood from a timber merchant or from some squalid man with a cart.

Yet Miss Emily never fails to drop hints about my wood, and how wonderful it must be to have it, and what could anybody possibly do with so much. It is always the same, whenever we walk in the garden together, and stroll out to the field where it is stacked in great heaps (I must admit, it *does* look rather like the yard of a timber merchant).

'Heavens!' she always cries, as though she were seeing it for the first time. 'Have you been cutting down any *more* trees?'

I deny this suggestion.

'But there's enough wood here to last you for the rest of your life!'

'I hope there is.'

This does not, as I had intended, close the conversation. 'In fact,' she continues, 'it would be absolutely impossible to burn all this in one house in under fifty years. *Absolutely*.'

'All the same, I shall have a good try.'

'I wonder you don't sell some of it.'

Silence.

'I really do.'

More silence.

We go indoors. A huge fire is blazing in the music-room. It is a glorious fire, that warms the soul as well as the body; it has a crimson heart and a mass of golden flames that dance upwards like ribbons streaming in the wind. It is a fire to fill Miss Emily's heart with the bitterest envy; you can almost see her mouth watering.

She pretends to shrink back in alarm.

'Oh dear!' she murmurs, 'don't you think it is rather dangerous?'

'I don't think so. Do come nearer. You must be frozen.'

She shrinks back still further, as though retreating from a roaring beast. An acid smile and a shake of the head. 'Thank you, no. I should be scorched.' A pause and a sudden exclamation of warning. 'Oh be careful! I think that log is . . . no . . . perhaps not . . . I thought that log was going to overbalance.'

I ignore these obvious machinations.

'Of course,' she continues, '*some* people would say you were *burning* money. If we were in London . . .'

'But we aren't . . .'

'If we were in London each of those logs would be cut up into at least six smaller logs and sold for sixpence each. And as there are six giant logs on that fire alone, it means that at this moment you are burning more than a pound's worth of timber.'

Which immediately gives me my opportunity. 'If those six logs are *really* worth more than a pound, I *might* consider selling some of them.'

'Oh, but you wouldn't *get* anything like that,' she

interposes, with great haste. 'One never does, does one? I mean, when one tries to *sell* anything. . . .'

And then she pauses, because she sees that she has walked into her own trap. She has walked into it so often before that I am always amazed when I see her walking into it again. But she always does. I can only conclude that she likes it.

I like it too, this mimic battle by the fireside. It is one of those 'encores' that give to life a pattern and a sense of continuity. And it always ends in the same way – by Miss Emily departing with a bundle of logs, gratis, in the boot of her car.

And as I bid her goodbye I tell her to make sure that there are no spiders left on them when she sets them alight.

Which leads us automatically to chapter fourteen.

CHAPTER XIV

NOT FOR THE TOUGH

THIS chapter, as I suggested before, should be skipped by all tough-minded persons, who will find it of considerable repulsion.

All the same, it goes in, for perhaps there may be, somewhere in the world, somebody who is as silly as I am on these matters, somebody who worries beyond all reason about the trials and tribulations of very small – and often unalluring – creatures who are regarded by 'normal' people as only fit to be trodden underfoot. There might even be somebody who can tell me what we can do about it.

We will begin where we left off, with Miss Emily and the logs and the spiders.

1 *Spiders that get left on logs that you have put on the fire*

This perennial worry is enough to stop one having log fires at all, and to make one turn the whole house over to gas. It happens over and over again. You collect a beautiful bundle of logs from the orchard; you carefully examine each log to see that it is spiderless, that there are no ladybirds hiding in the bark and no other insects lurking anywhere; you bring it indoors, arrange it, and set it alight; and then, all of a sudden, out comes rushing some wretched spider that has been overlooked, and darts to and fro with the flames flickering nearer and nearer. And you are struck with panic and push aside one of the logs, which nearly upsets the spider, and push aside another, which starts rolling out towards the carpet, and by the time you have caught it the spider has disappeared beyond all hope of rescue, and there is nothing to do but to pile the logs back again and hope, rather dubiously, that the spider has had a quick death and has not left too many dependants.

2 *Cutting worms in half with a spade*

How one is to avoid this, unless one is to stop digging altogether I really cannot imagine. But I cannot say that I like it, and I refuse to believe that the worms like it, either. Of course, there are all sorts of people who will tell you that worms do not mind being cut in half at all because both halves go on living – that the worms laugh it off with an airy shrug of the shoulders, exclaiming 'Oh *look*! This funny man has cut me in *half*! How *amusing*! Now I can go away for a week-end with myself!' But I suggest that the people who tell you that the worms like it are the same people who tell you that the foxes like it and that the lobsters like it – (being boiled, I mean) – and these are not the sort of people whose judgment I care to trust.

But what is one to *do*? It is all extraordinarily difficult, and one should have been born a cow.

3 *Disturbing hedgehogs*

I always seem to be disturbing hedgehogs, and always at the wrong time of year, and I wish there were some means of assuring the hedgehogs that this conduct is inadvertent.

I shall never forget the first time we disturbed a hedgehog. It was after one of the smaller elms had been cut down, at the very end of the field, on the edge of the coppice. I went out to see how the foresters were getting on, and found them bending over a small object on the ground. It was a hedgehog.

'The nest's over there,' said the head man, pointing to the hedge, 'with two littl'uns in it. And one of the big'uns is with them. They seem all right. But this one's acting a bit queer.'

They drifted away. I stood looking at the hedgehog. It was panting desperately, as though it had been running a race. Up and down, up and down went its little sides, as though it were struggling for breath. I felt that it was in the grip of some hideous nightmare; for when its world had suddenly come crashing down, it had been wrapped in a deep hedgehog sleep, a sweet, prickly slumber that would have endured – but for me – through the snows and the frosts and the rains. And now we had torn it back into the great world, and it was in hell.

The hedgehog went on panting. You would have thought its lungs were bursting. There was nothing whatever I could do about it, except to tell the men not to go near it.

When I went up again, a couple of hours later, it was dead.

So that was that. And I am afraid I have told the story very badly because . . . well . . . I suppose it isn't a story at all.

4 *Spraying*

I wish I had never read the advertisement on the tin. (It was a well-known brand of insecticide.) The advertisement said that the flies, or whatever one happened to be after, were killed by suffocation; the stuff coated their respiratory passages and choked them.

Which was not at all amusing. It did not seem to

matter so much with mosquitos, because mosquitos give a single gulp of the stuff and then gently collapse, so that they can be squashed straight away. (Which is probably a pleasanter death than most of us are heading for.) But it does seem to matter with flies, particularly a certain large 'bumble-fly' that gets into the music-room on summer afternoons. They take a dreadful time to expire, and buzz about in their death throes for ten minutes. And though few insects are less alluring, though they are an infernal nuisance and are probably a mass of germs, that is not the point. However unpleasant they may be, God made them that way, and somehow I feel that it is all wrong to assume this role of mass torturer.

It is the same with all the other sprays and washes and powders which one must use in any garden which is not to degenerate into a wilderness. If one really thinks about it, one must be causing endless misery and suffering every time one goes out with a sprayer. But again, what is one to do? The only logical conclusion would seem to be to join the Jains. In case you are not familiar with the Jains, it should be explained that they are a Hindu sect with such a dread of killing that they wear gauze veils in front of their mouths lest they should swallow a gnat.

5 *Destroying ant-heaps*

Well, one must, mustn't one? If you could have seen *our* ant-heaps, you would have agreed that the situation was desperate. The lawn resembled a lunar landscape. It was either us or the ants.

But how has one any right to wring one's hands over the folly and wickedness of the atomic bomb when one is personally and annually responsible for the death of millions of highly intelligent and industrious little creatures? Does it make sense? It does not.

There are four methods of destroying ants' nests, and they are all pretty grim.

There is the method by which you wait till the rain has softened the earth, and then go out to bang the nest on the head with the heavy thing they call a 'beetle'. This is the way I find the least repulsive – maybe through cowardice, because what goes on under the earth is not seen. Somehow I have a feeling that the ants, if they could be consulted, would also prefer it.

They would certainly prefer it to the boiling water method, which, if you have the least imagination, must recall the last days of Pompeii; or the digging-up-with-a-fork method, which must have all the horror of an earthquake. And I should think – though one cannot be sure – that they would prefer it to the powder method, for that is another of the asphixiants.

6 *Investing flowers with human sentiments*

This, to the tough-minded, will be the most completely nauseating confession of all. O.K. They cannot say that they were not warned.

Nauseating or not, this particular kink, if you like to call it such, is a drawback in a gardener, and a quite unaffected one. It means, for example, that if you are picking a bunch of mixed flowers, and if you happen to see, over in a corner, a small, sad, neglected-looking pink or paeony that is all by itself and has obviously never had a chance in life, you have not the heart to pass it by, to leave it to mourn alone, while the night comes on. You have to go back and pick it, very carefully, and put it in the centre of the bunch among its fair companions, in the place of honour.

That is only one form of the folly to which this kink can lead you. There are many others, and they nearly always involve the flowers which, by rights, ought to be thrown away. It is always the misfits that go to one's heart, the crippled, the straggling, the under-dogs.

Here is an example of what I mean.

Do you know what occupies the most important place in my whole garden? It is a small, stunted pine. It is the commonest form of pine in Europe; it is far from robust; it is not even straight, having been damaged in its infancy. And that involves a story.

Three or four years ago I went to Austria with two delightful companions. It was a dream of a holiday, which recalls itself as a medley of fantastic castles gleaming in the rain, calm blue lakes with the storks gliding over them, Mozart in little coffee-houses to the accompaniment of wines as cool and golden as his melodies . . . and pine trees. Mountains of pines and valleys of pines and long dark avenues of pines. I have, as you may gather, a 'thing' about pines.

On the final day of the holiday we found ourselves on a mountain road near Innsbruck. We had an hour to spare before catching the train. I said: 'Let's get out of the car and sit under the pines and have a last breath of mountain air before we get into that ghastly wagon-lit.'

So we did. We got out and sat down on the moss and listened to the silence, which is always a good thing to do. But it wasn't really silence at all, for there was a faint wind in the pines, and far below, a ghostly echo from the river – and nearer at hand, the tinkle of cow-bells. C sharp, A flat, D natural . . . tinkle, tinkle, tinkle . . .

soft and bittersweet. I thought how nice it would be to die to such a symphony . . . the sigh of the pines and the gentle laughter of the bells.

Then I noticed the pine seedlings. Naturally I had been conscious of them before, but only in the background; now I saw that not only were we sitting under some of the finest trees I had ever seen, but we were surrounded by a positive nursery of their little ones. They popped up everywhere, lifting sturdy heads through the bracken, thrusting their roots among the rocks and the moss.

'I'm going to dig up some pines and take them back,' I said.

Groans from my companions. 'You *can't* take back anything more in the vegetable line.' (This was an unkind reference to the fact that I had already taken over a considerable space in our suitcases for various forms of plants which had caught my eye. There were ferns, wrapped up in tissue paper, and geranium cuttings, and quantities of seed pods, and the root of a single yellow rose and a great many other things.)

'It won't take a minute.'

'Well, you'll have to put them in your own bag. I'm not going to have a lot of blasted pine trees in the pants of my pyjamas,' said one.

'What's more,' added the other, 'when we get to the Customs kindly remember that all these things belong to *you*. I don't want to be had up for importing some awful sort of beetle.'

'All the men at the Customs are fans of mine,' I said haughtily. 'If I tell them these are for the garden they won't examine anything at all.'

So I began scrabbling away among the rocks. There

was a fine clump of three seedlings, with a feeble little fourth one on the edge, and I devoted my energies to digging up these three. They came fairly easily, with plenty of root and a nice lot of earth, and I spread out a handkerchief on the moss to wrap them in. Then I noticed the feeble one. And – (here the tough-minded had better cover their eyes) – I felt that it could not possibly be left like that. Half its roots were exposed, and it was leaning over in an attitude of the greatest dejection. But even if it survived in a physical sense, it would be lonely; its brothers would have gone; there would be nobody to talk to, nothing to do but listen to the wind and the tinkling of bells. So I went back and lifted the feeble one out, with an especially large clump of earth, and laid it with its brothers.

I need hardly say that I did not mention these sentiments to my friends, who would almost certainly have been sick.

Well, by the time we came home, the feeble one had a very special place in my affections. It had suffered on the journey. One of its tiny branches had been snapped off, and a tube of toothpaste had exploded over its roots. When it was taken out into the garden and dipped in the water-butt, it looked more dead than alive. It was really only fit for the dustbin, and it would need a miracle to save it.

Very well, we would try to work the miracle. I made a mixture of the richest loam, with plenty of leaf mould and fine sand. I cut a strong stake. So much for the material side. What about the moral? Where should we put it, in order to make it feel important?

There was only one place. It was on the lawn, a few yards from the south wall. It was a place that had been reserved for a specimen tree, such as a double white cherry or a ghinko, because in time it would grow up and look into the bedroom window.

That was where it went, in a hole most carefully dug and drained, and when the stake had been driven in I put a paper flag on top of it so that it should not be trodden on.

The little tree is still a little tree, and still a feeble tree. But last year, for the first time, it seemed to perk up, and lift its head and put on an inch or two's growth, so I am still hoping that in time it will thrust skywards, till it will be as high as my bedroom window. It would be nice to hear the wind in its branches, and to remember the tinkling of those bells that had rung long ago on a day of happiness.

CHAPTER XV

FLOWERS AND THE WOMAN

WHILE this story has been slowly unfolding itself, only two women have drifted through its pages – Our Rose and Miss Emily. There have been others, of course, for what would a garden be if women had not graced it? What colour would your memories have, if you could not remember a white dress under the copper beech, or recall how lovely the lilacs looked when a pair of pretty hands was reaching towards them?

These ladies must remain anonymous. They would prefer it, you would prefer it, and I would certainly prefer it. Whatever opinion I may have of my talents, I have never taken them to include the power to write a love story. A normal love story, that is to say. A passionate interlude with a crocus, maybe; an enslavement to a Siamese cat or a heartbreak over a cocker spaniel. Yes. One day I might even describe the very peculiar feelings I have about a certain Chippendale chair; when anybody sits on it I feel as if I were witnessing the rape of a beloved. But normal boy-meets-girl stuff . . . no. It would all be most tiresome and embarrassing.

Besides, it would prevent me from saying the many very acid things which I wish to say, in all sincerity, about women and flowers. If I were to be fatally ensnared by the owner of the pretty hands that reached towards the lilac, I might be tempted to forget the monstrosities she performs with that lilac when she has picked it. If she were Our Rose she would probably tear it to pieces and float it in a Lalique bowl with a pineapple in the middle.

But Our Rose, though she is straining at the leash at the back of my mind, must be kept in abeyance for a few moments. It is of women and flowers in general that I wish to speak. Our Rose, where flowers are concerned, is only femininity raised to the *nth* degree. She and her many imitators nearly all commit the same crimes, chopping off stalks, twisting heads, tearing open petals, and using countless spikes and wires and instruments of torture to ensure that no flower can possibly look as God intended it to look.

To prove the callousness of most women in this matter of flower decoration, you only have to spend a week at a nursing home.

You lie in bed, hopefully waiting for somebody to send you a bunch of something, and eventually somebody does. In hurtles Nurse Fortescue, with a swish of tissue paper and a fragrance of roses or narcissi or whatever it may be, crying: '*Look* what somebody has sent us! Aren't we spoiled? I'll pop them into fresh water straight away!'

And before you can stop her she has flounced away, to return a few minutes later with the wretched flowers half throttled, stuffed bolt upright into something which looks like the neck of a glass giraffe. That is the nursing-home vase, *par excellence*, the giraffe-neck variety, which is totally unsuitable for any form of vegetation except, possibly, a single red-hot poker. However, there are many variations. There are vases in a sickly oxy-dized green, and vases with gross bulges in the middle, and – in the extra expensive nursing homes – there are fan-shaped plaster things filled with coils of wire which twist even the most malleable blossoms out of shape.

But the giraffe-neck is the nurse's pride and joy. She will use it even for a bunch of Parma violets, sticking the stalks into the narrow aperture at the top, so that the poor little flowers look as though they were balancing on the top of a pole.

You may tell me that it is not the nurse's fault – that she has to use whatever material comes to hand, and that there is nothing but these horrors in the vase cup-board on the landing. That argument will not work at all. *Some* woman bought those horrors in the first place. And it is the nurses who continue to use them, year in and year out, without a protest and without even a hint of a strike. One is forced to the conclusion that they must really like them.

Please do not regard these remarks as an attack on the nursing profession. Nurses are skilled, heroic creatures, who are sadly underpaid and grossly overworked. Any man who does not marry his nurse is a fool – myself included. I am merely pointing out the fact that nurses do these terrible things with flowers, not because they are nurses, but because they are women.

May we therefore diverge for a few moments, and be very practical indeed?

§ 11

First, let me sing the praises of the common basket, for almost all the flowers that blow. It is strange that one can go through half one's life without realizing the importance of putting flowers in baskets, but there it is. Life is like that.

Take an ordinary wicker basket, fairly shallow, with a nice sensible handle, and paint it glossy white, inside and out. If you do it yourself it will probably look rather repulsive, and will stick to the table-cloth, but if you give it to your local Mr. So-and-So, he will charge you only a few shillings, and when he brings it back it will look like the finest Belique china. It really *will.* I have a lovely plate in lattice-work Belique, and when you put the painted basket next to it you can hardly tell the difference.

Nor is white the only colour for the baskets. A very deep blue, the blue of old Worcester china, is as effective, and you can get pretty effects with pale yellow, very pale green and – for sweet peas – the palest possible blue.

While your Mr. So-and-So is painting the baskets – which he will greatly enjoy, because it is one of those jobs which are out-of-the-rut – you must also instruct him to make zinc containers for them. These will be rather more expensive; I think mine were about eight shillings each. Fill these with fine sand, to within about an inch of the edge. And then pour water on the sand, so that the whole of it is saturated, with just a thin layer of water on the top. That is all.

I cannot tell you how much brighter your life will seem if you carry out these instructions, how much more colourful your days, and how much less tedious your rheumatism. The baskets sit there *asking* to be filled. Whatever flowers you put in them are invariably on their best behaviour; they stand up straight in the sand as though they were growing. Or they will droop prettily over the edges, if you wish, or lean as though they really wanted to, against the support of the handle. The handle itself is the greatest fun of all, because there are dozens of long sprays that you can twine around it – jasmine or clematis or rambling roses – or, best of all, I sometimes think, the common ivy, which in this formal setting suddenly discloses itself as a lovely, carven jewel, wrought by the hand of a master.

After the baskets I would stress the importance of conch vases, large and small, in glass or china, or even plaster, because the shape of the conch seems to have been specially designed by nature to fit almost all the flowers in the world, spreading them out in a delicate fan of blossom that enhances their most lovely qualities. It is astonishing to reflect how many women, outwardly respectable women too, stumble through life without the assistance of a single conch. They go about their ways with an apparently clear conscience, they smile as they trip down the street, they stand in queues and chat with their neighbours, and all the time, if one only knew it, there is this terrible secret – they are conchless. Such women should look up the word 'conch' in the *Oxford Dictionary*, where they will find a very fitting description of themselves. After describing the shell, its trumpet shape and origins, the dictionary adds: 'Also colloquially, *conk*. A nickname for the lowest class of inhabitants of the Bahamas, from their use of conches as food.'

If you, gentle reader, are a conk, it is to be hoped that you will do something about it without delay.

Seriously, however, the main thing to remember is that you cannot possibly have too many vases, jugs, bowls, glasses, figures and ornaments in general; you ought to be constantly adding to them; and you ought never to pass a junk-shop without going in to see if there is something that will give you an idea. Sometimes it is quite an unlikely object which suggests itself, like my small white Worcester figure of a girl holding out her apron. Every spring I pour a wineglassful of water into the apron and fill it with buttercups. Or my little negro carrying the bucket on his head. In January the bucket always holds a bunch of snowdrops. Or my Sheraton box of old rosewood, which is lined with lead, and makes a very beautiful container for the first Parma violets. I have no doubt that I often 'go too far', as the saying is, because there is practically nothing capable of bearing water which does not seem to me to demand to be filled with flowers. Indeed, on one occasion when we found a hole in the blue Venetian chandelier, I climbed up and trailed clematis around it, which looked very nasty indeed, dropped spiders down one's neck, and eventually fused the lights.

But at least I have been faithful to one principle; I have always tried to let the flowers speak for themselves; I have never asked them to say things which Nature never intended them to say; I have never chopped off their stems, nor twisted their heads, nor tortured their leaves, nor throttled them with wires, nor used any of the loathsome Gestapo tricks of the fashionable florist.

And since this sort of thing was the main occupation and delight of Our Rose, you may imagine that our relations were often somewhat strained.

§ III

The climax came on a very hot day in September when I was invited to luncheon at her intensely Tudor Cottage, 'The Weathercocke'. I was suspicious of this invitation from the first, because of the elaborately casual manner of its delivery – just a note pushed through the letter-box on the night before, asking me to come and take 'pot luck' – (pronounced 'potty lucky'). However, I accepted, because I had a morbid curiosity to find out what she had been up to.

When I arrived the other two guests – Miss Emily and Marius – were already there, and cocktails were being served, in long-stemmed Venetian glasses. On the top of each cocktail floated a single flower of the blue monkshood. 'Such a pretty idea,' proclaimed Miss Emily.

As I sipped my cocktail I wondered, not for the first time, what Our Rose could possibly have put in it to produce so staggering an effect of sobriety. And it seemed that Marius wondered too. For he held up his glass, blinked at it, and said:

'I have been making a little calculation. And I have come to the conclusion that it would take at least two hundred of these to produce an effect of paralysis.'

Rose went through the process known as 'drawing herself up'. 'Really . . .' she began.

'You think less?' interrupted Marius, blissfully unaware of her reaction. 'Perhaps. Vomiting would certainly begin after the hundredth.'

She could only stare at him in pink indignation.

'Personally,' snapped Miss Emily, 'I find the cocktail delicious!'

'So do I,' agreed Marius, with a puzzled blink. Light

suddenly dawned on him. 'Surely, my dear Miss Fenton, you realized that I was referring, not to the cocktail, but to the flower?'

There were two embarrassed giggles, and from myself a sigh of relief.

'Not, of course, that it is as poisonous as the root, but it certainly *is* poisonous. In fact, my dear Miss Fenton, we might almost be justified in calling you Miss Medea. For I imagine that nobody could deny that it *was* aconite which filled the cup which she prepared for Theseus?'

Nobody could. So we went in to luncheon.

And as we entered the dining-room, the whole deep plot was immediately apparent. For the table was loaded with such an elaborate floral display that there was hardly any space left for plates or glasses. The *pièce de resistance* was a huge mound of dahlias, with their heads, as usual, chopped off a few inches below the blossom. In the heat they were already beginning to wilt. Around these was arranged a fringe of elderberries, which, I must admit, would have looked rather pretty, with their dark wine-coloured fruit, had they not been jostled by a quantity of miscellaneous vegetable objects, including purple heads of kale, seeding dandelions, and one scarlet toadstool.

'My dear Rose,' cried Miss Emily. 'Exquisite!'

Rose looked around her in surprise. To what could Miss Emily possibly be referring?

'The table, my dear. A positive picture.'

'Oh – the *flowers*,' laughed Rose, with sudden understanding. 'Marius dear, would you sit on my right? Yes, I just threw them on the table before mixing the cocktails.'

This was obviously such a howling lie that I tripped

over a Tudory Hassocky that was lurking under the refectory table, and was thereby excused from replying to Miss Emily's next exclamation, which was addressed to me, and was to ask if I did not think that Rose had created a masterpiece, and *what* would one not give to have such a talent as hers?

However, Rose was not going to let me escape scot-free.

She pointed to the scarlet toadstool.

'I think *he's* rather twee, don't you?'

I agreed that 'twee' was the word, which it certainly was.

She gave one of her silvery laughs. 'I picked him off an old log in the lane. He was just what I wanted. I felt he would *do* something to the dahlias. And I do think he does, don't you?'

It was fortunate that once again I was saved from replying to this question by the advent of the grapey fruity, which was brought in, with some resentment, by Rose's Czechoslovakian maid, who was a 'displaced person'. Never has an adjective been more apposite, at least from a domestic point of view. Whenever she ought to have been on the left she was on the right, and there were so many signs and hints and nudges to her from our hostess that she grew more resentful than ever, and conversation flagged.

The silence was broken by Marius. 'This stinking elder,' he murmured.

'I *beg* your pardon?'

'Stinking. Is not that the word?'

A faint flush suffused Our Rose's cheeks. 'I'm *so* sorry. Perhaps you would like it removed?'

'Removed? But why? Surely it was the *flower* to

which Shakespeare was referring in *Cymbeline* . . . not the berry?' He blinked at her in all innocence.

Another laugh, not so silvery this time. 'Of course. I had forgotten.'

'Our Marius is *so* erudite,' observed Miss Emily, with some acidity, helping herself to a very disorderly portion of spaghetti.

'But that is the very *last* word to apply to one,' protested Marius, in all sincerity. 'One is merely interested in things, and a few of them stick in one's head. What does one know about the common elder? Nothing. Or practically nothing.' He turned to me. 'What says my Hesculapius? My Galen? My heart of Elder?'

It was so long since I had read *Merry Wives of Windsor* that I was not equipped to answer this question.

'All one knows,' continued Marius, 'is that Judas was supposed to have hanged himself on an elder. In the Middle Ages that was universally accepted. And again, that the Cross of Calvary was made of it.' His voice grew melancholy. 'A gloomy, twisted tree, one is inclined to think' – flicking one of the clusters before him. And here he murmured a couplet which he afterwards informed me – (astonished that it had 'escaped my memory') – was from Spenser's *Shepheards Calender.*

> The Muses that were wont green Baies to weave
> Now bringen bittre Eldre braunches seare.

'Oh dear,' exclaimed Our Rose. 'I really feel quite depressed. My *pretty* berries. Such mournful associations. I shall certainly never use them again.'

'But please . . .' protested Marius . . . '*please* continue to use them. They are delightful. And just as much has been said in their favour as against them, if one could only remember it. But for the moment all I can recall is Lord Bacon's use of it for *warts* . . . so strange that so great a brain should have seriously believed that after rubbing the wart with the elder one must bury the stick in the ground. And, of course, that great physician Boerhaave, who never passed an elder without raising his hat, because he had so high an esteem of its medicinal properties. But what does one know of Boerhaave? Nothing. Nothing at all. It is enough to make one weep.

'And please . . .' he concluded, turning to Miss Emily, and carefully rolling a dollop of spaghetti round his fork . . . 'please do not be alarmed by that quite harmless little insect that at this moment is walking up your sleeve.'

'Insect?' cried Miss Emily sharply, looking downwards. 'Sleeve?'

'I refer,' observed Marius, swallowing his spaghetti with great deliberation, 'to the small specimen of *forficula auricularia* which appears to have adopted you. Vulgarly known as the earwig. The important thing to bear in mind is that it is *not* aiming at your ear. One of the commonest errors . . .'

But what one of the commonest errors may have been was drowned in an immediate pandemonium. For there was a shrill scream from Miss Emily, who leapt to her feet, shaking herself, and even shriller screams from Our Rose and the displaced person. And out of the dahlias we saw advancing a small army of earwigs, dropping from the edges of the petals, scurrying round in circles, shooting over the edge of the table, and falling on the floor. The rest of the luncheon was not a triumphant success.

That is why, whenever I see one of Rose's 'creations' in the lounge of a smart restaurant, or spread over the pages of a glossy magazine, I always have the creeps. It makes me think of earwigs.

§ IV

I have said so many acid things about females and flowers in the past few pages that it is perhaps too much to hope that I can persuade them to join me in learning a new game. They will probably sulk, and go off to the other end of the recreation yard, and toss their heads, and mutter that they don't want to play any more, not with that horrid man.

If, however, they could possibly be lured back, and induced to listen for a little while longer, I believe they would agree that their time had not been wasted, and that the game I want to teach them is really rather fun. And so, on the assumption that there are still a few listeners, I will proceed to explain the game of . . .

THE LIVING FLOWER PICTURE

But first, I shall have to ask you to do two things – to look at a picture, and to listen to a story. Three stories, in fact, if you can bear it.

The picture hangs over my desk as I write. It is a flower picture – one of the prettiest you ever saw, a riot of roses and paeonies and irises and carnations and trailing vines, with bunches of grapes and curling leaves of kale with the dew on them . . . a rich, glowing carnival of a flower piece. It is only a coloured print, but I have never had much sympathy for people who despise coloured prints. If you cannot afford Corots and Van Goghs, to say nothing of Botticellis, why should you necessarily be regarded as a monster for putting up with the next best thing?

This picture, which was one of the few of my possessions to survive the blitz, was conceived by an artist called Joseph Nigg, who painted it in the suburbs of Vienna in the spring of the year which witnessed Napoleon's retreat from Moscow. One would not have thought that Central Europe was a very flowery place at that time, but Nigg found his flowers, immortalized them, and handed them down, as it were, to me.

Well, one cold winter evening, before the war, I was standing by the fire, staring up at the picture, when for the hundredth time I noticed something new about it. There always *was* something new to be found, even if it was only a very tiny thing, such as a dewdrop on the petal of an iris or an ant crawling along the stem of a vine. But this time the thing I noticed was not small–it was, indeed, the very vase in which the flowers were arranged, and the only reason it had not previously caught my attention was because it was in deep shadow, and almost concealed by the leaves and petals which tumbled over its edge. As I peered more closely, it seemed slowly to catch the light, to come into focus, and suddenly I saw to my astonishment that it was the exact replica of a vase which I had owned for years – an old terra-cotta urn with a frieze of classical figures which I had picked up in Athens years before. You could just see a dim glow of terra-cotta through the leaves, and the very faint profile of a nymph which decorated one of the handles.

And then I had an idea. Here was a picture that I had learned to love, a picture that had given me many hours of delight and consolation, as it hung there on the wall, in its frame of black and gold.

Why not bring it to life?

I had the same vase. I had the same flowers – or access to them – and if they were not already in the garden I could plant them. And all through the spring I could watch them growing, hurrying some along and keeping others back, in order that they should all be out together when the time came to arrange them as Nigg had arranged them, a hundred and forty years ago. For at the outset it was obvious that if one was going to get the most out of this delectable game one must play it honourably; there must be no cheating, no saying to oneself . . . 'well, I haven't got any of those striped pinks so I'll put in a couple of white ones instead'. Every detail must be scrupulously correct. There were thirty-six grapes showing in the bunch which Nigg had painted; there would be thirty-six in mine. I would even try to do something about the insects. If a small green caterpillar were not available, like the one which Nigg had put on to his leaf of kale, I should get a stuffed one.

There and then I ran up to the attic, and brought down the vase, which was badly cracked, but could be repaired. And there and then I made an exhaustive list of every flower and leaf in the picture – the paeonies, the early lilies, the old-fashioned roses, the pinks, the irises, the vines. Most of them were already in the garden, and those which were not could easily be obtained from the nurserymen.

But there were three flowers missing; and that is why you are asked to listen to the three stories. For the search for those three flowers led to three separate adventures.

The three flowers were:

1 A dark, purple Iris, reminiscent of a Susiana, but much smaller.
2 A small white tulip with pink stripes.
3 A humble convolvulus with a white centre and a blue edge.

These three flowers seemed to have vanished from the face of the earth. This is the story of how they were found.

§ V

It was in the spring of 1938 that I went, for the second time, to Palestine. It seemed a good idea, the world being what it was. You do not have to be a specially religious man to feel cleansed by Palestine; it is a country where sky and earth seem to meet; the heavens brood so closely over the hills that you feel you could stretch up your hands and just manage to touch the golden gates. In the year of Munich I wanted that sort of inspiration.

And I wanted the flowers. Unless you have roamed through Palestine in the spring you have never seen wild flowers; like rivers of blood the scarlet anemones tumble down from the highlands that lead to the Jordan; near Nazareth there are fields so thick with crocuses that you would say the hills were draped with tapestries of blue; and only a few miles from Jerusalem there are quiet places where the little violet sword-lily – *gladiolus atroviolaceus* – grows so freely that you can pick an armful of it in a couple of minutes.

And always, as you walk, you remember that on these same flowers the shadow of Jesus might have fallen; the poppy that you pluck for your buttonhole may be a direct descendant of some flower that His hands had touched as He wandered through the cornfields. Even the anemones, that riot so profusely throughout the land, may be the 'lilies of the field' which He made to shine so brightly in the loveliest of the parables. So, at least, maintain the majority of the scholars, and they quote the Song of Solomon to prove their contention – 'My love is like a lily among the thorns'. For the tallest of the anemones, which are indeed of the lily family, are always to be found among the thorn bushes, struggling towards the light.

Palestine can raise you to the heights of spiritual ecstasy at one moment, and plunge you to the depths of spiritual depression at the next. So it was in Nazareth, which was my final port of call. The old part of the city is a living miracle; here you may wander through the narrow streets and courtyards, and find dozens of barn-like rooms which must correspond, in every detail, to the room in which Christ was born. There are even carpenters' shops which have not changed in the two thousand years since He learned His trade. But the tourists seldom bother about the old city; they prefer to gape at the architectural monstrosities of the new, which are crammed with bogus relics and hideous frescoes.

It was this new city that drove me out into the hills, outside the city. There were three hours to spare, and I wanted to think. After an hour or so I sat down in the shade of a rock, and idly tugged at the grass by my side. Suddenly I noticed a purple stain on my fingers. I looked down. I had been pulling at a tiny clump of irises, of the exact shade of royal purple which I had so long been seeking.

It is not much of a story, though it has an epilogue. When the irises had been dug up – no easy business – I hurried back to the town. I lost my way in the side streets, and found myself walking towards a rough stone fountain from which there flowed a stream of diamond-clear water, icy cold. I thought it would be as well to sprinkle the roots of the iris with this water, for the earth around them was parched and hot. As I was doing so I suddenly realized that this was Mary's Well, the only well in Nazareth, which must have been used by the mother of Our Lord. Not *could* have been, but *must* have been. 'Now I know that my irises will live,' I said to myself. 'Now I know that they will flower again.'

And they did.

§ VI

1939. War. And an end to flowers, to say nothing of flower pictures, for an indefinite period, maybe for ever.

And yet, from time to time, the flower picture still glowed at the back of my mind, and sometimes, when things were very bad, I would dream about it, take it out from its mental storage and reconstruct it in my imagination. On the rare occasions when it was possible to leave the city and get down to the garden – not, of course, the garden of Merry Hall, which was not yet mine – I would always pay a first visit to those flowers and shrubs which were essential to the picture. I thanked God that they were flourishing – in particular the little clump of iris.

1940. 1941. 1942. All the time the world was growing darker; shadows were falling over the picture, too, so that it was growing more and more difficult to remember. But there came a certain evening in March 1943, when suddenly it seemed to live again before me, in all its exquisite detail.

It was in one of the wildest parts of the world that this happened – the Swat valley, on the North-West Frontier of India, a desolate no-man's-land that lurks in the shadow of the Himalayas. I had been sent to India as a war correspondent; I had been stricken with a mysterious illness; and after a generous blood-letting I was being jogged down a mountain track on an improvised stretcher, on the way to the military hospital at Peshawar.

I lay on that stretcher trying to behave like an English gentleman, without any marked success. The pain was excruciating; the flies buzzed round a wound in my foot; and I was consumed with a torturing thirst, for the water-bottles had long been drained. Then, all of a sudden, we swung round a sharp corner, under a jagged rock. The movement was so rough that it forced me to sit upright, and as I did so I gasped, not only with pain but with delight. For there before us, lit by the last gold of the sun, was a great drift of the striped tulips which I had been seeking all these years. They swept through the fields like an avalanche, they tumbled over cliffs and spilled into the forest, and as the breeze caught them they seemed to dance in welcome.

'Hussein! Hussein!' I cried to my bearer. 'Flowers! Get sahib flowers!'

'Yes, Sahib.' He motioned to the others to set down the stretcher, which they dropped with a bump on the hard road. There was a clump of the tulips just beside me. I stretched out my hand and picked one. Yes, there could be no doubt about it. It was the right tulip, snow white, with six stripes of coral pink, the tulip which Joseph Nigg had painted in the year that Napoleon had retreated from Moscow.

Well, this might also be my own Moscow, but I wasn't going to retreat without a good supply of those tulips. So I set Hussein to work to dig them up, taking deep clods of soil with them, so that the roots should not be disturbed. When we continued our journey it was by moonlight; the weight of the stretcher had perceptibly increased, and when we reached the military hospital it was some time before the sleepy Muslim sentries would let us pass, for they assumed – not without reason – that they were being asked to admit a flower-laden corpse. An assumption in which they were very nearly correct.

It would need a whole chapter to tell you how we saved those tulips, how they were stowed away under a bed in which two murderers were sleeping, chained to the wall, how they were transported to yet another hospital in Bombay – how, in the delirium that accompanied my final operation, I entrusted them to an American pilot who was flying home, and how, at length, true to his trust, he planted them in the cool English loam of my deserted garden. All that matters is that a year later, when at last I reached home and went down to the country, they were blooming merrily in the shade of a copper beech – pink and white, with the thrushes singing all around them, as though England had always been their home.

The flower picture was almost complete.

§ VII

The war was over, but still the morning glory evaded me.

It was ridiculous to be thwarted like this, by a simple convolvulus with a white centre and a blue edge, but there it was – or rather, there it was not. I wrote to all the seed merchants asking what they could do about it, with no result at all. They offered morning glories of dazzling azure and burning ultramarine, morning glories the size of your hat, morning glories that would climb to the roof, but they did not offer a simple convolvulus with a white centre and a blue edge. It was far, far beneath them.

And then one morning – yes, it *was* in the morning, and a glorious one at that – I found it.

If you do not know the Chateau d'Horizon at Cannes you have probably heard of it. It is the most fabulous villa on the Mediterranean, and it was built by an equally fabulous person – the late Maxine Elliott, a statuesque Edwardian beauty, who broke a great many hearts and created a great many reputations. When Maxine was alive I used to visit the villa a great deal, and to say that there was never a dull moment would be an understatement. The place bristled with celebrities. If you saw an old sun hat on the rocks you might safely assume that Winston Churchill was underneath it; if you saw an old man with white hair and a tennis racquet it was always the King of Sweden; and if you encountered a young man with blond hair and two tennis racquets it was fairly certain to be the Duke of Windsor – or rather, the Prince of Wales. It was that sort of place.

(No, I have not forgotten the morning glory.)

After the war the villa was bought by Prince Aly Khan, as a fitting setting for the delightful Rita Hayworth, and one morning last spring I went to luncheon with them and found myself walking once again down the long drive under the pine trees, with the Mediterranean gleaming before me like a peacock's tail. I felt as though I were walking in a dream; in the past ten years the face of most of Europe had changed beyond recognition; yet here was the villa, still standing in the sunlight, a monument to a vanished age of gaiety, of luxury, of folly. What would it be like inside? What would Prince Aly have done to it?

There was no time to answer those questions. Suddenly, in front of me there was a flash of blue. In the centre of the blue, a ring of white. It was a solitary plant of the missing convolvulus, clambering merrily over the red rocks. How it had come there, what frolic wind had blown it from the mountains, I neither knew nor cared. All that mattered was that it was here . . . just one flower that had bloomed late, and a whole cluster of seed-pods.

With trembling fingers I gathered a couple of those seed-pods, wrapped them in a thousand-franc note – (they were worth a great deal more to me than that) – and tucked them away in my wallet. When I eventually faced His Highness I felt as though I were carrying the whole fantastic treasury of the Aga Khan in my hip pocket. I never dared to tell him, and it is to be hoped that if he reads these words he will not prosecute me for theft.

So there it was. The wheel had come full circle. The final petal was in place, the flower picture could at last be painted.

And painted it was. Not in the first year at Merry Hall. Nor the second, nor the third. It was only last summer that I attained anything like perfection, and even then the caterpillar was missing, and I had to do a little cheating with the grapes. But I think that Joseph Nigg, if he were able to look down through the clouds of a hundred and fifty years ago, would certainly recognize it; he might even be tempted to take up his brush and paint it again, in celestial colours that would never fade.

Our Rose, needless to say, would throw it on the rubbish heap.

CHAPTER XVI

LAUGHING WATER

WE are now about to enter an entirely new world, as different as the one which Alice entered when she stepped through the looking-glass. The simile is not inapt, for we too shall be stepping, in imagination, through a mirrored surface . . . the surface of a pool; nor will it be only on our imagination that we shall be relying, for we shall be able to see, quite clearly, the strange life that unfolds itself below, the fantastic creatures that glide and dart through the green shadows, the curious stems and roots that weave and wave, like fingers groping.

And all this silent, secret drama is played beneath a ceiling of liquid beauty, a ceiling that is sometimes gold and sometimes silver and sometimes ebony, according to the waxing and waning of the sun and the moon above; a ceiling, too, that is often as rich as a rainbow with the flickering shadows of the flowers that float on the surface, the roses and crimsons of the lilies, the blues of the water hyacinths, the purple of the irises on the bank. So that the fishes, as they look upwards, must feel that they are gazing through a stained glass window.

In any form of creation one's approach is all-important – a statement that is meaningless without an example. Here is a very simple one. If you are building a rock-garden your approach must be Lilliputian. You must shrink, drastically. It is no use standing over a heap of rocks, like Hercules at Rhodes, glaring down on little patches of pink and mauve. That is likely to be a bore for you, and it may possibly be intimidating for the aubretias. What you must do is to kneel down, close your eyes, take a deep breath, and suddenly become a midget. Please do not start to argue and say that nobody taught you to do this at school. It is quite simple and needs very little practice. I can become an excellent midget, of between two and three inches, in a space of from ten to fifteen seconds, and if there are any questions about it I am prepared to prove it to all challengers.

When you have become a midget you can really enjoy your rock garden, gazing with awe into the giant trumpets of tiny daffodils, battling through foaming cataracts of pinks, scaling lichen-covered cliffs the size of a man's head.

So it is with a water garden. The approach is all-important. You begin by thinking of it as a mirror, which gives to the life of the garden an extra dimension, creating depths and distances which did not exist before. And that, as a beginning, is fair enough; for just as a room without a mirror is dead, so a garden without water is never quite alive. In a mirror the fire flickers again, and the flowers give birth to a ghostly progeny; there, in a golden frame, a mimic world awaits you, a world even more magical than this one, because it has the quality of a dream. So it is with the water in the pool. It is not only a mirror but a magnet, with a power that reaches to the ends of space. It can pluck the moon from the sky and float it like a lily; it can reach up to the dark night to draw down the stars and hold them shining to its breast; and through all the seasons it paints its pictures of the flowers that lean over it; the steely engravings of the snowdrops on some grey day of February, the rich flush of the lilacs in May, the blood-red ripples that it catches from the maples in October. Even in the heart of winter, when it is black and still and sullen, it is not sleeping; there is life in it; it is watching – watching and recording. And all the pictures that have ever flashed across its surface are still there, I think, held in its crystal heart.

But that is only a beginning; as the pool matures, as the green carpet of leaves spreads, as it were, over the bare and shining floor of the surface, as summer scatters its rosettes of blossom, and as the water grows to know your shadow – for surely, in some subtle way, that shadow must slowly colour it, affect it, give to it some personal quality? – so you are caught with a desire to dive below, to step through the mirror, to glide in and out among those strange stems and roots that once you held in your hand.

You must, in short, become a fish. And once again I trust that there will be no mutterings and poutings from the back of the class. The art of transforming oneself into a fish may not be as easily mastered as the art of transforming oneself into a midget, but mastered it must be. I myself can become a quite passable golden orfe within the space of thirty seconds, and I am at this moment practising to be a *barbus conchonius*, in which guise I expect to pass many pleasing hours. According to the catalogues the *barbus conchonius* is a very satisfactory species, and 'during the breeding season the male assumes a rose-toned sheen'.

All this, however, is for the advanced classes. And we – that is to say, you and I – are still standing on the threshold of it all. The pool is not yet dug, nor even thought of; we do not know the difference between a Laydekeri and an Oderata; we are miserable, earthbound creatures, shut out from a world of enchantment. It is high time that we entered that world.

Which is the cue for Cupid.

§ II

Cupid began it all. If I had not gone to Crowther's, on that hot summer afternoon, I should never have met Cupid, and should not have been tempted by his extravagant suggestions. When I went there I had no intention of buying anything; I merely wanted to renew acquaintance with a slender Palladian temple, to pay respects to a few nymphs, and in particular to pass the time of day with a most disreputable bronze satyr, who for years had leered from a hedge of myrtle with such suggestiveness that nobody had ever had the courage to buy him.

But the temple had gone, and the nymphs had nothing much to say for themselves, and it was very hot; and on the way to the satyr I found myself in a courtyard heavily shadowed with mulberries and magnolias. In the centre of the courtyard was a small, shallow pool, and in the pool stood this graceful Cupid. He was delicately fashioned in lead; one leg rested on a marble plinth, the other danced high behind him. Over his head he held a little snake, which had curled itself round his wrist in a curiously affectionate manner, and out of the snake's mouth spurted a jet of water which fell with a soothing plash on to the dark surface of the pool.

'Now this,' I thought, 'is very nice. And you . . .' mentally addressing the Cupid, 'are also very nice, though when one looks more closely at you, your resemblance to Mr. Winston Churchill is almost uncanny.' Nor was there anything disrespectful in such a thought, for it was Mr. Churchill himself who once observed: 'I look like all babies, and all babies look like me.'

The more I studied Cupid, the more I liked him. There was a tap by the edge of the pool, and I turned it on to see what happened. What happened was a terrific spurt of water from the snake's mouth, shooting up into the magnolias and making thunderstorm noises on the broad flat leaves. That was most satisfactory. Then I turned the tap very low so that only the faintest trickle came out of the snake, and the surface of the water was scarcely disturbed, and one could see the magnolia blossom shimmering in reflection, like cream spilt on a dark tray. Better and better. 'One' and 'Four' would find endless diversion in such a pool; there would be leanings over, and wettings of tails, and dabbings at water-beetles, and . . . oh Lord, here we are again, buying things, letting ourselves in for vast expense, and trouble, and agony . . . and delight.

For of course, Cupid had to be bought.

After a long search for an assistant – as usual, at Crowther's, everybody seemed to be drifting down distant avenues, propelled by secret dreams – I found a young man who unscrewed Cupid and carried him out to the car. He was a heavy boy, and on the way home, whenever we were caught in a traffic block, he seemed to give great pleasure to the occupants of buses. But soon the cities were left behind, and the fields and woods surrounded us, and when at last we reached home, and carried Cupid out on to the lawn, he looked as though he had been standing there for centuries.

§III

Sometimes in a garden it takes quite a while to find exactly the right place for an ornament; one staggers about for weeks with urns and busts and pillars, ruining the lawn and cricking one's back to no effect. But we found the right place for Cupid – or maybe he found it for himself – within a few minutes of his arrival.

It was on the small square lawn outside the music-room. At this point the house forms the shape of an L, so that one has the effect of a little courtyard, which I have enhanced by two low walls of heather on the open sides.

Cupid was placed in the centre of this lawn, and as soon as he took his stand it was obvious that it was the perfect place not only for us, but for him too . . . for him, I mean, as an individual. If you think it tiresome to personify statues, to invest them with souls of their own, then that is your affair; I myself would take scant interest in a statue which I felt was only a block of marble or of lead; and if I were ever lucky enough to own the wicked satyr, I should consider myself swindled if I were ever to suspect that he did *not* creep off at night and misbehave in the laurels.

So it was with Cupid; it was important that he should not be bored, and from where he stood he would have a perfect view of the *va et vient* of the house. He would be able to peer into the music-room and listen to me practising the waterfalls – if that could be considered an advantage; he would be able to watch Oldfield as he disappeared into the cellars every morning, to stoke up the fires; he would also have a perfect view of the conservatory, in which there is never a dull moment throughout the year, from the pinks and scarlets of the geraniums in January, through the long pale blue months of the plumbago, up to the snowy piles of chrysanthemums at Christmas.

I will not write a long saga about the pool we made round Cupid; it is enough to say that it was oblong, four feet by two and a half, and about a foot deep; it was lined with some very old terracotta tiles that had been lying in the woodshed. It is the sort of thing which the *Daily Herald* will tell you can be dug over the week-end by a not very bright child with a not very sharp spade. I need hardly say that in fact it required an army of workmen and cost the earth.

It was not long before we discovered that this tiny stretch of water, not much bigger than a tea-tray, was rapidly developing into one of the focal points of the garden.

Marius really began it. One hot summer evening I came home to find the pool had apparently blossomed out with water lilies; there were about a dozen of them, pink and white, lying on their broad flat leaves. As I came nearer I saw that they were in fact nasturtium leaves; and that in the centre of each of them somebody had placed a cosmos flower, with its stalk cunningly concealed and dipping an inch below the leaf into the water. There was a step behind me, and Marius was revealed as the culprit – though that is an ungrateful word for the inventor of so charming a conceit.

'I came out to see if your nose was convulsed,' he observed blandly.

'No erudition, Marius, please. It's too hot.'

'One can hardly call that "erudition"; it is merely translation. The nasturtium is a pungent plant. Pungency convulses the nose. What is the Latin for convulsed nose?'

'*Nosus convulsus* for all I know.'

'I ought to send you to the bottom of the class. It is *nasus tortus*. From which it is the simplest of steps to the word nasturtium.'

'Simple or not, I think your idea is enchanting. Let's do some more.'

We did lots more, on the surface of the pool, not only then, but in the long sultry days to come. We floated the leaves of camellias, and blended them with heavy, creamy stocks. When they had faded we picked quantities of little white dianthus; in a light breeze they all joined together and waltzed round the edge like the maidens in *Les Sylphides*. Sometimes we would try a single dramatic effect, such as a big tiger-lily glowering out of a cluster of dark laurel; but this was never really a success; it looked artificial. It was more fun with the tiny things. (One of the most charming effects was obtained by covering the water with a sheet of buttercups; they looked like a tapestry of sequins when the sun was shining). The pool was too small for any of the garden's ampler glories.

Yes, the pool was too small. In spite of all the delights it afforded us, it was much too small.

Awful thoughts began to possess me. Thoughts of pools ten times the size, fifty times the size, a hundred times the size. I did not dare confide them to Gaskin, for already the overdraft was in a state of acute inflammation, and my last remaining shares, which were in some sort of oil – and I should think a very peculiar sort, judging by the latest prospectus – had sunk so low that the gentleman in the *Financial Times* called them 'nominal'. I could have called them several better names than that. But when your reserves are 'nominal' it is inadvisable to go in for landscape gardening on a considerable scale.

Yet this was precisely what I proceeded to do.

§ IV

It was done with bamboos in secret.

That is to say, the design was marked out with bamboo canes, which were, in themselves, a sort of camouflage. If I had tackled the job with pegs and tapes, Gaskin would have guessed that something was up and would have gone about dropping hints of ruin. Ted, my secretary, with careless cunning, would have left bank statements lying on the sofa, showing sinister figures in bright scarlet. What Oldfield would have done is best left to the imagination.

But people were so used to seeing me darting about with bundles of bamboo canes that they would not think

WATER

twice about it. They had learned from long experience that the bamboos were, in fact, tree-markers. I would look out of the window, some bright morning, and see the snow of the pear-blossom, and think how delightful it would be if there could be still more snow in the distance. And that meant an immediate raid on the tool shed, a seizing of bamboo canes, a rush to the orchard, and a most enjoyable hour sticking in bamboos in the right place. If you concentrated, and half shut your eyes, you could almost make the bamboos burst into ghostly blossom.

Or I would be especially enchanted by some group that had been planted the year before, and feel an urge to make it much bigger. When the first mock oranges came out, I cursed myself for being so niggardly; there were only three when there should have been a dozen. Off to the tool shed for more bamboos. It was the same with the *rhus cotinus.* They had leaves the colour of Chambertin and masses of tiny fluffy beards, as if a swarm of midget Abrahams were hiding in the branches on some secret game of their own. One could not have too many of them. More bamboos. This went on all the year; indeed, one of the priority jobs in the garden is a weekly inspection tour of the bamboo sticks, to see that nobody has been fiddling about with them. You would be surprised how many people *do* fiddle about with them, particularly men with scythes, who refuse to realize that the bamboos are potential pears, maples, silver birches, lilacs and so forth.

Therefore it was possible to do a great deal of prowling round with bamboo sticks, without anybody suspecting that one was doing anything more expensive than plant another orchard.

The first thing to do was to choose the site. 'In for a penny, in for at least twenty pounds,' has always seemed to me a sound economic basis on which to plan one's gardening career, and so I decided to put the water-garden bang in the centre of the lawn, where, at the back of it, there was already planted a line of white weeping cherries. To the right a group of maples was well established, and to the left some irregular clusters of flowering crabs. As I stuck in the bamboos it seemed that the green grass turned to a sheet of water in which was reflected the white of the cherries, and the rich, trembling reds and pinks of the maples and the crabs.

Below the site for the water garden there was a dip in the lawn, over which one might eventually run a cascade, which could fall into a huge stone shell and spout out again from the mouth of a dolphin – and probably flood the lane. It was enough to make one feel quite sick and giddy with delight, and also with alarm, because dolphins, like everything else, had almost certainly 'gone up'. However, the dolphin was not an absolute necessity; it could wait; and I made a mental resolution that if I ever met any dolphins in the near future I would look the other way. Besides, the actual shape of the pool was not yet decided.

In went the bamboos, and out again, and in and out, and every time I altered them the pool grew bigger. The first design had been very modest indeed, a slender oblong about thirteen feet by four and only a foot deep; but when I walked away from it and studied it from a distance it looked so insignificant that I hurried back and made it nearly double. That was better – twenty-five feet by seven. Even so, was it the sort of pool that a dolphin, a really exquisite dolphin that had possibly been used to lolling about in the perfumed cascades of Versailles, was entitled to expect? Not, of course, that there *was* any dolphin for the moment – dolphins, as we had already decided, being 'out'. Still, one must look to the future, and if – or rather when – the dolphin took up residence, and began to spout, it might well complain that it had practically nothing to spout into. Which, in its turn, would involve a complete reconstruction of the pool at enormous expense.

In short, I argued, it would be a real economy to make the pool at least twice the size.

And so, in the interests of economy, out came the bamboos once more, and the skeleton of the pool now measured fifty feet by twelve.

But as I stood back and surveyed this phantom lake, I began to have serious doubts as to whether I had, in fact, been economical enough. It was that dolphin again. One could hardly ask it – when the time came – to spout in a sort of vacuum, without any sort of company; it would feel absurd, doing all the work alone. There would have to be something, or somebody, doing a bit of spouting too, probably into the pool itself. Perhaps a Triton. That would be a very nice compliment to the dolphin, if, when it arrived, it were to find a Triton already established, spouting away like mad.

But if there were a Triton – and it seemed practically impossible to imagine any conditions in which there should *not* be a Triton – he could not just be stuck on the edge of the pool, without any sort of ceremony. People who would treat Tritons like that deserve to go through life without Tritons. He would demand a setting, some sort of niche or alcove. This, in its turn, would mean a good deal of brickwork in curves, and anybody who has ever had anything to do with bricklayers will agree that when you ask them to do anything with curves, which you nearly always do, they become very petulant, and put up their prices.

Therefore, I argued, it would be a real economy – as curves would obviously be soon among the things that were 'going up' – to prepare the alcove for the Triton in advance, indeed, at this very moment. With which I removed the bamboos once more, and made the alcove. It was just the sort of alcove a Triton would like. I could almost hear him blowing his wreathed horn.

And now it really is time that we drew a plan. This was now the design for the pool, and this was how, after endless troubles and difficulties, it was finally built:

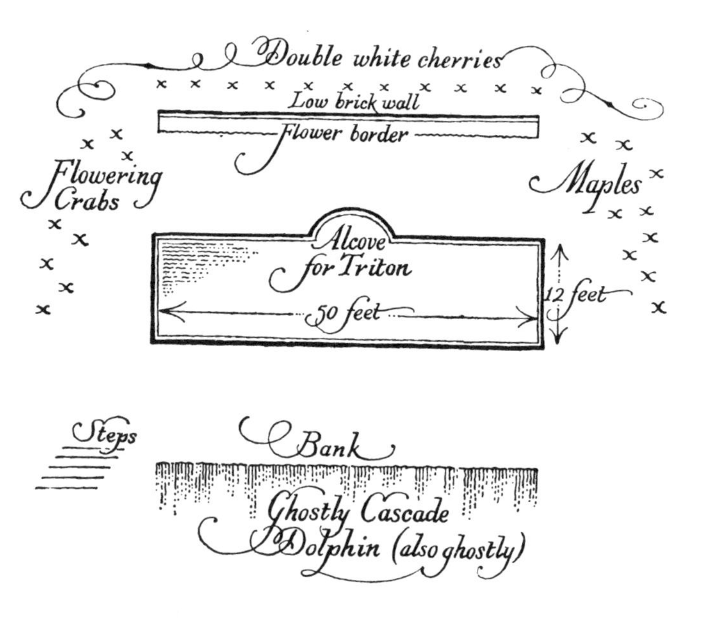

CHAPTER XVII

RIPPLES AND REFLECTIONS

WE will skip the painful story of how the news of this latest financial folly was broken to the household. Gaskin, for days, did one of his Silences. These are accompanied by raised eyebrows, tight lips, and sinister shrugs of the shoulders. Coupled by acid insinuations such as: 'We're down to the last three bottles of white wine . . . perhaps you won't be ordering any more?' Ted, the aforesaid secretary, went about the house leaving a positive paper-chase of bills, and uttering, from time to time, the most ghastly predictions about the oil shares. One would think that nobody was ever going to use any oil again, from the way he went on.

Oldfield's comment was summed up in one word.

Floodz.

The cellars, he pointed out, were already flooded badly enough in the winter. They would now be flooded far more. There would be floodz. *And* floodz.

'But *why*?' I protested. 'If we make the water garden – I mean *when* we make the water garden – it will all be properly drained. There will be dozens of drains to take it all away.'

'Drains is funny things,' said Oldfield. 'You never know where you are with drains. That's one thing Mr. Stebbing always said. You never knew where you were with drains, he said.'

I had a very shrewd suspicion where Mr. Stebbing would be with a drain if I had any say in the matter. He would be down it, good and proper.

'But Oldfield,' I said, 'this is just a question of a pipe . . .'

'There's t'land drains as well,' he interrupted. 'All drains that come down from t'copse, and through orchard, and across lawns. There's a powerful lot o' land drains been put in this place in past forty years. You'll be cutting right across them. Water'll have to go somewhere.'

He paused, and in this pause I had a momentary, fleeting idea . . . a very pleasant idea, too, which I kept to myself. I will explain it when the time comes.

'*Somewhere*,' repeated Oldfield. 'And in my view, it'll be t'cellar. There'll be floodz.'

In spite of the spectral floodz, I went ahead. Mr. Young, who is the local builder, joiner and decorator, and the nicest possible man, arrived, and spent long hours with me tramping over the lawn, arranging the final details. Curves, it seemed, had not 'gone up' nearly as much as might have been expected, so there would be no difficulty about the alcove. Nor was there any trouble about getting the bricks, which were to be of a soft, pretty red that would look pleasantly faded even before the water got at them. Indeed, Mr. Young was so co-operative that I decided, when the time came, to reward him by showing him some of the simpler methods of turning himself into a fish.

So we began. And once again the garden at Merry Hall began to look like a mixture between a quarry and a railway station. Immense wagons rolled up the drive, scraping the overhanging branches of the copper beech; pyramids of bricks rose on the grass; mountains of cement sacks were piled outside the tool shed; every path was littered with pipes; and 'One' and 'Four' were kept so hard at work, inspecting every new development, prowling from heap to heap, sniffing, testing, jumping up and down, that by the end of the day they both looked quite exhausted.

Needless to say, Miss Emily and Our Rose were soon at hand.

Their visit coincided with an accident to one of the lorries in the lane. As it was turning into the drive all the bricks fell out, causing a temporary traffic block. There is so little traffic down the lane that this hold-up did not reach any considerable proportions; indeed, at the end of ten minutes it consisted only of the butcher's boy, who could quite well have lifted his bicycle over the bricks, and a woman with a perambulator, who seemed delighted at the break in the monotony. However, the peace was suddenly disturbed by the sharp, repeated tooting of a motor-horn, so I hurried out to see what was happening.

Miss Emily was the hooter, and Our Rose was by her side. Neither lady looked very gruntled. Miss Emily leaned out of the window with somewhat too sweet a smile. 'Good morning. Will this be long, do you think?'

'The lorry driver's just gone to fetch his mate.'

A theatrical sigh. 'In that case we must wait.'

'As they may be a little while, won't you come inside?' They would have to be let into the secret sooner or later, so I might as well get it over. 'I'm making a water garden.'

The eyes of the two ladies met, as though rolled on swivels. 'So *that's* what's going on!' they seemed to be saying.

'How kind. Well . . . just for a few moments.'

They stayed a good deal longer than a few moments,

and in the course of their visit they did their utmost, in the nicest possible way, to convince me of the vulgarity, folly and indeed criminality of my behaviour. After the first conventional compliments, delivered with low hisses and expressionless faces – 'So charming . . . lilies of course? . . . delightful in the summer, if we ever have any summer . . . and fish? . . . he must have fish, Emily dear, don't you think? . . . no, I don't suppose the cats would eat them *all* . . . and a fountain?' – after these encouraging preliminaries, Our Rose opened the attack.

'I don't quite *see* it yet,' she observed, with her head on one side.

'As there's nothing to see, that's not surprising.'

She ignored this tactless misinterpretation of her meaning. As we have already observed, it is generally accepted, among her admirers, that when Our Rose 'sees' or does not 'see', it is with the psychic eye.

'I should have thought you would have something less severe,' she said.

'I don't know why you should call it severe.'

'No?' She gave one of her 'teasing' little laughs, and sketched the outline of the pool by holding her hands rigidly in front of her. 'Rather formal, don't you think?'

'It's intended to be formal. The house is formal. The lawn is formal. The pool is in the middle of the lawn. If it were anything but formal it would be quite ridiculous.' And if I were anything but formal, I thought, I should be quite rude.

'Of course, I'm not really the one to speak,' she said. 'I like *natural* beauty. A little curving pool . . . a stream trickling . . . stones covered with moss . . . yes. All very simple, I'm afraid. But Nature's good enough for little *me*!'

Only by clenching my teeth and holding them in a vice-like grip was I able to refrain from commenting on this outrageous statement. I thought of the last series of Our Rose's 'creations' which had been published in a woman's magazine. There was no abuse to which she had not subjected the unfortunate flowers which had fallen into her hands. She had even taken tulips and wrenched open their petals so that their lovely shapes were maimed and distorted. If there is any justice in the after-life, I thought, Our Rose will be condemned to spend several years purgatory in a herbaceous border, where all the flowers she has tortured on earth will be empowered to torture her in return. She will be throttled by lupins and speared by irises and banged on the head by red-hot-pokers.

It was lucky that at this point there was an interruption from Miss Emily, who had been prowling about among the bricks and the pipes with a most sinister expression. She turned to me and said:

'Of course, you have Spoken to the Authorities?' (I have put it in capitals, because that was how she said it, with an awful echo of doom.)

'Which Authorities?'

'Well . . .' and here she shrugged her shoulders as if my question were really too trite . . . 'the *Necessary* Authorities.'

'I didn't know there were any.' This was only half true, for constantly in these past weeks I had been haunted by the uncomfortable reflection that I was a citizen of a Welfare State, and as such was liable at any moment to be forcibly prevented from doing anything whatsoever that could be described as creative or original.

'Of whom were you thinking?'

'Surely the Water Board will have Something to Say?'

'I don't see what it can have to say except to tell me that I'm using some of its water. If it does, I shall reply that that is presumably what it is paid for.'

'It was more the Housing Authorities that I was thinking of. All these bricks. So very strict they are nowadays, about bricks. So many poor people without homes.'

'In our village,' said Rose, in crocodile tones, 'there are whole families living in stables.' She turned to Miss Emily. 'Did you hear about poor Mrs. Canning?'

'Yes. A converted cow-shed.'

'What has Mrs. Canning's converted cow-shed got to do with *me*?'

'Oh nothing. Nothing at all!' replied Miss Emily, though she said it as if I were personally responsible for pushing Mrs. Canning into an immense heap of manure. 'It's merely that the Authorities . . .'

But what the Authorities might or might not be up to must remain a mystery. For at that moment the lanky figure of Marius was observed loping across the lawn. And Marius frightens the two ladies. They like him, they respect him, but he fills them with alarm. Why I can never quite understand. Maybe it is because they feel that when he fixes them with that dreamy eye they are being 'seen through'.

At any rate, he caused them to flee. After a few more twitters, and double-edged compliments, and swivel-eyed 'looks', we were left alone.

§ II

'Everybody's against me, Marius,' I said, sitting down on a pile of bricks and taking 'One' on my knee. 'Those two women depressed me beyond words. They made me feel that the pool was too square and too large and too everything.'

'It is a pity,' said Marius, 'that it did not occur to you to remind them of the activities of King Amenhotep the Fourth.'

'It is indeed. And I should certainly have done so if I had the faintest idea who he was or what he did. What *did* he do?'

'He was so enraptured by the beauty of the lotus that he built a pool in his garden that was nearly three quarters of a mile long and over a hundred yards wide.'

'Miss Emily would have had a fit.'

'He went even further than that. The whole of his immense bedroom was decorated to give the illusion of a water garden, with fish swimming in mosaic over the floor, and painted water-lilies floating on the ceiling.'

'Better and better. Tell me more.'

'But my dear fellow, I know nothing, but *nothing*, about water-lilies. And yet, their history must be of incredible antiquity. I cannot remember the name of the Japanese scientist who germinated lotus seeds which had been lying dormant for fifty thousand years, but the evidence struck me as irrefutable. And for all those fifty thousand years legends must have been gathering around them. Have you ever seen a figure of the god Nefer-tem without a lotus flower on his head?'

As I had never seen a figure of the god Nefer-tem,

with or without a lotus flower on any part of his anatomy, it was easy to reply with a firm negative.

'Or the god Horus, sitting on anything but a lotus leaf?'

Certainly not. If one ever caught Horus sitting on anything but a lotus leaf one would feel that he had forgotten himself.

'Horus and Nefer-tem date from only 2500 B.C. What other gods must there be in the dim past, dancing about among the lilies – gods of whom one has not even heard?' He heaved a long sigh. 'I suppose one must fall back, as usual, on Herodotus.'

'If I were to fall back on Herodotus I should fall into space.'

He did not seem to hear me. 'I always think that one of the most charming passages in all Herodotus is his picture of the Nile in flood, when it had turned the plains into an inland sea and when the waters were white with lilies. And his description of the multitudes of men and women sitting on the hot sands, gathering the flowers and drying the seeds in the sun. He spoke very highly of the bread they baked from those seeds, but I wonder if he had ever tasted it? One can never be too sure of such details with Herodotus. It might be amusing to make the experiment when your lilies ripen.'

'It might indeed. We could try the bread out on Miss Emily, and if she got a pain we would tell her that it was all in the interests of historical research.'

The thought of baking lily bread for Miss Emily was so inspiring that we stopped our chatter and went off to help mix the cement.

All through October the work went on, and some of it was highly technical. Although I am all for dreaming, and although I think that it is important to spend a reasonable portion of one's life drifting about in a trance, waving wands and muttering, there are also times when it is equally important to wake up. One day I woke up with a bang and went off to the Royal Horticultural Society's Gardens at Wisley, and routed out everybody who could conceivably be suspected of knowing anything about water gardens. They told me a lot. When they were exhausted – in every sense of the word – they sent me off to Enfield, to the fabulous institution of Messrs. Perry's, whose partners live in a strange, aqueous world of their own, studying and tending and propagating all the miraculous flora and fauna of the lakes and rivers of the world. They taught me even more, and sent me away with a catalogue which is one of the classics of English garden literature.

Of all the horticultural catalogues I have ever read – and they have always been my favourite form of literature – Perry's *Water Plants* has given me the greatest measure of delight. On that first night I sat up with it till the small hours, exploring the contours of a new world, tasting the savour of an unknown element, spelling out the syllables of a new tongue . . . a strange language of unearthly beauty. There was a liquid music in the very names of these things; it was as though the water had washed away all dissonance and whispered to them its own sweet titles . . . willow-moss, water-violet, spire reed, water-mint, mermaid-weed, floating-heart. There was humour too; the chaffer and the chuckle of the stream was echoed in the names of the plants that danced around it . . . brass buttons, elephant's ear, hose-in-hose, umbrella grass and lizard's tail.

And there were mysteries abounding. It would have needed a Blake, fresh from the discovery of the awful symmetry of his immortal tiger, to do justice to the floating water hyacinth. This incredible creation is furnished with bladders, which act as water-wings to the swimmer. From these bladders stretch the tiny white tendrils of the roots, tipped with black, very frail, yet so acquisitive that they need no soil, but suck from the water the vital essences that are drawn through the stems to emerge as flowers of a lavender blue, that stare up to the sky with the eye of a peacock.

But this was dreaming again, and though it was nearly four o'clock when I reluctantly closed the catalogue and staggered off to bed I was up at the crack of dawn, back at work, not only on that day but on many days that followed. Back to build brick pockets in the four corners, and six brick baskets for the lilies, and nine brick pans for the under-water plants. Back to fill up the pool, and scatter it with permanganate of potash, so that it turned into a lake of claret. When the leaves from the copper beech began to fall, and were blown on to the water, they were stained the colour of wine, and drifted over the surface like the petals of dark red roses. Back to study temperatures and charts and soils and levels. . . .

Only one thing worried me. I did not like the idea of the water coming out of a tap. It seemed faintly suburban. Though there were fields and woods around us, though the wind blew untainted from the uplands, and though, in a strictly horticultural sense, tap-water was just as good as rain-water, I still did not like it. I could not forget that at the other end of the tap, miles away, lurked a Necessary Authority. I thought of him as a lantern-jawed creature with a top-hat, sitting on top of a tank, watching me through a telescope. This was a problem that would have to be solved somehow or other, sooner or later, for I did not want even the faintest shadow from the outside world to mar the smooth surface of the pool.

Then the rains came; and something happened.

§III

It rained and rained and rained. All through December, all through January, all through the early days of spring. The new trees stood in pools of water; a small lake spread in the hollows of the lawn; gurgling torrents ran day and night down the lane; Oldfield's face was black. All his broad beans and early peas were growing rank and root-bound in their frames; in such a swamp they could not be planted out.

But the rains did not discourage me, for they solved the problem of the pool. Not by filling it directly from the heavens – it would have needed a series of cloud-bursts to do that. But by the unexpected source of the land-drains, to which Oldfield had referred in such gloomy tones when the pool was being built. As he reminded me, the old garden was honeycombed with them; they ran down from the coppice, circled the field, joined hands in the orchard, and then crossed the lawns till they emptied themselves at some mysterious destination near the lane. That is to say, this is what they *had* done, before the pool was built. But now, we had set a barrier in their way, and every time it rained, the waters came hurrying down their secret channels to meet this barrier and be thwarted, and then to rise to the surface in an angry flood and pour over the edges into the pool.

At first this was depressing. It meant a muddy torrent falling haphazard over a design that should have been clean and formal. It also meant that all the earth was being washed away from the daffodils that I had massed round this design, leaving their roots bare and exposed. But it needed only a little imagination to realize that there must be ways in which all this water could be canalized and gathered together and made to flow into the pool . . . to the discomfiture of the Necessary Authority. And lest the expression 'land drains' sounds distasteful to you, suggesting dregs and unpleasantness, let me assure you that the water that runs down these ancient grooves is the purest in the world, that it is fragrant and filtered by the final antiseptic, the good earth itself.

It needed some persuasion to 'sell' this idea to Oldfield. One dripping morning we squelched out together to survey the prospect, which was like a scene from that gloriously gloomy Victorian novel *The House on the Marsh.*

'Well, I told you it'd be floodz,' he observed, with sombre satisfaction. 'And floodz it is.'

'Yes Oldfield, I know. But that's only for the moment. All we've got to do is to dig round the pond, connect all these drains together, and make them run into one pipe. Then if we knock a hole in the brickwork, two inches below the top, all the water will pour through it, and that'll be an end of it.'

'It'll cost a pretty penny.'

'I don't see why. Anyway, we can't . . .' I was going to say 'We can't spoil the ship for a ha'porth of tar', but I had been saying it so often in the past few months, on so many and such varied occasions, that it was becoming a sort of theme song. So I ended, rather lamely, 'we can't help ourselves.'

'And it won't look too grand,' he continued relentlessly, 'all that water pouring through a hole in the wall.'

'Perhaps it won't. But . . .'

I did not finish the sentence. For at that instant there was a tug at my sleeve. A spectral tug, but a distinct tug – though perhaps it would be better described as a nibble.

It was the dolphin again.

§ IV

I did not turn round. There was no need to do so. The dolphin, quite obviously, was there, though being of an astral variety, it cast no shadow, and Oldfield could not be expected to see it.

'Perhaps it won't. But. . .'

Not only Oldfield, but the dolphin, was waiting for me to go on. And really, why there was this long pause I cannot imagine, it was not only discourteous but unnecessary, for the dolphin knew as well as I did that its hour had come. I suppose the hesitation was due to the fact that for so long, out of mistaken notions of economy, I had been thrusting dolphins from me; hastily turning the page when they cropped up in literature, averting my eyes when they stared at me from the pages of a magazine or from the canvas of a picture, and, whenever I went down to Brighton for a breath of sea-air, positively whizzing past the Royal Pavilion which, as you may or may not know, abounds in the most amiable dolphins of all sizes, shapes and colours. It was really too foolish; it made me feel mean and pinched; and if Oldfield had not been there I should have turned to the dolphin and begged its pardon.

As it was I said:

'Perhaps it won't. But . . . but there'll be a . . . there'll be an ornament.'

With which the dolphin disappeared. It was not too sure whether it cared for being called an 'ornament'. It would have to think it over, in the spectral regions in which it would linger till its moment came.

It did not have to wait long. That very afternoon I was off to Crowther's. And if I were to tell you that I was 'led' to a special dolphin, that was waiting in the shadow of a special mulberry, with a gleam of raindrops in its eyes, and a mouth that was wide open and longing to spout . . . if I were to indulge in such conceits, there are many who would scoff and sneer. But there might be some who would believe that it is true. Anyway, that was how it was . . . and, to come down to earth . . . I have the bill to prove it.

It was growing dark when the dolphin and I arrived at Merry Hall, and for the moment I did not recognize a shadowy figure who was standing on the steps. Then I saw that it was Miss Emily.

She came towards me. 'So lucky to have caught you,' she said. 'I was just passing and I thought . . .' Then she started and stepped back. 'Whatever is *that*?'

'It's the new dolphin.'

'Dear me!' She gave a nervous laugh. 'For a moment I thought it was alive.'

I had a good mind to tell her that of course it was alive. And that if she did not take care, it would bite. However, that might have led to prolonged arguments and discussions, and I wanted to be alone.

'What a curious creature!' she murmured, peering at it through the window of the car. 'Why did you get it?'

'To spout.'

'*Does* it spout?'

'It spouts like mad.'

'How?'

'Through the mouth.' What a silly woman she was. How did she expect it to spout? Out of its tail?

'Oh I *see*! The water garden!'

'Yes. The water garden.'

The terse nature of these replies conveyed to Miss Emily the message I had intended, which was that there were moments when two is company and three is none and that this was one of them. So she came quickly to the point, which was a very boring one, about opening a Sale of Work. Opening Sales of Work is my idea of hell; nobody but a professional writer knows how large they loom on his horizon and how darkly they shadow his sky. But I was so anxious to get rid of Miss Emily that if she had suggested it, I would have promised to open a zoo, so I said yes, that would be delightful. The twenty-third at three o'clock? Splendid. Yes, it looked as if we were in for more rain tomorrow. The forecast says . . . Good-night. And she was gone.

I went to the car, and lifted out the dolphin. The twilight was almost gone; there was a watery moon that seemed to race across the sky; it was a magic hour. As I staggered across the lawn I could hear a plash of water falling on to the empty floor of the pool, and when I reached the edge I saw that Oldfield had dug a small trench to canalize the floodz, so that they fell in a steady stream, like a fountain.

I set the dolphin down on the grass, and jumped on to the floor of the pool. There were still some loose bricks lying about, and it was the work of a moment to build a little platform where the water was falling. Then I climbed back again, lifted up the dolphin, carried him over, knelt down and set him on the platform. There was an opening under one of his fins, and the water fell directly on it, tinkling inside him and filling him up. As he grew fuller he began to gurgle and make happy bubbling noises, suggestive of delight. I stepped back, waiting, watching. There were several moments of agonizing suspense, and then – it happened. Out of his mouth shot a thread of diamond clear water. It formed a tiny arc that sparkled like a necklace in the light of the rising moon.

He was spouting.

How long I stood there watching I do not know. I felt that I never wanted to go away. For this was one of those moments in life when a thousand frustrations and fights and pains and problems seem to be explained and resolved and justified in one simple symbol. I had struggled very hard for Merry Hall and its garden. It had not been easy, in a harshly competitive world. There had been times when one wondered if it was really worth while. All this was forgotten now; I had my reward in that silver thread of water, sparkling in the moonlight.

For you see, it really is a magic water. How otherwise could you describe it? Is it not the essence of all the garden's sweetness? There is the dew of white violets in it, and the raindrops from their dark green leaves. There is the juice of apples in it and the savour of all the pears and plums that fell into the long grass in September, and were forgotten and grew as brown as the earth with which they mingled. There is the scent of snow in it – for snow, as you should be aware, has a distinct scent, and so, for that matter, has the North wind. And there is the tang of ice . . . the ice that laid out its little mirrors of glass all through the orchard in the clear days of January, so that the sky might lean close and see its face.

Yes, it is a magic water, and many flowers have coloured and enriched it. Down the long border in June, after a shower, each leaf of the lupins bears a watery diamond in its centre; if you bend closely over the leaves you can see the blues and purples of the petals reflected in these liquid jewels, so that for a moment they seem to turn into sapphires and amethysts. All those jewels have fallen, sooner or later, into the earth, and sparkled their way down to the pool. The roses in the morning wind have shaken their golden faces, and shed their tears, and the white cherries, and the irises, and the eternal dewy waterfall of the weeping willows.

There are secrets in it too, dark and earthy secrets. As it has run down its ancient courses, in the dead of night, moles have been burrowing around it, and hedgehogs have scurried overhead, and it has heard the whispers of ants and beetles and centipedes. One would have thought that when at last it reached the end of its journey, and flashed with a silver gesture on to the pool's surface, like a dancer alighting on a ballroom floor, it would have shown some signs of these adventures, that it would have been dim or tarnished. But it is still innocent and crystalline as though it had known only the high white snows.

So do you wonder that I call it a magic water? And that the dolphin, as he spouted away on that unforgettable evening, seemed to laugh and gurgle and glisten, as though he were spouting not water, but wine?

§ V

And there we will draw a line, and go our separate ways. Not because there is nothing left to say, but because there is far too much. If we were to set out together on those few square yards of water which now, in their first year, are beginning to break into blossom, we might find that we had embarked on a voyage from which there would be no returning.

We should be ensnared by the fragrance of the water hawthorn which, as I write, is lifting its first white flowers above the water; yesterday, when the sun was shining, the scent of it was so compelling that if you closed your eyes you would think you were standing under a hedge in full bloom. We should lean over, and gaze deep down, and lose ourselves in the strange underworld beneath us, where feathery tendrils and tenuous fingers are beginning to twist and turn in a hundred shades of green, from the fantastic plumes of the water thyme, that is so sensitive that it trembles if you breathe on the surface, to the curious, spectral branches of the tape grass, so pale that it is almost translucent, so avid for air that its thin spiral stems are hung with perpetually changing clusters of diamonds.

We should follow the pink and silver gleam of the golden orfe, as they dart hither and thither on their mysterious ways, marching and counter-marching like a squad of submarine soldiers, drilling in strict formation, as though they were obeying the commands of an unseen sergeant-major. It was only a few months ago that I first emptied these charming little creatures into the pool, and already they have given me hours of amusement and delight. Nor am I the only person whom they have entertained. I regret to say that 'One' and 'Four'. . .

And that reminds me of something. Yes, we really must throw down the pen, this very minute. If you would rise from the desk with me, and peer through the window, you would understand why. You see over there? Yes, that is the pool. Even from here you can observe that the first of the lily buds are just turning pink. But this is no time for considering the lilies. Look again; now perhaps you will realize what I mean. A small beige shape is disposed at one end of the pool, and a small black shape at the other. 'One' and 'Four', it is to be feared, are at action stations.

Quickly. I think that 'One' is beginning to lift his paw. . . .

INDEX

The index of plant names was prepared by Roy C. Dicks, formerly reference librarian at the Wake County Public Library, Raleigh, North Carolina. Plants are indexed by currently accepted botanical name. A cross-reference has been provided wherever the author used a common name or outdated Latin name.